A Wealth of Wildlife

Alan Stewart is a retired police inspector who, after 6 hours' retirement in 1997, went on to be the force wildlife crime officer in a civilian capacity, the first full-time post in Scotland. His interest in wildlife crime stemmed from dealing with salmon and deer poaching cases early in his career, and from an interest in farming, shooting, fishing and the countryside in general. Retiring from this role in 2011, he continued wildlife crime-related work as an intelligence officer with the UK National Wildlife Crime Unit, finally retiring in 2015. Alan was presented with several prestigious awards during his policing career, including in 2001 the MBE for services to policing wildlife crime and is the author of four books on that subject. He lives with his wife, dog, ducks and hens on the edge of a Perthshire village.

By the same author:

Wildlife Detective
The Thin Green Line
A Lone Furrow
Wildlife and the Law

A Wealth of Wildlife

A Year on a Highland Perthshire Estate

ALAN STEWART

THIRSTY BOOKS
EDINBURGH

Published in 2015 by Thirsty Books, Edinburgh
thirstybooks.com

ISBN: 978-0-9932828-3-6

The paper used in this book is recyclable. It is made from low chlorine pulps produced in a low energy, low emission manner from renewable forests.

Printed and bound by Bell & Bain Ltd., Glasgow

Typeset by Main Point Books, Edinburgh

For David

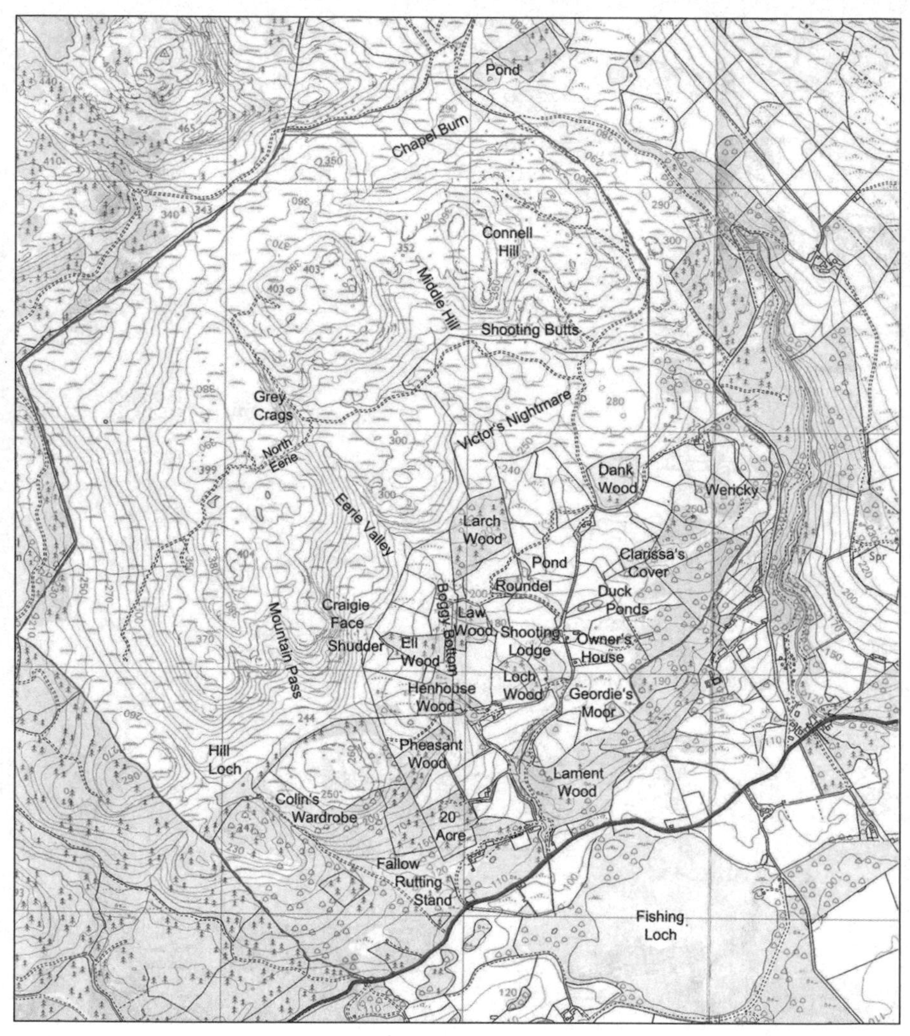

Map of the Estate

Introduction

Shooting estates get bad press because of the manner in which some are run. For many years a high proportion of landowners and their gamekeepers virtually disregarded the law. Legislation has protected some birds of prey since the early 1900s, many more since 1954 and all of them from 1981. Yet all species were shot, trapped and poisoned, even in some cases kestrels, which feed predominantly on mice and voles. White-tailed eagles were exterminated in the UK (though some responsibility for this lies with sheep farmers). The same eradication befell goshawks, while buzzards, golden eagles, peregrines and hen harriers were reduced to a fraction of what their numbers should have been. Police officers were not switched on to this type of criminality, and the few who were took scant regard of the legislation. It was not until the advent of designated police wildlife crime officers in the late 1980s, and encouragement and cajoling from the RSPB and statutory agencies such as Scottish Natural Heritage and Natural England, that inroads were gradually made to a whole range of crime committed against wildlife.

We now live in more enlightened times and most – but certainly not all – low-ground shooting estates stay within the law. Unfortunately the same cannot be said of some upland estates that specialise in driven grouse shooting, with particularly disreputable sporting agents ensuring that their gamekeepers wipe out any species that pose a threat to grouse. It is noticeable on these moors that there is an almost complete absence of wildlife apart from red grouse. On one grouse moor in the north of England, early in the month of September, the head gamekeeper instructed guns to shoot any pheasant that came through the line on a grouse drive, even though the pheasant shooting season did not open until

1 October. The guns were told that if they failed to comply they would be subject to a fine! The reason given was that the pheasants that had come on to the moor might carry disease to the grouse. It is therefore hardly surprising that the aversion towards sporting shooting and the associated practices felt by a high proportion of the public has not lessened.

It is against this background that a good friend of mine who owns an estate in Highland Perthshire hosting driven pheasant and red-legged partridge shooting asked me if I would carry out a wildlife survey of the estate. For many years he has been proud of the fact that as wide a variety of species as possible can be seen on the estate, and I have seen over the years while on the estate that it boasts just about every species of bird and animal that can be found in Highland Perthshire habitat. He normally has one or sometimes two gamekeepers and the first instruction they get before they are hired is that if they break the law they will be fired. On some occasions I have assisted by ensuring that the keepers are acquainted with the legislation that allows them to use traps and snares, which has become more complex due, rightly, to improved animal welfare concerns.

To support biodiversity the gamekeeper mixes wild bird seed with grain for the game bird hoppers, ensuring that in winter time small seed-eating birds can benefit. This is the first time I have seen this on such a scale and is a costly addition to the feed bill. The bird seed is mixed through the pheasant feed in a cement mixer, a simple but ingenious initiative. Scores of garden birds also feed on the selection of bird feeders in the landowner's garden, and at least 20 pairs of house martins nest under the eaves of his house.

Species that are considered a threat to game and nesting birds are controlled so far as the law allows. A springtime offensive is carried out against carrion crows by means of shooting, multi-catch crow cages and Larsen traps, and a reduction on rook and jackdaw numbers is carried out using multi-catch cage traps, as much to save on the feeding provided for game birds and ducks as to limit their predation on eggs and chicks of game birds and waders. Foxes are shot and snared, and a springtime check is made on known dens for any cubs that are missed. A trapping regime is also carried out against stoats, weasels and feral ferrets using tunnel traps, though these mustelids are not in high numbers in any case. Some people may not like the idea of these culls but they are a legitimate part of estate management.

To reduce partridges kills by birds of prey such as the sparrowhawk and buzzard, there are dozens of shelters dotted over the hill. These consist of a couple of sheets of corrugated iron covered in heather turf and placed about 18 inches above the ground. Partridges under threat from an aerial predator can find safety under these shelters. This is an innovative approach and they have proved to be a success.

I carried out the survey over the course of a year, starting on 18 July 2011 and finishing on 25 July 2012. I made 33 visits during the course of the year, normally of four to six hours' duration and walking up to 10 miles. I varied my route every visit, with the part of the estate covered sometimes influenced by season or weather. The estate extends to 2000 acres and is roughly 50% hill, 35% mixed woodland and 15% pasture. There are two main lochs on the estate and several ponds. At the time of the survey a large commercial fishing loch adjacent to the estate was owned by the estate but has since been sold. During the survey I noted 89 species of birds, though I have seen an additional four since: golden eagle, peregrine, merlin and grey wagtail. I also noted 10 species of mammals.

The landowner had strong views on wildlife crime associated with driven grouse shooting and was keen to buy a grouse moor to demonstrate that reasonable numbers of grouse could be shown over the guns without the need to break the law. He visited upland areas that were on the market but none of those available was suitable. He never realised his dream, as sadly he passed away in February 2015 after a long illness. He was a man who disliked fuss and though he appreciated he had a unique estate he was keen to quietly keep improving the biodiversity rather than brag about it. For that reason I have not identified the estate.

I am sure that his family will continue running the estate in the same tradition and that in time birds much persecuted elsewhere such as the golden eagle and hen harrier may nest there.

CHAPTER 1

Monday 18 July. Weather: dry and dull, with the odd sunny spell.

The first day of my wildlife survey and I started my walk at the Hill Loch, which is at the west end of the estate, having been dropped off there by the estate owner. Apart from a large loch open to the public to fish on payment, the Hill Loch is the biggest of the lochs on the estate, and is stocked with decent sized brown trout. It is secluded, with woodland round the south and west shores, and the remainder of the loch bordering the hill. There is a boathouse on the south east corner, and the four resident mute swans on the loch help to keep it the water free of weed (I don't count them as wild birds as they are semi-domestic Polish versions of mute swan and fed regularly in winter). The setting for the loch is simply idyllic.

The first thing I saw at the boathouse was a buzzard circling and calling over the woodland to the west of the loch near the boundary with the estate that borders to the west. It was soon joined by another that flew westwards over the north shore of the loch and both landed in trees on the estate boundary, still mewing loudly. This was a great start, as on many shooting estates birds of prey are either absent or scarce. A tiny wren was singing loudly from somewhere on the south shore of the loch, invisible but easily distinguished by its lovely song that, volume-wise, would do credit to a bird 10 times its size. The song began with a rather metallic *tic, tic*, developed into a melodious warble, and finished with a trilling *chip, chip, chip, chip, chip*. Within a few minutes here I had seen one of the largest birds on the estate and one of the smallest, both with distinctive calls that can be easily identified.

I walked past the pheasant pen in Creag Bheag wood to the east of the loch. This is a long narrow wood of predominantly mature conifers with a good mix of larch and Douglas fir. It was full of inquisitive pheasant poults that had not long been bought from the game farm, though red-legged partridges will not be bought and put out on to the hill till mid-August. The poults have an element of (though not complete) safety in the pen, but it is not long before they start to fly over the eight feet high netting fence. They tend to stay in the vicinity of the pen while they are young and can re-enter the pen at any time through a system of netting funnels. Until the pheasants begin to roost up in trees they are very vulnerable to ground predators: foxes and, to a lesser extent, stoats. As poults they can also be vulnerable to buzzard and sparrowhawk predation. It is natural that if there is an abundant food supply for predators they will take advantage of it. This and some other well-run sporting estates live with this, controlling species they are legally entitled to, and trying to limit predation by protected species through a series of legal measures. Regretfully this is not the approach taken by all estates.

A jay, by far the most colourful member of the corvids, began screeching loudly, annoyed at my intrusion. Its loud shriek reminded me of the noise a young piglet makes if picked up. Ignoring the jay's warning, a male blackbird was feeding on the ground at an open gate leading from the hill land to Creag Bheag wood, only a few feet away from a three-quarter grown rabbit. I quietly walked closer to the rabbit, taking a step or two forward when its head was down feeding, and remaining motionless when it was on the alert, inky black eye watching and velvety nose twitching. I was almost right up to it, only about 12 feet away, before it hopped unconcernedly through the gate and into the wood. It had been aware of my presence but had not yet learned of the dangerous relationship with humans.

A woodpigeon clattered out of the wood as I walked along the outer edge, disturbed off a twiggy low-level nest. A woodpigeon can lay its pair of almost-round white eggs throughout the year, though the main breeding period in Scotland is between June and September. In this case the nest contained chicks, not eggs; two gargoyle-like squabs with down beginning to be replaced with embryonic feathers. Woodpigeons are the most handsome of birds when adult, but at this stage they certainly wouldn't win any beautiful baby competitions. They have a varied, mostly vegetarian, diet. I used to shoot quite a lot of woodpigeons when I was younger, in fact roast pigeon is one of my favourite meals. When I plucked them, sometimes the crop was full of grain, other days it was peas, or brassica leaves, and when they were eating clover their crops were usually full to bursting. Further on, a male wheatear bobbed a couple of times in typical fashion on top of the stone dyke of an old sheep pen, before flying off, white rump flashing, to study me from the safety of a distant rock in the heather. Wheatears are summer visitors, nesting in crevices amongst rocks or even in rabbit burrows. The drystane dykes of the old fank – the old Scots name for this type of sheep pen – would probably have been its mate's nesting place. I think male wheatears are one of our smartest-looking birds, with their grey crown and back, black eyestripe and wings and light orange breast. The males always remind me of a groom or best man at a posh wedding. They just lack the top hat!

Leaving the wood, I cut left up a track through a very steep mini 'mountain pass'. There were meadow pipits in abundance, showing their distinctive white outer tail feathers in flight. One began to fly round me, probably in protection of a late or second nest. Meadow pipits are the most common moorland birds and, along with voles, are the main food source of moorland raptors such as hen harrier and merlin. Further up the mountain pass there was a dead but still fresh adult frog. It was partly predated and probably the victim of a buzzard. It seemed incongruous away out on the hill, but there was a small burn with sparklingly clear water nearby, so that may have been its origin. A buzzard behind me, probably one of the pair I saw earlier, was gliding from the direction of the Hill Loch over Creag Bheag wood, to land on the top of a high tree at a point half way along. It may have been attracted by the pheasant poults in the pen, but it certainly made no effort to investigate any more closely than from this lofty vantage point.

Near the top of the hill a small brown bird was flitting about on the heather, feeding on insects. It clearly wasn't a meadow pipit, and after a decent view through the binoculars and a quick look at my bird reference book (the RSPB Handbook of Scottish Birds), I confirmed it as a willow warbler. It was surprisingly tolerant of my presence and was in what I considered an unusual place for such a bird. I'm not too good on an instant ID of warblers, but yellow eyebrows, white underparts and pale coloured legs fitted the wee willow warbler perfectly. A very pale yellow colour at the top of the breast made it more likely to be an immature bird, which was probably also the reason it allowed me so close. At the very top of the hill I looked westwards down on three small lochs in a line on the neighbouring estate. On the largest loch there were two dark-coloured geese, which could only have been Canada geese. There was also a handful of ducks, probably mallard, but unfortunately at the maximum range for my binoculars.

From the top of the hill I walked down the steep and narrow gorge bounding North Eerie and on to Middle Hill, where there were two buzzards mewing and circling. A female kestrel, which came from an area to the east of Middle Hill where there is a single small tree, started to mob one of the buzzards. It continued mobbing for five to 10 minutes, but backed off when the target buzzard turned as if to retaliate. Having lost some of its confidence, the kestrel flew back and landed on some large rocks to the left of the single tree. The buzzards disappeared, though one continued to call from somewhere above and to the left of the single tree. I looked for ages with the binoculars to try to locate it but couldn't find it and gave up, deciding to rest on a trackside rock and eat part of my lunch. The still-hidden buzzard continued to call for 10 to 15 minutes, at which point the second buzzard returned and was immediately mobbed again by the feisty kestrel, which came off the rocks at the single tree, its courage recharged. The buzzard seemed to tire of the continued pestering by this much smaller raptor and landed on a rock 200 yards below the single tree. I thought the kestrel would have continued to mob it on the rock but no, it returned to the rocks at the tree and kept watch. Ten minutes later the buzzard took off and was mobbed again by the kestrel till it moved away from the area, and the kestrel returned to its lookout post. I suspected this to be a territorial defence and the area at the tree may have been a nesting place earlier in the year, though there was no sign of fledged young or of a male kestrel. It was an interesting encounter while I was 'at lunch'.

I headed back the hill road towards a partridge drive called 'The Shooting Butts', and after a mile or so passed Dank Wood on my left, which effectively is the boundary between the hill and the grass fields of the lower ground. Dank Wood is a smallish square-shaped wood of mainly mature sitka spruce, with the trees more widely spaced than in a commercial plantation. The trees at the far (north-east) side of the wood have been harvested, though the clear-felled area has not yet been replanted. An adult red squirrel was on the ground at the west edge of Dank Wood eating what I thought was a woodpigeon's egg. I watched it through the binoculars for a few minutes, and saw that a coal tit was as fascinated with the squirrel's activities as I was, studying it from a branch just above. Having had enough of a feed, the squirrel headed, still on the ground, further in to the wood. My closer investigation showed it had been eating a toadstool or mushroom. There was no sign of the mushroom cap, but the squirrel had eaten down the white stalk to ground level, and maybe had eaten the cap as well. It obviously had a varied diet, and there were lots of cones on the ground, stripped in typical red squirrel fashion to relinquish their prize of seeds. I regularly see toadstools – even some of the poisonous red ones – with chunks nibbled out of them, but I had always put this down to mice or rabbits. Red squirrels forming part of the nibbling team was an interesting discovery.

When I left Dank Wood behind me about a hundred rooks and jackdaws, and also three oystercatchers, were busy in a grass field above the duck pond. There were sheep in this field, which I'll refer to regularly and call the 'sheep field', so the birds were probably getting invertebrates around the dung. Several rooks were feeding at the edge of the duck pond, and I assumed the prize there would be barley or wheat put out for the ducks. The corvids at the pond edge were having it their own way, as I could only see a single adult mallard drake in residence.

Back at the estate owner's house the air was filled with house martins and swallows. The martins had half a dozen nests under the eaves of the house, and I could see well-grown martin heads peeping out from most of them. The swallows were more intent on the inside of the adjoining farm buildings and no doubt had nests there. I hoped that both species were having a good breeding season and that their incredibly risky two-way journey over the vast Sahara Desert had been worthwhile.

My day finished with the steady *pink-pink, pink-pink* alarm-call of a male chaffinch from telephone wires at the front of the farm buildings. I looked to see what was causing it concern, but it was clearly aware of something I couldn't see. A chaffinch at home, with its partner on a nest among *Hydrangea petiolaris,* a climbing hydrangea on the west wall of the house, does the very same every time I go into the garden, so the problem with the estate chaffinch might well just have been my presence. When I was thinking about the species of birds I had seen, it suddenly struck me I'd been out on the hill for about five hours and had not seen, or even heard, a carrion crow. George, the keeper, would be pleased at that!

Birds identified that day: common buzzard; wren; pheasant; jay; blackbird; woodpigeon; wheatear; meadow pipit; willow warbler; kestrel; coal tit; rook; jackdaw; oystercatcher; mallard; house martin; swallow; chaffinch
Mammals identified that day: red squirrel

Chapter 2

Monday 25 July. Weather: Sunny in morning but cloudy in afternoon.

The west gable of the estate owner's house is completely covered with ivy, and this morning it seemed that it contained a house sparrow for every ivy leaf. They were chirping incessantly from deep within the ivy, with only the odd one visible nearer the outside. One particular cock sparrow looked really smart, with his grey crown, white cheeks and huge black bib. Those with large black bibs are meant to be the more dominant birds, puffing out their feathers to make the bib even larger if the need arises to assert authority over a rival male. He was a handsome bird though his song, a monotonous *chirp, chirp, chirp, chirp* would certainly not win any birdsong competitions. Sparrows – a species on the decline – in such numbers is fantastic to see and, for someone my age, nostalgic, bringing back memories of when they were universally common.

Despite the estate owner's offer of a quad bike to get me out the hill I much preferred Shank's pony. I needed the exercise and in any case I thought that the noise from a quad bike might frighten off some of the species I wanted see. Swallows and house martins were everywhere as I started off up the hill road, including sitting on the telephone wires above my head. Mostly it was swallows on the wires, with a ratio of young to old of at least three to one, the lack of long ribbons on their tails giving the youngsters away. The twittering of swallows is a lovely sound and, like the sparrows, takes me back to my youth when swallows – in fact all hirundines – were far more numerous than now. Anyway two members of the genus were certainly doing well on this estate.

There were plenty ducks in the pond today, though all were the ubiquitous mallard. They're interesting to watch; I can vouch for this having had mallard regularly visit my khaki Campbells at home. They were dabbling away in the shallows with upturned tails, but I was too far away to hear any of the vocals as they quietly chattered to each other, which is the most intriguing part. In the sheep field above the pond, though there were still 30 or so rooks and jackdaws, they had largely been replaced by lapwings and oystercatchers. The lapwing numbers were higher than that of their pied neighbours, which is good to see as it is usually the opposite. Many of the lapwings were youngsters, lacking the smart crest of their parents. They also seemed to lack the purpose of the adult birds, which were busying away looking for invertebrates, while their offspring seemed much less focussed. Dotted amongst the birds, rabbits were lazily stretched out on the grass outside their burrows enjoying the morning sun.

Though lapwings appear to be black and white at a distance, the adult lapwing in fact has an almost iridescent green over its back with white cheeks and breast, a black face and chest, and a lovely orange–brown under the tail. Its black crest is striking, giving the bird a real air of grace and superiority. It looks much more black and white in flight, since the wing tips, above and below, are black. I feel better now that I've done one of my favourite birds justice. They are such fantastic birds and it is a great pity that their numbers have crashed, mainly because of a change in farming methods.

I raised my binoculars higher and a roe doe and pair of fawns came into view at the side of a roundel beyond the pond. They were having a last bite of dew-laden grass before adjourning to the cool of the woodland, but it showed the difference in colour between the two age groups. The doe was a real foxy-red in its summer coat, while the fawns were considerably darker. They looked totally relaxed, and would be even more stress-free within the next half hour once they settled down for the day amongst the trees.

The mewing of buzzards had been constant, but I'd never

looked at them till now with so much else going on. There were five soaring high in the sky, probably a family group. They did well to rear three youngsters considering the very wet and windy spring we had, however young rabbits, their most important food source at this time of the year, were plentiful. They appeared at different times during the morning, in woodland and at different levels in the sky but always in the same area, which was clearly their territory. As I scanned round to the south a magnificent red kite came in to view, hugging the edge of the woodland to the east of the estate farm buildings and not far from the march with the neighbouring estate to the east. A pair bred successfully this year and last year on the estate. About three years ago the owner had told me that he had seen a pair of kites and wondered how he could keep them on the estate to breed. I suggested leaving out plenty of dead rabbits as carrion for them, which he did. Hopefully this was a factor in their making this estate their home.

I walked up past a cottage just below Dank Wood, which had 20 or so hens and cockerels, mostly either white with black neck and tail feathers or a lovely grey/purplish colour. They were scraping contentedly in a determined search for worms or other invertebrates on a rough piece of ground beside the cottage. The land around the hens was ideal habitat for small birds and I was not disappointed. Two willow warblers (identified this time without reference to my book – I hope to gain much more experience in identifying the more unusual birds during the coming year) flitted from one tree to the next. I kept my binoculars trained on the tree and got some good – and fairly close up – views. I'm always very aware of birds when out walking but this is the first time I've really *looked* for them. Between the cottage and Dank Wood I had a lovely surprise to see a pair of whinchats, which also settled on a fence long enough for me to make the positive ID. They're lovely wee birds, with the male being slightly darker than the female and both having a white stripe above the eye. The male's breast was more noticeably pinky-orange than that of his mate. I'm more accustomed to stonechats, which I regularly saw when holidaying in Brittany.

I moved further up to Dank Wood, where last week I had watched a red squirrel. This time I walked round the wood in an anti-clockwise direction. There was a grassy track between the wood and the dyke bordering the field, which made a lovely walk. I watched a bird land on some bracken and as it flew away I was sure I saw a red tail. Redstart came to mind but I only had a fleeting glimpse. I stood for a few minutes and saw it again. When it flew away this time I didn't see its tail because of the sun, but the wee bird gave me a third chance which clinched it: definitely a redstart, though with the millisecond I had it in view I wasn't able to say if it was male, female or immature. I've seen black redstarts in Germany but very few redstarts in Scotland, with the last ones being in Glenesk, Angus, in late April this year. There was no doubt that this was my most interesting sighting so far.

Beyond the redstart, on a pile of large stones in the field, I watched a bird flitting from stone to stone. This one seemed larger than the small birds I had just been watching, but I had been misled by its very upright stance, as if it was on guard. It was an immature wheatear, still with tufts of down, like ears, sticking up from its head. At that age it would probably still be dependent on its parents, though they were nowhere to be seen. The remainder of the walk round the wood was through the clear felled part and was quiet bird-wise.

I was now on the road out to the hill and before long watched two dark coloured fallow deer with calves of the same colour trot in line down a track in the heather. They were aware of me but not unduly bothered as I was several hundred yards away. They were followed shortly after by an almost black buck, its short antlers, maybe four inches long, still in velvet. It was a beautiful beast and I marvelled at the variety of colours of fallow deer, from pure white right through to jet black. The colour variation was exemplified a few minutes later when I saw another group. This time there were two dark coloured does, one with a dark calf, followed by a beautiful light coloured dappled doe with an identical calf. I wondered if the calves were always the same colour as their mother, which was what

I had seen so far, but this didn't make sense as black is normally the dominant gene. (I had hoped that the internet or relevant books I had could help with this puzzle, but could find no reference to fallow parent – offspring colour.)

I cut right-handed off the main hill track on to a less-used one which went round near the boundary with the estate to the east. A heather fire had gone out of control here earlier in the year and burned more than it should have, but blaeberries were already coming back, so the fire had not gone in too deeply to the peat. Blaeberries were the clue to numerous purple bird droppings on the track, but with an apparent scarcity of birds on the burned ground I wondered who had been eating the blaeberries. Between the track I was on and the march dyke was a strip of heather about 100 yards wide, widening as I went round, and which held plenty of meadow pipits. I noted several varieties of wild flowers, three yellow and one white, which I failed to identify. My 1970s copy of *The Observers Book of Wild Flowers* is dated, and every second page is black and white – not much help in identifying flowers. An investment is needed here!

I followed the track round the hill, which finished at a turning place, but which was replaced by quad bike tracks leading off up to the top of Connell Hill. I followed those to near the top but they also disappeared and I was left with a choice of going back or trudging through knee high heather and waist high bracken. The moor is managed for red-legged partridge rather than grouse. They seem to prefer bracken, where they can get plenty of cover yet move about on the ground with relative ease. The bracken also allows the birds to be flushed more easily on shooting days. Bracken is disliked almost everywhere else but it suits both the wildlife and the shooting on this estate. My walk over the hill to again re-join a civilised track flushed three red grouse, two adults and one well-grown chick, which rose in front of me and landed only a short distance away. It is good to see there are still some grouse around, though it was a pity there was only the one offspring. A pair of wheatears also kept me amused, observing me observing them. The difference was that I wasn't bobbing up and down.

I was now back on Middle Hill, where I lunched on a track-side rock in the same place as last week. As I sat down I saw a roe doe munching contentedly on grass in a boggy area 300 yards away. I say contentedly, though her ears never stopped flicking to try to keep the flies off. I spied round about looking for the ears of twin fawns sticking up above the grass, but no sign. The doe munched and I munched, still hoping to see the elusive fawns. By the time I'd finished my sandwiches she had moved out of sight behind a knoll so I'll never know if she had fawns there or not.

I took the right fork of the track and moved off up Grey Crags, where half-way up the hill I was aware I was being scolded by a decidedly angry or alarmed wren. It was 10 yards away atop some heather and as I stopped to look at it (without the need for binoculars for once) I was aware of more tiny wrens also sitting on the tops of heather tufts. In fact there were seven others in total, probably all fledglings as no other wren was chattering at me. Like the wheatear earlier they still had tiny wisps of down sticking out of their head and they could not have long fledged. It was a good brood, and a very welcome sight after the hard 2010/11 winter the adult wrens must have come through. Hopefully most of them would make it through the next winter to try to bring the beleaguered wren numbers back to near normal in 2012.

I walked to the top of Grey Crags, and sat down to watch some pond skaters on a pool at the track side. They never fail to amaze me with their ability to literally walk on water. Their body and legs are covered with dense velvety hairs to prevent them sinking, nevertheless the fact that they don't sink is just incredible. There were probably 40 or 50, and some reacted by racing in the direction of a petal off a clover flower I threw into the water, but seemed to realise before they reached it that it was a hoax, and that no tiny struggling insect was available for lunch. I turned and went back down Grey Crags, disturbing a roe buck with two points on each antler, which ran up the steep west side, looked at me from the hilltop, then ran off barking its *buff, buff* call at me. Unlike the fallow with antlers still in velvet, the roe antlers are clear of velvet and ready for the rut just starting. They mate much earlier in the year than red and fallow deer but there is little embryo development until the following year, a phenomenon, strangely, they have in common with our mustelids.

With embryonic diapause, giving the strategy its biological name, the females are fertilised when in peak bodily condition as a result of a plentiful supply of food. The tiny embryos are virtually in a state of limbo over winter, ensuring the female maintains sufficient reserves to see her through till spring. It is then that the embryos speed up development, at a time when food is more readily found. Nature – and species evolution and survival – at its best!

I made my way back in the direction of the shooting lodge, following the hill road down. I was keen to have another look at Dank Wood where I saw the redstart, but before I got there I watched a family group of birds, five of them flitting about on the heather stems just too far away for good identification even with binoculars. I sat for a while hoping they'd come closer but they were getting further away. I tried to walk in on them and got close enough to *think* that they were whinchats, but couldn't be positive. Frustrating.

Back at the wood the activity there had gone quiet, with only a young robin, freckles instead of red on its breast, being visible. It must have been siesta time. Further down the track, near the cottage with the hens, a bird sat on a fencepost long enough for me to get detail enough to consult the book and identify it as a chiffchaff. Birds are much more easily identified in springtime when they are singing, even when they are hidden in dense cover. This one would have been easy to identify as it sings its name – *chiff-chaff, chiff-chaff, chiff-chaff.* It was almost identical in every respect to a willow warbler but dark coloured legs, as opposed to the willow warbler's pale legs, were the deciding factor this time. Noting all the features of a bird for identification is much more interesting – and more of a challenge – than what I used to do, saying 'that's a warbler of some sort'.

Back at the shooting lodge I relaxed on a seat on the veranda overlooking the loch. There was obviously a feast of flies over the water for the swallows and house martins, which were there in abundance. I was amazed how often they took a fly from the surface of the water, so that the flat-calm loch became a tapestry of concentric circles, some made by rising trout, but most by birds. One of the rings was made by a very sizeable trout, far bigger than anything I have ever caught, and having it on the end of a line, then roasting it in the oven in some garlic butter would have been very satisfying. Many of the swallows were flying in and out of the boathouse, most likely nesting there. They were joined in their sojourns to the boathouse by a pied flycatcher, maybe also with a nest. The scene was peaceful, with three highland cattle contentedly grazing in front of me, and rabbits, including a black one, feeding quietly on the far shore. It was a relaxing end to the day. I had seen carrion crows on this visit, not a lot but maybe nine or 10. I had also been looking out for evidence of foxes, but all I saw was a very old and dried-out fox scat. Maybe George, the keeper, with the release of red-legged partridges imminent, will still be quite pleased.

New birds identified: house sparrow; lapwing; red kite; whinchat; redstart; red grouse; robin; chiffchaff; pied wagtail
New mammals identified: roe deer; fallow deer; rabbit

Chapter 3

Monday 1 August. Weather: Cloudy all day with a couple of very light showers. Warm and no wind at all.

There was a great show of lapwings in the sheep field above the duck pond this morning. The sheep are still in the field and are clearly the vector for the invertebrates attracting this flock of birds. Looking round the crests – or lack of crests – there are a high proportion of immature lapwings. If they all originated on this estate they must have had a very successful breeding season this year. It demonstrates the advantage to wildlife on land where there is very little cultivation apart from an odd field being re-seeded in grass or game crop; no tractors and implements flattening eggs or chicks; few predatory carrion crows or foxes to feast on clutches of eggs or chicks, and, probably most importantly, no chemicals used to kill off weeds and insects. Lapwings need insects, and insects need flowers and weeds. I'm looking forward to next spring to see the lapwings' breeding success developing for myself.

Across the track from the sheep field some old pasture has just been ploughed, limed and re-seeded. The confederation of rooks and jackdaws that were with the lapwings last week are now foraging in this field. They've been joined by a dozen or so common gulls, some of them in immature brownish plumage, and all busy harvesting whatever has attracted them to this new breakfast table. They're also accompanied by 50 or so pheasant poults, much less sure of what they should be doing but trying to find something to eat in any case. The scene was completed by a couple of dozen rabbits sitting round the grassy end-rigs of the field; merely spectators providing a more elaborate frame to the picture.

I wanted to have a look at Eerie Valley. I've twice been a gun on the Eerie Return drive – when the birds are driven roughly from north to south across the valley, rather than in the other direction, in which the drive is called Eerie Valley. It is a drive in which I've yet to hit anything, as the partridges (and some pheasants) come over the crest of the hill so high and fast that, as a once-a-year shooter they are beyond my capability (and that of many of the more experienced guns). As I walked up the hill from the shooting lodge towards Larch Wood on my way to Eerie Valley, the rabbit runs, where the rabbits had knocked the dew from the grass, were dark green ribbons on a sea of silvery-green shimmering and soaking wet grass. At the top of the field I spied a rabbit burrow that would have young rabbits of less than two weeks old inside. To most people it would seem like an oval-shaped flattened molehill but at one end there was a circular area of small shiny, earthy balls about the size and shape of rabbit droppings. These balls disguised the burrow entrance and are formed by the damp earth constantly being pushed forward by the doe to block the hole, preventing access by weasels and other small mammalian predators, then later re-opened so that the doe can get in to feed the kits. The burrow would only be three or four feet long, with a nest of dried grass and rabbit fur at the end, keeping a litter of probably six or seven young rabbits cosy. After a couple of weeks the doe leaves the entrance open, though it is invariably smaller in circumference than the entrances to larger warrens. The young in this burrow were quite late in the season and might have less chance of survival than some of their earlier siblings if we have a hard winter.

I made my way up the hill, noticing a dark coloured fallow doe and calf at the edge of the top end of Law Wood off to my left. They slipped quietly into the trees as I continued. I passed the wood and began the descent that would lead to a grass field and then the hill at Eerie Valley. As I approached the field I decided just to spy out the hill with the binoculars, as I would still see most of what wildlife was present from there rather than walk out the track that leads to the different pins for the partridge drives in Eerie Valley.

Everything was soaking after a shower, but I found a suitable rock, put my rucksack on it and sat on the dry and comfy rucksack. Three cattle and two calves were in the grass field, while the rest of the herd had gone through the open gate to the hill. In their unexciting world I became an object of curiosity. Despite my being 200 yards away, they all stood up to get a better view and gradually made their way towards me, the ones in the field being separated from the rest by a fence. I also became the object of attention for pheasant poults, which came out of the bracken on to the drier track, studied me with querulous squeaks, and slowly came up the hill to get a better view. Next to join the audience was a great tit that studied me from the branches of an elder bush just yards away.

The cattle were getting closer. They were a mix of creamy coloured Simmental, deep red Limousin and some crosses, a couple being pure black like Aberdeen Angus and one black with a white Hereford-type head. Some had yellow ear tags, some had blue and most of the calves had both. I amused myself trying visually to pair the well-grown calves with their mothers, confirming the pairings by reading the tag numbers through the binoculars. The calves were a similar mix of colours. I noticed that the mother of black calf number 58 was in the field, while the calf was with the rest of the group on the hill. It was well past needing a constant milk supply and, like most adolescents, probably preferred its pals' company to that of its mother.

The list of intrigued onlookers increased by one as a small brown bird landed on the fence about a hundred yards away. At first I thought it was a young robin, but it had its back to me and I couldn't be sure. Its head was slightly darker than its back and I wondered if it might be a female whitethroat. All was revealed when its mate appeared and perched beside it: they were Mr and Mrs Stonechat. When the male arrived the female turned round. I could clearly see the darker head of the male and a larger, clearer, white band at the side it its neck, much less obvious on its mate. The pinky-orange colour of its breast was also much more pronounced than that of the female. As I studied these birds I was aware of the cattle getting closer, with their attendant clouds of flies. I'd no wish to share the flies with them, since they are often very hard to shake off, so made my exit.

I walked eastwards along Boggy Bottom, a marshy strip of land, with the top end of the Law Wood on my left and heading in the direction of Ell Wood (the wood was originally L shaped, though now rectangular) which was 300 yards distant on my right. A buzzard was circling lazily high above, being mobbed by half a dozen house martins, which gave up as the buzzard soared higher. Three small brownish birds (it would be much easier if all birds were completely different colours) flew into a tree. I had a job locating them with the binoculars and when I did they weren't brown at all; they were green. Greenfinches. I put off little time with them as they are probably the most common bird in my garden, and anyway my attention was taken by two oystercatchers alarm-calling, *peep-peep, peep-peep, peep-peep,* in a field just beyond Ell Wood that had been re-seeded the previous year and had a lush crop of grass. I could only hear them, as trees blocked my view, but I went to the field gate to investigate. The birds had quietened down and there was nothing obvious, though I watched a roe doe and a single fawn grazing busily in a marshy square of land adjacent and to the east of the field.

Just then a flock of a couple of hundred jackdaws rose from some scree on Craigie Face, to my south-west, where they nest among the rocks. The concentrated *chak, chak, chak* of the birds was deafening as they left the hillside and swept westwards. I could see the cause: a female (or possibly an immature) goshawk was flying eastwards from the direction of the jackdaws towards the north end of Creag Bheag Wood. I followed it with the binoculars, seeing clearly its barred tail and its equally large but more streamlined shape compared with a buzzard. It flew with ease through the trees, typical of a goshawk, and at the same time a cloud of small passerines exploded out of the wood. As it went further in to the trees I lost it, but kept the binoculars trained on the trees as this was the first wild goshawk I had seen in Scotland, the only other being in south Germany. In due course I saw it again in the trees, and watched it landing on a branch, though at the distance it was still impossible to say whether it was an adult. I was thrilled with the sighting, which had made my day. I knew that George, the keeper, wouldn't touch the goshawk, but equally I knew that it could be a major threat to his partridges if it decided to take them rather than the numerous rabbits and jackdaws. Hopefully it would balance its diet and not draw too much adverse attention to itself.

I'd now to go back down the hill through a grass field to cross and come up on the far side of the Henhouse Wood. After I turned to start the slight descent I looked back, to see five buzzards wheeling at the highest point of the Craigie Face. I'm sure it was not the same five as I'd seen the previous week, as they were in a completely different part of the estate, and I assumed it was a new family group. Just at that point I glanced into the Henhouse Wood and saw a buzzard nest high in one of the trees. I wondered initially if that might have been their nest from earlier, but it was rather battered and worn and looked more like one from the previous year.

I skirted the bottom of the Henhouse Wood and began back up the other side. I watched an adult pair of red-legged partridges and wondered if they had chicks. The male flew off and landed nearby in a field, but the female remained in longish grass. I watched for a while, though I was fairly sure it had no chicks. Minutes after, as I walked on up the west side of the Pheasant Wood, I encountered my first unfortunate rabbit of the season with myxomatosis. It is a vile disease, man-made and causing what must be painful pussy swellings round the eyes, base of the ears and genitals. Many rabbits survive myxy, but this wouldn't be one of them. It had a dull, dark, staring coat, was completely blind, thin and swarming with flies. I tried to creep closer so that I could despatch it, but it still managed to detect my presence and blundered off into the bracken. While I was distracted by the doomed rabbit, another mammal had noticed my presence: a roe buck in the Pheasant Wood. I didn't see it but its barking indignation at being disturbed was clear identification as it bounded deeper into the trees.

At the top of the Pheasant Wood the area into which the goshawk had flown was on my immediate right. It was quite mature, open woodland, but I could see no trace of the magnificent raptor. I looked across to the Craigie Face where I had seen the five buzzards circling earlier, and their number had swelled to eight. This was much more than a family group; more an extended family gathering. I suspect with the heat of the day it was the thermals in which they were interested. They seemed to be enjoying themselves, and I watched two gripping each other's claws and spinning head over heels in a manner probably more common to golden eagles.

I cut round behind the top of the Pheasant Wood and stopped half-way down the other side to have the second half of my piece, repeating my earlier exercise with rucksack on top of rock. As I munched, a bird landed on the branch of a tree further down the wood edge. It then flitted out a few yards from the wood to catch a fly, then back to a branch again. I've seen this at home regularly with a pair of spotted flycatchers that nest in the *Hydrangea petiolaris.* The bird's second foray comprised a few quick flips of its wings, a fly was caught and back it came to its perch, where it sat in a very upright pose, I had the bird positively identified. The fact that it repeated this many more times while I sat there left no room for doubt. The spotted flycatcher seems to be one of the latest birds to arrive here from Africa, not usually with me at home till the end of May or even the beginning of June, so this one may still have been feeding dependent young. Its grey brown upper parts and light coloured, slightly speckled, breast makes it similar in looks to many other wee brownish migrants but the feeding habits set it apart. As I was finishing my piece a young pied wagtail landed at the dyke-side near me, a misty grey and white colour unlike the distinct black and white of adults. It wagged its tail a few times in true wagtail style, then flew off along the dyke. Flies are also its main diet but it does not compete for food with the spotted flycatcher as the wagtail takes most of its flies from the ground.

I made my way back towards the shooting lodge to have a look round the loch shore. As I passed the south side of the Loch Wood I stopped to look at a bush with bright red berries. They hung in bunches rather like rowans or cotoneaster, but were neither. I think (having looked up a book) that they were the berries from a guelder rose. I have seen them from time to time in the countryside and suspect that they are not eaten by birds, as they often hang on the bush long after the leaves have fallen. My eyes dropped down to a burdock, thinking how often I have brushed past one and found my clothes covered in the sticky bracts that are damnably hard to remove. It is a good seed dispersal tactic. Alongside the burdock, and partly hidden behind it was what I was quite sure was a single giant hogweed plant. It may have been ordinary hogweed but the leaves looked too large for that. In any event I told the estate owner so that he could have it checked and dealt with. Having looked it up, I see that one of these non-native, extremely invasive, plants can produce 50,000 seeds, though it still had a bit to go to the flowering stage.

On the other side of the Loch Wood, bordering the loch, there was a veritable feast of wee birds. Robins, young and old, were everywhere, as were great tits, and a song thrush flew into the wood in front of me. I could see several small brown (brown again!) birds just inside the wood so I sat on a tree trunk in a clearing for a while. One of the wee brown birds landed on a branch above me and as I was scanning up with the binoculars a tree creeper appeared in view before I had got to the never-to-be-identified 'wee brown bird'. I watched it hop up the tree with great ease, pecking at lichen to dislodge or uncover any insect morsels below. The tree creeper is yet another brown bird, this time with a white breast and a longish curved beak that has been adapted over thousands of years to secure it this specialised feeding niche. Its most unique feature is its extremely stiff tail, which it sits back on and uses to balance as it lands on or climbs a tree. Because of this rough usage, its tail feathers often look very tatty. It flew down to near the bottom of an adjacent tree and started its ascent all over again.

The birds seemed to be getting used to me sitting there quietly and I got good views of many of them quite close up for a change. Many were willow warblers. I'm getting better at identifying warblers, with one of the key points of a willow warbler being its very pointed beak. I was also aware of a redstart in the distance. It gradually came closer and for a while it was on the ground quite close to me so that I could easily watch it without binoculars. Its name, redstart, is completely appropriate, as when it flies off the display of rust-red on its tail is 'startling'. My half hour on the log was an absolute treat.

As I made my way back again round the lochside I thought that would be it for the day, but at the outflow from the loch there was a chocolate brown dipper feeding. It was on one of the concrete walls separating the different channels at the overflow when I saw it first. It bobbed two or three times, showing off its white bib, then hopped into the shallow water of the overflow. I was not sure whether there would be much food for it there as the dam and overflow were reinforced in 2010 and the bottom of the channel might still be quite sterile, but I doubt it would be wasting its time if there was nothing edible. Interestingly, I had a lot of dippers in the burn that runs through my property until the visiting mallards multiplied to quite high numbers (I had as many as 70 mallards some years). The dipper numbers crashed, most likely because the mallard were eating the caddis fly larvae, but now that mallard numbers have decreased I'm seeing dippers much more often.

The red-legged partridges will be delivered to the estate in the next couple of weeks, weather permitting. I'm looking forward to seeing and hearing them on the hill again.

New birds identified: common gull; great tit; stonechat; greenfinch; goshawk; red-legged partridge; spotted flycatcher; song thrush; tree creeper; dipper
New mammals identified: none

Chapter 4

Monday 8 August. Weather: Cloudy but with lots of bright intervals. Very windy.

No red-legged partridges yet. The weather had been so bad that their delivery was delayed. Forecast for this week is no better, with heavy rain from mid-week onwards.

Birds were spectacularly absent today, probably because of the very strong wind. There were 40 or 50 mallard on the pond above the shooting lodge, and still some rooks and jackdaws in the sheep field, though they had abandoned the re-seeded field where they were foraging on my previous visit. There were still some lapwings, probably 30 or so, intermingled with the rooks. At this time of year they are silent, but I'm really looking forward to hearing their lovely *peeeee-weep, weep-weep, peeeee-weep* calls next spring as they skydance in the manner of a male hen harrier over their chosen nesting area.

I walked out the hill road, and past Dank Wood without seeing or hearing a bird apart from the distant chattering *chak-chak* of jackdaws. At least there were deer about, and I sat and watched three fallow does with one calf, and what I thought was a buck. The reason I was not sure was that I couldn't keep the binoculars steady in the wind, and couldn't be sure that what I thought were two thin antler spikes weren't in fact ears. All of this group of fallow were the lovely light dappled colour. They moved slowly through the bracken, making their way up a gully. Their light colour made them stick out like beacons when they were against a heather background, but when they were in bracken they blended and seemed to just disappear. The (suspected) buck was ahead of the rest of the group and I thought if I continued on round the corner of the hill road I might just meet him coming up the gully. As it turned out my timing was not bad and he crossed the track just in front of me. It was indeed a buck, with short spikes of antlers more like a young red deer staggie. He got a fright – I think from a blue-coloured pheasant feed bin he suddenly passed on his left – and came running towards me, but got a bigger fright when he saw me and took off through the heather. I waited for a bit to see if the rest of the deer would come up the gully, but the wind would now be carrying my scent to them and I suspect they would have doubled back.

I marched on up the hill road, admiring the heather now in full bloom and creating a lovely purple carpet intersected by ribbons and patches of mid-green bracken. Occasionally the sward of green was broken by a frond or two of brown, dead bracken. One of these tiny patches caught my eye high up on Middle Hill. For some reason it looked slightly different. Maybe it was just instinct, but I put the binoculars on it… and it was a lovely russet-red roe doe. It was barely moving, so was either enjoying a very rich patch of grass, or was watching me. I could only see the back-end behind a lone holly bush under a crag on the hill, but it was moving, though almost imperceptibly. Eventually its head showed, and it had indeed been feeding. I found a trackside rock and sat to watch for a while, keen to see if it had a fawn – or even a pair of fawns – at foot. After 15 minutes my opinion was that it had no fawns. It was in remarkable condition, fat and sleek. Those I had seen nursing fawns were noticeably thinner, with coats that had nothing like the gloss of this doe. I left it, undisturbed, browsing on the jagged leaves of the bush beside which it had earlier been feeding.

I heard my first buzzard of the day. It was circling at the bottom of Grey Crags and most likely one of Middle Hill pair (or trio) I had seen on previous visits. It mewed for 10 minutes or so as I walked through Middle Hill, then disappeared. With the heather in full bloom, I was amazed how many honey bees were out and about, especially considering the wind. There are a dozen or so beehives on the hill in the middle of the drive named Victor's Nightmare. Victor is a friend of the estate owner, and I can only assume that Victor was shooting on this drive one day and despite being a good shot had an extremely low cartridges-to-kills ratio (and no doubt was mocked relentlessly by the rest of the guns). When I looked across at the beehives with the binoculars there were literally thousands of busy bees swarming about outside the hives, coming and going in their endless task of gathering pollen. There would be no shortage of pollen today. A lone small tortoiseshell butterfly captured my attention as it landed on a patch of mud at the roadside ditch. It sat for a long time with its wings fully out, relishing both some shelter from the wind and the blink of sunshine. This is one of the most common butterflies in the UK, with the top of its wings bright orange and black, and with a row of light blue triangles round the edges. The short stop to watch it gave me time to appreciate just how many honey bees were in the heather within a few feet of it. This area might have been the bee restaurant of the day, though I suspect the heather all around would be just as popular.

I walked a further mile or so to the top of the gorge bordering North Eerie, then turned left to explore an interesting-looking quad bike track that headed south over the hill. The first part was boggy, but further on as it became slightly drier I spied a single fox pad in the mud. It had been torrential rain the day before, so the fox must have passed this way during the night. As I walked along the quad bike track there were another couple of probable fox pads, but not clear enough for me to be certain. I went over the top of the hill and started the descent on the other side, but the track came to an end at an old derelict partridge pen. I learned later from the keeper that partridges seemed to hate this particular bit of hill and this pen was no longer used. My meanderings disturbed a roe doe, which ran off up the hill behind me. Like the last one it had no fawns and was in superb condition. I wondered if the incredibly cold and snowy winter had made roe deer lose condition so that only those that had fared the best had managed to produce milk for fawns when they were born in May. Those, like this one, that didn't have fawns would gain condition quickly once the snow had gone and there was a welcome new flush of grass. I also wondered if, like rabbits, deer can re-absorb foetuses back into the body during adverse conditions, but I can find nothing to confirm this.

Now that I had run out of track I had lunch on top of a huge flat rock to consider my next move. I'd a great view to the south of the estate, over the big fishing loch in the distance. Through the binoculars I could see that there were at least five boats out, with the anglers preferring the north shore, which was the lee shore, rather than battling the waves in the centre. Two pairs of swans didn't mind the waves, and were feeding near to the south shore. A pair of buzzards was circling over a pheasant release pen in the Henhouse Wood, and I watched for a while to see if there would be any attack on poults, but the buzzards seemed uninterested and eventually drifted off over the Pheasant Wood. Unusually, according to the owner and keeper, hardly any poults had been killed by any kind of predator so far this year. Buzzards feed a lot on rabbits and voles, on frogs and lizards, and on invertebrates like worms and beetles, and with the wet summer there would be no shortage of those. Though there are sparrowhawks on the estate, which I have seen regularly in past years, I had seen none since I started this survey. Neither had I seen any further sightings of the goshawk or any evidence of its kills.

As I contemplated my route I remembered from my first visit to the gully now somewhere to my west, which ran from one side of the hill to the other, the 'mini-mountain pass' I'd cut across though travelling in the other direction. I could see a gully on my right and walked west along the ridge of the hill to have a look, but it was a different gully. It certainly would have taken me off the hill and to the Creag Bheag Wood to the south, but I didn't fancy going through the waist high bracken in and below the gully to get there. I crossed the next ridge of hill and realised that I was now at the pass I was seeking, except there was a frighteningly steep decline to get down to it. I began the descent, through knee-high heather, and the further I went down the slope the steeper it became. I had to move right a bit as I could see the route straight ahead was vertical. I continued down and right, to find that the last 20 yards were still near vertical. I thought about going up again, but when I looked up, the thought of going through the high heather 'against the grain' as it were, meant that I quickly binned that option. With great care, I slithered and scrambled this last few yards down. There was a real risk of falling, but I thought, with the relatively short distance, at least I wouldn't be killed! I made it (otherwise I wouldn't be typing this) but reflected that at my age I should really be past this sort of bravado and foolhardiness.

Now that I was on the mountain pass my journey was easier, but with the scree on the steep path rolling and sliding beneath every step I took I would have much preferred walking uphill rather than down. A single ragwort plant swayed in the wind at the path-side. I pulled it out of the ground, thinking that I was doing my bit to prevent this plant, poisonous to horses, to seed and spread. My efforts were wasted, however, as when I passed a bush in the centre of the path which had been blocking my view of what was beyond, there were another 100 ragwort plants! On the positive side most of them were hosts to hoverflies, which are beneficial in being voracious predators of aphids and of pollinating plants.

Creag Bheag Wood, the long narrow wood running from the Hill Loch at the western boundary of the estate back towards the centre, was now in front of me. The east end of the wood is where the goshawk flew to on my previous visit. At the time it had disturbed a cloud of wee birds, so I thought I'd make for there to see if I could find out what species they might be. I walked along the quad bike track in the centre of the wood and found a rock to sit on at the far end. I sat for about 15 minutes but saw not a single bird. It was as if they had all been drowned in yesterday's downpour, or blown away by today's wind! There was a huge nest high in the tree above where I was sitting. I wondered if it had been the goshawk's nest, though could well have been a buzzard's. In any event there were no prey remains underneath or any 'whitewash' from the young birds squirting their faeces over the edge of the nest, so it most probably hadn't been used this year.

I left the wood and sat on a nice grassy sward that was surprisingly dry considering the excessive rain not 12 hours earlier. In front of me was the marshy area where I had watched a roe doe and single calf on an earlier visit (just before I had seen the goshawk). Running along the top of the marshy area is the Craigie Face, and directly ahead of me, between the marsh and the Ell Wood, is a grass field which had been re-seeded the previous year and had a lush crop of grass. The only occupants of the field were a dark-coloured fallow doe and its calf. The doe was dark on top and light underneath, with the division being a virtually straight horizontal line similar to that of a 'high trace' clip given to some horses in winter to stop them sweating when exercised. Those who have seen this can now imagine exactly what the doe looked like. Its calf was light brown with a really dark coloured head. I don't know if this dual colour is common but it's something I'll look out for.

After my rest I cut along the bottom of the Craigie Face towards a pheasant and partridge drive called 'The Shudder'. This took me round the top of Ell Wood, which is where the largest number of pheasants are reared on the estate. It is an extremely boggy wood and not at all pleasant to walk through, but for some reason the pheasants seem to love it. There were 50 or so in the field on the far side of the wood, and almost as many rabbits. One curious female poult came up to me, stopping only three or four feet away and looking at me as if I were its long lost pal. I stood still, and it walked round me to get a better – or different – view. I told it that it better sharpen its wits if it wanted to see the New Year, and left it to ponder my advice.

So no new birds had been seen to add to my list today. I headed back towards my car, having probably walked about 10 miles, but first had a look in the Larch Wood en route back to see if any wild birds were visiting the feeders. None were, as it was probably too early in the year, with plenty food still about. The only bird – apart from pheasants – I saw in the wood was a song thrush. But I *heard* a bird I can add to my list: a great spotted woodpecker. These are frequently in my garden and I am well acquainted with their call, which is usually a single '*chik*'. In spring birds are more often heard than seen. Though there are as many birds about in August, by and large they are silent, with the just the odd exception, which in this case gave the game away… and saved me having a day without a new bird being identified.

New birds identified: great-spotted woodpecker
New mammals identified: none

Chapter 5

Monday 15 August. Weather: Sunny with some cloud cover from time to time. Light wind.

Apart from the ubiquitous pheasant poults that were scurrying about all the way up the estate drive the first birds I saw today as I arrived were two dippers. They whirred across the loch at the shooting lodge close to the surface, one of them at one point touching the water, and landed at the edge of the loch just out of my sight. It's more unusual seeing dippers at lochs rather than at running water, but the water at the edge might just have been shallow enough for them to have an underwater exploration for caddis fly larvae and other aquatic insects.. I'm sure they'll nest somewhere along the burn that runs from the loch, which has waterfalls and in places has carved a deep gorge out of the rock. I'll be interested to see if I can spot their nesting place in the spring.

Half of the partridges are now out in the pens on the hill, but I decided against a walk to the hill today as it is a perfect day for a sail. The estate has the adjacent large fishing loch, long-famed for its quality of fishing and, from what I gather, improving daily. I had a coffee with the owner at his newly-built café/restaurant/boardroom/office at the east end of the loch, and admired two of the fish recently caught, now stuffed and displayed in glass cases on the wall of the fisherman's café. Both were brown trout, one of 14 pounds and the other slightly bigger. The owner's daughter showed me a photo of a 22.5 pound rainbow newly caught and about to join its salmonid cousins on the wall.

I had boat No. 11, one of the fleet of three-seater boats 12 feet long and made of glass fibre-reinforced plastic. I think it is the first boat I have used on a loch that hasn't been sloshing with several inches of water *inside!* The boat is powered by battery, with a very easy-to-operate control on the tiller: turn one way to go forward and the other way to go backwards. The further the handle is turned the faster it goes – in either direction. It was a pleasure to drive (if that's the nautical term), and something a five-year-old could easily master. Twelve boats were already out on the loch and I was ready to join the fleet, though with different purpose.

The loch is about three quarters of a mile long by just over quarter of a mile wide. It was not the flat calm I had expected as a breeze had got up while we were having coffee, but the slight ripple caused a delightful lapping sound as the bow of the boat pushed ahead through the water, reminiscent of gentle waves gently vying with each other to be first to come ashore on a sandy beach (it was as close as I'd had to a seaside holiday this year). Apart from the low electrical hum of the engine and the pleasant sound of water there was hardly another sound to be heard. Anglers on a loch, in common with most folks who enjoy the country, make little noise. Even when I passed quite close to another boat the quiet chat of its occupants was barely audible. It was simply heavenly, and as far removed from noisy city traffic or rowdy football crowds as could possibly be imagined.

There was a raft of a couple of dozen tufted ducks ahead. (It's almost impossible to count diving ducks as you can never be sure how many are under water.) They are well used to the boats and tolerate them quite close, swimming away rather than taking off if they feel the boat is getting *too* close. The males were smart wee fellows, with their predominantly black plumage with a large patch of white on each side and white bellies. Like the goldeneye, with which they are sometimes confused, they have a bright yellow eye, but their black crest at the back of the head, rather like that of a lapwing, is their trademark. They lack the white spot on the cheek, which is the main identifying feature of the rarer goldeneye. The females, in common with most female birds, are fairly drab, being a dark brown all over, with a shorter and less imposing crest. They bobbed about like corks, more intent on resting than feeding.

Near the tufties there was a group of five mallard, probably a female and the grown-up survivors of a brood reared earlier in the year round the loch edge. There were reeds of different kinds skirting most of the loch's edge and I'm sure this would be perfect for many species of nesting birds, though mallard might be more inclined to nest further into the woodland. I had gone right to the far end of the loch to get away from most of the anglers, and cut the engine to drift for a while as the owner had told me an otter was quite often seen at the quieter top end. No otter today, but another competent fisher came into view: an osprey quartered the loch for about 20 minutes looking for a late piscine breakfast or early lunch. It was definitely keen on fishing and flew quite low for much of the time. Several times, looking through the binoculars, I thought it was within touching distance, but when I lowered them it was still several hundred yards off. Like the tufted ducks, it seemed used to the boats and did not consider them a threat. I've never seen an osprey catch a fish, and I was disappointed when it gradually drifted across to a nearby loch. This area of Highland Perthshire has lots of nesting ospreys and this one could have been from any one of around 10 nests. Many of the trout in the loch will be too big for the osprey to tackle, but the owner told me at coffee that he regularly stocks the loch with several hundred smaller trout of about a pound in weight especially for the osprey, and tries to encourage the anglers to return these fish if they are caught. Considering the biggest trout I have ever caught was just over two pounds, and most have been little more than half a pound, I'd be very pleased with a 'pounder'.

There were four pairs of mute swans on the loch, spread out into what would probably be territories. Surprisingly none had grey/brown young in tow, and I was puzzled as to why this was. As I drifted, I watched an angler in the boat nearest to me play and land a trout. It was landed on the far side of the boat so I couldn't see what size it was but the relatively short time taken to land it indicated it could be one of the osprey snacks, especially when the angler returned it to the water. I could see that there was a great-crested grebe beyond the boat, so I gradually wended my aquatic way round the back of the neighbouring boat so as not to disturb the occupants' fishing. About 100 yards from the grebe I cut the motor and drifted quietly, watching the grebe and two chicks. The chicks were still quite young, maybe two weeks or so, but had gone past the stage of depending on hitching a ride on their mother's back. They were well out on the loch but seemed quite confident, sometimes exploring 15 yards away from their mother. Quite often they would roll over on their side to scratch their head with a foot, exposing their light grey bellies. But suddenly there was panic.

With having the binoculars to my eyes, I had a limited view of what was happening beyond the grebe family. The female alarm-called, making something between what I would describe as a growl and a '*churr*'. At the same time both chicks dived, and I heard splashing on the water which, when I took my binoculars down, was the male (which I hadn't seen up to this point) flapping over the surface to come to the assistance of his brood. The cause of the alarm was a cormorant flying low over the water directly towards the grebes. It passed over their heads and banked left as it approached me. The cormorant was behind me before the two grebe chicks surfaced. As fish eaters, I doubt if the cormorant would be a threat to young birds, but the grebes were taking no chances. With only two chicks, it's possible that earlier on they lost some of their brood to an avian predator, most likely one of the larger gull species, and their protective instinct had kicked in. I was impressed!

Though I was thoroughly enjoying myself on the boat, I now needed some exercise and started to head back to the mooring. On the way down the loch I passed another boat crewed by what looked like a father and son. The son had just hooked a fish, which seemed almost to be pulling him over the side of the boat. This was clearly more than an osprey snack and I cut the motor again to watch him play the fish for about 10 minutes, and eventually manoeuvre it over the landing net the father had waiting in the water. I'm not sure about the size because of the distance between their boat and mine, but it was certainly bigger than anything I've ever caught.

Having tied up the boat, I decided to go now to the mature woodland at the west end of the estate, referred to simply enough as the West End. I parked my car at the bottom of the track leading to the hill loch and donned my rucksack, lighter today as I was confident I wouldn't need waterproofs. I made my way quietly up the track through the wood that followed the course of the burn running from the Hill Loch. I met an elderly couple on holiday from England and had a chat. They had been up to the loch and were returning to their car. They were most impressed with Perthshire and so pleased that they could actually go and walk on the hills or through the woods, which they said they couldn't do in England. I told them I was bird watching and asked if they had seen any interesting birds or animals. 'Nothing,' they said. 'We've not seen any birds at all.' I walked on for another hundred yards, near where the guns are placed for the pheasant drive called the Fallow Rutting Stand, and sat in a clearing with my back wedged between the buttress roots of an old larch tree. It was the most comfortable seat I'd had so far on the estate. I could almost lie back and look at the trees and sky above me.

Despite the holidaymakers' view that there were no birds, I could see at least half a dozen birds flitting about from branch to branch at the top of nearby larches. Looking up at the sky, especially into the sun, all birds are just wee black dots and almost unidentifiable. However with some knowledge of their flocking and feeding strategy (they were extremely acrobatic, often upside down on larch cones) I suspected they were members of the tit family, though not long-tailed tits which are recognisable even in silhouette. The birds began to fly in groups to other trees, one landing to my left and slightly lower down. It was a coal tit, as were the rest of the flock. As I was looking up at them a much larger bird came into view: an osprey, my second of the day. It saw me and quickly veered off, but it gradually turned back again and seemed to be keen to come in to the wood. It is an ideal wood for an osprey to nest, though it may well just have been over-flying the wood to get to one of a number of nests that I know of on neighbouring estates.

The wood I was in was a fantastic mix of trees; predominantly oak, but with pine and several other types of coniferous trees (about which I'll need to learn more as I'm not great on trees). Oak trees mean jays, and I was not disappointed when families of jays regularly screeched at my presence. The burn ran alongside the track I was on, with a high number of ash trees and some rowan, many growing from the crags skirting the burn. It really is one of the most beautiful woods I've been in, though this is not surprising as this part of Perthshire is famed for its really old trees, and known as 'Big Tree Country'. At the top of the wood I stopped at the loch and had my 'piece'. The four resident (Polish) mute swans swam over to see me and I threw them some crusts. Swan feeding habits in Poland must be different as they ignored them, their stomachs probably full of weed from the loch.

I cut back to the centre of the estate through Creag Bheag Wood. When I came out in to the open at the far end of the wood I became aware of black ears down a grassy dip on my left – those of a fallow deer. I only saw its ears and it would be unable to see me, but it knew I was there. It stood for a minute or so, with ears twitching and forward-facing to catch the least sound that it might interpret as danger. Even though I never made a sound, the ears bounded off, gradually revealing a very dark fallow doe attached, and another mix of colours of fallow in tow. The owner had been surprised that I had still not seen Penelope, a pure white fallow doe that had been on the estate for many years, but she was in this bunch. There were another four does accompanying the black one and Penelope, with one of them being dappled. Three calves were in the group, amongst which was a beautiful very light sandy coloured one. I suspected it was Penelope's calf, a suspicion that was confirmed when momentarily the white doe broke from the group followed by the sandy calf. Fallow that grow up to be white are a creamy colour as calves so this one was destined either to be white or very light coloured. They stopped and turned to look at me for a few seconds, before walking quietly into the next bit of woodland, the Henhouse Wood.

I passed the duck pond in the Henhouse Wood – this time full of mallard whereas the last time it was empty – and cut along one of the estate roads in the direction of my car. My route took me past some sloe bushes, and I checked with interest, thinking of sloe gin for winter, but the crop was very poor. I walked past a cottage near to the estate house, a large house retained by the former owner of the estate, and stopped to watch a feeding frenzy of butterflies on a buddleia bush. I put my binoculars on them to get a better view, (I couldn't tramp over the occupant's garden) and saw that they were all peacocks. They were almost black when their wings were folded, but when they opened them they were a beautiful deep red, with circles of blue and bright red fore and aft, just like eyes – which of course they are meant to replicate in order to frighten off predators. While I was butterfly-watching, a willow warbler came into view (I'm definitely getting better at warbler identification) feeding off the insects on the buddleia, then a great tit. It was a really pleasant interlude.

When I got back to my car I reflected that I had just read a report on a nation-wide RSPB bird watch that said that a blue tit was the most commonly seen bird on the survey. Unbelievably I still hadn't seen one!

New birds identified: tufted duck; great-crested grebe; osprey; cormorant
New mammals identified: none

Chapter 6

Monday 22 August. Weather: Dry and cloudy, but mild, with a light breeze. Good shirt-sleeve day.

My observations started early today, with a young red squirrel running across in front of my car when I was just a few hundred yards up the estate road. It's a tremendous area for red squirrels and they seem to be doing well. The area is also great habitat for greys, though thankfully they are either scarce or absent, making the reds safe from the deadly squirrel parapox virus that greys can transmit. Grey squirrels had been present in considerable numbers when the present owner took over the estate, but he and his successive keepers carried out a control programme, so far as is possible with wildlife, to eliminate them. Now on the rare occasions one is spotted, George the keeper is on the scene quickly with cage traps. As I arrived at the top of the drive at the shooting lodge there was a flotilla of mallard on the loch, with a white one in amongst them. I looked to the far side of the loch and today there was not one but two black rabbits. A white duck and two black rabbits was a good start for more unusual sightings!

I parked my car and walked over to the top (west) end of the loch, crossing a new footbridge over the boggy area right at the head of the loch. I looked up the wee burn that feeds the loch, wondering if the trout in the loch might go up there to spawn, but, coming from a boggy area the bottom of the burn was muddy rather than the gravel-type habitat that fish need to spawn. I walked anti-clockwise round the Loch Wood at the south end of the loch. There's a great crop of rabbits this year, and bunnies of all sizes were scuttling everywhere. Myxomatosis thins them out most years, but is not nearly as damaging to the population as viral haemorrhagic disease (VHD) which seems to kill every rabbit in the area; they just suddenly vanish without trace, since most seem to die in the burrows. Thankfully, so far as I know, there has been no VHD on this estate. I noticed a buzzard tail feather on the ground, at the same time hearing a buzzard wheeling overhead. I'm sure this one would be the previous owner of the feather as it had moulted two from the centre of its tail, giving it a red kite-type silhouette.

There was a lot of activity from small birds in the Loch Wood. Unfortunately they were at the very top of the trees and difficult to identify. I picked out two as female chaffinches. I always had chaffinches down as seed eaters, but from their activity at the top of a fir tree they seemed also to be feeding on insects. (This was replicated by chaffinches later in the morning on an oak tree and on a birch tree.) I had another look at the plant I saw on an earlier walk and thought was giant hogweed. I could see now it wasn't on its own, and there were several others trying to poke through the bracken. I'm even more certain now that they are these foreign invasive plants, and need to be dealt with urgently.

I walked down the drive towards the public road for a bit, then turned left following quad bike tracks to a part of the estate I'd not been in before, across near the east march and part of the area called Geordie's Moor. It was real old-fashioned woodland, comprised mainly of large juniper bushes but interspersed with oak and birch. A very attractive white climbing plant was growing up round the edges of many of the junipers, giving the impression of the bush being surrounded by a low-lying mist. It was lovely woodland to be in, thronging with small birds and with rabbits and pheasant poults lining the grassy tracks criss-crossing it. Most of the birds seemed to be flying in groups between trees. They were certainly flying like finches, with typical undulating flight, and the ones that did stop on a branch long enough for me to get a look at them were mostly chaffinches. It seemed to be a chaffinch day. One, though, was a much more interesting bird: a female bullfinch. It stopped on top of a juniper long enough for me to get the binoculars on it, but even when it flew off its white rump would have clinched the ID. Coincidentally there was a bird on my roof at home two days earlier. It was chirping and I didn't recognise the sound. I thought of going back into the house for the binoculars, but was sure it would be gone before I came back. I did *think* it was a bullfinch, but never managed to confirm it… until the next morning. I was weeding at the gable of the house and it was lying dead on the ground; a female, having collided with a window. It was a plump wee bird, about house sparrow-sized, but with a much thicker neck and a pinkish-grey face and chest contrasting with jet black on the top of its head. Its black beak was short and broad and obviously suited to its specialist niche of feeding on a range of buds and seeds. What a great pity. They're not everyone's favourite bird due to their penchant for eating fruit buds, but they are just wee beauties.

One birch tree seemed to be full of birds, and I sat down to try to keep the binoculars a bit more steady, as the birds were in amongst the leaves and hard to identify. I looked for ages at two feeding together on the branch tips. I was 50 yards away but I could see they were a greeny-yellow colour. Initially I wondered about greenfinch, but they were smaller and more agile… and one had a black cap to its head. They were a pair of siskins. They were extremely busy on the birch branch, often hanging upside down, though it was hard to say if their target was seeds or insects. A couple of dozen birds flew out of that one tree, probably chaffinches again, but I kept my eye on the two siskins. Having been deserted, they thought they'd better join the flock – safety in numbers – and flew off in the same direction the finches had gone. I left the woodland across a marshy area, using the same tussocky 'stepping stones' that rabbits had been using. Their route was very clear, with the grass on the tussocks flattened and slightly muddy from the passage of many paws. They knew the area better than I did and if that route was good enough for them then it would do me as well.

Leaving Geordie's Moor I skirted the boundary with the estate to the east, making to cross the first of two parallel wooded ridges running from the boundary fence down towards the duck ponds.

As I came over the first ridge I spotted a small foxy-red patch near the bottom edge of the bracken on the second ridge. As always, these colour variations are worth investigating, and I brought the binoculars up. A roe deer was resting in the bracken, only 50 yards away. If I went any further it would see me and be up and away. It was time for a sandwich anyway so I quietly sat down on the grassy slope and opened my rucksack. The wind direction was good for me and provided I made only slow movements there was no way the deer would know I was there. By the time I had got my first bite of a salmon sandwich the deer was on its feet. It was a young buck with only one small branching spike near the top of each antler. It stood for a minute, then turned and sat down facing the other direction. Before it sat down I briefly saw that its left front leg was curled up and I wondered if it was injured. It was only down for a few minutes when it got up again, visibly uncomfortable. It was difficult to see clearly through the bracken but its left leg was curled up again.

The buck started to munch at some grass and gradually limped out of the bracken onto better grass at the edge of the ridge. The leg couldn't be broken or dislocated since the beast was able to curl it up, but it was not keen to put weight on it and moved only on three legs. I had a good look at its body when it was in the open, and it seemed in reasonable condition; no clapped-in flanks or dull, staring, coat. It may have been a recent injury, caused either when jumping a fence or dyke, or maybe more likely a stab from a stronger rival buck, as the rutting season was just ending. I finished my sandwich and had a drink of juice, wondering if there was any way I could get away from there without forcing the beast to run. It was in enough pain without my inducing the panic of a dreaded human suddenly appearing so close to it. Watching the deer flicking its ears in annoyance at pestering flies I was thinking I would try to slowly creep backwards over the ridge. In a way the flies were its saviour as, to get away from them, it took four or five faltering steps into dense bracken. I would be safe enough back-tracking now since, even if the deer saw me, it would consider itself safe in the bracken and remain there. I was glad my dilemma was solved.

In the 20 minutes or so I had been sitting on the grass, three dark-coloured fallow deer had appeared behind me. We saw each other at the same time and I froze, but the wind was blowing towards the deer and they took off. The group consisted of a doe and a calf, with a young buck also in tow, maybe last year's calf. It was a great corner for deer. When I skirted the bottom of the first ridge two roe deer took off from a large patch of reeds above the duck ponds and bolted towards the second ridge. Simultaneously all the ducks took off from the ponds and flew round in a wide circle. They were not alarmed at me as they are well used to humans; they probably just needed to stretch their wings. The exercise was infectious, because the flock of lapwings feeding in the sheep field also got up for some aerial exercise. Strangely they were joined by four starlings that mimicked every bank and twist with them. Starlings are clearly mimics in more than one way.

As I climbed the fence to go up the far side of the second ridge I picked up two owl pellets from the ground beside a fence post leading up to the wood known as Wericky, which is just across from Dank Wood. Without dissecting the tangle of fur and bones I've no idea what mix of small mammals the owl had been eating, nor what species of owl it had been, but owls are about and will hopefully be added to my list in due course. Before I headed out to the hill I sat and watched George feeding the ducks on the ponds now far below me. He scattered two bags of grain along the edge of the pond and he had hardly turned his back when the ducks descended on the feast. From the slightly different colours of the two lines of grain I assumed one might have been wheat and the other barley. Well-fed ducks!

Out on the hill I was momentarily surprised at the sound of red-legged partridges calling from every quarter. I had forgotten they'd now been released and was pleased to listen to their *ko-chic* and *chuk-chuk-chukaaar* calls in quadrophonic sound. I headed out the main hill road, then after quarter of a mile turned right along the track that skirts the march dyke with the estate to the east. I hadn't gone far when I spotted a red kite above me, so sat down to watch what it was doing. It circled a few times, and, though I was not quite ready for it, I had another sandwich since I'd found a comfy place on the bank at the edge of the track on which to sit, but the kite gradually drifted off north-west, roughly in the direction I was heading. My sit-down was short-lived, as I needed home a bit earlier than usual and I knew the circuit on which I was embarking was at least another two hours, so rucksack on again.

A few hundred yards further on there was a wet muddy patch on the road, and these are always worth investigating. Plenty bird tracks, probably pheasant poults, but there was another interesting one that I didn't recognise right away. The feet were mammalian, smallish – about three-quarters of an inch in length – and the claws at the front were quite clear. The foot marks were quite close together, much more so than a rabbit, and the beastie had been ambling, not hopping. I went through the possibilities: stoat – prints far too large; mink and pine marten – maybe the right size but the wrong gait, as both these animals lop along, and sometimes their trailing tail is also visible in mud. Any other creature had to be too small or too big. Except a hedgehog. Hedgehogs are less common out on the hill, preferring more arable or wooded land, but I'm sure there would be some around. I'd just read a report that hedgehog numbers have fallen drastically, possibly because of the number of road kills and the lack of insects through agri-spraying. Any that feel threatened elsewhere are welcome to make their way to my garden, as they are incredible slug controllers!

I continued round the track, at one point looking back just in time to see a lovely mature dappled fallow buck with huge palmated antlers studying me, before jumping the dyke over to the estate to the east. Further on there were two yearling dappled bucks, and I wondered if I'd just seen their father. I continued on to the end of the track, where there is a gate leading on to the neighbouring estate. I climbed the gate to avoid a boggy patch, and walked along the private road up towards the neighbouring house. I had to share the road with a herd of pedigree Aberdeen Angus cows, calves and a bull, which were convinced they had more right to it than me, and were reluctant to make space for my passage. They are lovely quiet cattle, and it's a pity that they have largely been replaced by faster-growing and much more flighty continental breeds, though I understand there is a renaissance in their popularity. Once past the cattle I climbed the fence back on to 'my' estate and started a mile-long uphill battle.

I was fascinated by the first part, which was through a flat boggy section beside the Chapel Burn before the climb proper began. I walked over mosses of every colour, from deep red, pink, bright green and yellow. It really was a great display of nature and I wished I knew a bit more about bryology. I then came on a mix of bell and ling heather, intermingled with a great crop of blaeberries. I collected a good handful of the dark blue berries and sat on a flat rock to relish their sweet taste. As I was picking them I saw red berries, but they were attached to the same plants and could only have been the unripe blaeberry fruits, which I avoided.

The climb-in-earnest began through heather that had been burnt in the runaway fire. I noticed that blaeberries and some bracken were already beginning to grow again. Most were growing through an underlay of moss and grass. This had probably been damp at the time of the fire and had prevented the fire going down into the peat. Though a large expanse was burnt, little real damage seems to have been done because of this underlay, and new heather will follow shortly. Several years ago I walked over an area near Amulree in Perthshire where there was a similar runaway fire, though in that case it had gone deep down in to the peat. A decade after that fire there was still little sign of heather re-growth. Where I was now the burnt heather had been long, rank heather, and the dry, hard stalks still remained. Naturally, all were lying facing downhill, and it was really tough going. At one point I looked down at my light-coloured trousers and for nearly a foot above the top of my gaiters it looked as if an undisciplined face painter with a black charcoal brush had gone mad painting cats' whiskers. Many youngsters would have been delighted with the design across their cheeks. At one point on the climb I nearly fell over three young dark-coloured yearling fallow deer resting in a patch of yellow grass. They scampered off for a few yards then, typically, stopped to look back at me. They seemed relatively unperturbed and trotted off up the hill. At one point they stopped in line astern, an equal distance between each deer, all looking back over their left shoulder at me. Their balletic and symmetrical pose would have done justice to a scene in *Swan Lake*.

Near the top of the hill I found and followed a path of heather that had been swiped by a specialised machine, sometimes used as an alternative to heather-burning. It ran along the edge of a ridge on my left, and I hoped it might lead up on to the top of the ridge, as that was the direction I wanted to go. A fox had made use of the easy going as well, and there were three fox scats in the centre of the path within a distance of about 20 yards. Two were old and desiccated, but when I picked the third up (I'd finished all my sandwiches by this time) it was more recent, but still more than a couple of weeks old. From the fur and small bones in the scats, and with minute jawbones visible, young rabbits and rodents seemed to have made up the recent diet. A small covey of grouse had spent the night on the path, and the piles of grouse droppings, like inch-long cylindrical pieces of brown minced heather, were more recent deposits than those of the fox. The path started to veer to the right, and downhill – not the direction in which I wanted to go – bringing my easy walking to an end. I could see a quad bike track in the distance, which seemed to go in the direction I wanted, but I was not sure that the two would meet. Somewhat reluctantly, I struck left up the long unburnt heather towards the ridge. This was even tougher going than through the burnt heather, and clouds of pollen came off the heather and dried my mouth. I was surprised to see honey bees working the heather. Though I didn't know at that time *exactly* where I was, I was sure that their hives were at least a mile away as the bee flies.

At the top of the hill the heather was shorter due to regular exposure to the wind. It was also growing vertically rather than down towards me, so going was a lot easier. I walked along the ridge hoping to have come out at the top of Grey Crags, but I was 300 yards short. Looking back from my position of height I could also now see that the swiped path had gone downhill, but had turned uphill again and met the bloody quad bike track. If only I had kept going...

I scrambled down to the track at Grey Crags and sat on a trackside rock to get my wind back. I scanned North Eerie and saw a red kite gliding along the ridge, something I hadn't seen with the naked eye. I watched for a minute or two then scanned left, to see a second red kite flying at almost ground level, then landing. It had a white wing tag on the right wing, though I couldn't see its left wing. Kites tagged in this way usually have different colours on each wing, but even after it took off it never offered me a view of its other wing. They are one of the most graceful of birds of prey, and one of the most easily identified, even at a distance or in silhouette, because of their forked tail.

I was pleased to be going downhill now, and marched down to Middle Hill. Only one buzzard was 'on duty' there today, but its actions were different to those I'd watched on earlier visits. Formerly they were soaring lazily high in the sky, but today the buzzard was actively hunting at a much lower level, quartering the hill like a springer spaniel. Might this now be because the partridges are out and about? With the bracken cover they will certainly be hard to catch, and in any case the buzzard can't be grudged what is its natural prey. Partridge kills by a variety of predators are inevitable and are accepted by the owner and keeper, though they have noticed that, like pheasant predation, partridge predation is much lower than normal this year. This is possibly because the birds were a bit older when they were released, and consequently more switched-on to danger.

I encountered three of the partridges on the track as I walked towards my car at the shooting lodge. They were dusting and enjoying their freedom. As I got closer they trotted down the track for a few yards then diverted into the thick bracken at the trackside, where they would be absolutely safe from avian predators at least. The industrious bees were in their thousands round the hives, and if the work I'd seen them carrying out gathering pollen is anything to go by it should be a good honey season. All the way down the track to the more arable land the hills resonated with *chuk-chuk-chukaaar*. It is an alien sound, as these partridges are not native to the UK, but extremely pleasant nonetheless.

New birds identified: bullfinch; siskin
New mammals identified: hedgehog

Chapter 7

Monday 29 August. Weather: Dry and cloudy with some sunshine. Stiff breeze.

When I arrived on the estate and parked at the shooting lodge there was a feeling of autumn in the air, reinforced by lines of swallows perched on telephone wires. A high proportion still didn't have long streamers on their tails, being this year's young. It seems to have been a successful breeding season. I checked the house martin nests under the eaves of the estate owner's house. All were empty, and that will certainly be their last brood of the year. Like the swallows, they will now be building up their strength for the long and perilous flight back to Africa.

I made my way towards the hill, noticing that there was still a large flock of lapwings in the sheep field above the ponds. A group of six starlings were feeding with them, and no doubt would join them again in a circuit of the field if the lapwings deigned to do so. I spied away across to the hill to the Craigie Face and watched a kestrel mobbing what I initially thought was a buzzard, but after a minute or two I saw white above one of its wings, which a buzzard doesn't have. As the bird turned I could just make out the forked tail, though the bird was a mile or more away. The white on the top of its wing was a tag, and confirmed the bird as a red kite. The kestrel pestered it for a good five minutes (though I've no idea how long it had been mobbing it before I picked them up on the binoculars). It then gave up and the kite drifted north-westwards along the hill and landed on a rock.

I walked round Dank Wood, but, apart from two buzzards, things were quiet bird-wise as August always is. It could be that many of the summer migrants had begun to make their way south in readiness for crossing the English Channel in due course, and it would be another month before the winter migrants started to arrive. At the top of the wood I found an antler cast by a red deer stag. It had three points, so had been a young beast. The antler was partly chewed, a practice in which many deer indulge to recover some of their calcium. I'd still to see red deer on the estate, though this was certainly evidence of their presence.

I met a pack of about 40 red-legged partridges on the hill road. They had been dusting, and stood looking at me for a few minutes before trotting off further down the road then into the bracken. The hill was quiet. No deer about and no birds except for the many meadow pipits that flew ahead of me; short flights, landing every so often on heather or bracken at the side of the track until they were out of their comfort zone at my approach, then curling back over my head. Even the bees were quiet, and must have been at home. It maybe was too windy for them and when I put the binoculars on the hives there was not a bee to be seen. Just when I thought that Middle Hill had even been deserted by the buzzards I heard them mewing far above me. I scanned round and saw them lifting off from rocks and come sailing across at a high level. I couldn't help but think they'd been watching me and it was my presence, more than half a mile away that had caused them to move. I watched them for a while. One glided right down towards the lower ground, while the second circled round to its right and landed on a rock half way up Grey Crags.

In any case I was making for the left hand fork in the road, the shallow gorge that led up the side of North Eerie (rather than the right fork up Grey Crags), but didn't see or hear the buzzards again. There were some feathers of a male pheasant poult on the track just after the fork, which must have been a kill by some predator, maybe one of the Middle Hill buzzards, or maybe a golden eagle that the owner and keeper had both seen several times but which had always been absent when I was there. The chances are the eagle would be an immature bird, as satellite tagging has shown that they drift round Scotland (and sometimes even into the north of England) until they are of breeding age at around four years of age and have claimed a territory. I walked a further hundred yards up the gorge and sat on a track-side rock where I'd a good view back in the direction I'd come. I sat for a good half hour, passing the time by having the first of my slices of pizza. A pheasant poult jumping in alarm straight out of the bracken took my attention and I watched to see if it had been a fox that had been the cause. Other poults were pecking away quite contentedly not too far away, so it seemed to have been a false alarm.

Nearer the top of the North Eerie ridge, past the gorge at the bottom end where I'd just come up and where the sides open up a bit, there were another 40 or so red-legged partridges on the road ahead of me. They trotted along on the road and seemed reluctant to move into the long heather at the track sides. They were beginning to get too far from where they had been released and I was a bit concerned they would take off and finish up on the neighbouring estate to the west, so I cut left through the heather to get ahead of them. When I re-joined the track I could see them scurrying away back to where they'd come from. Right at the top of North Eerie I sat on another rock with a view across the boundary. I scanned the three lochs far below on the neighbouring estate, but if any water birds were on them the white-topped frothy waves hid them from view.

I had intended to return back down the gorge and cut along behind the beehives, but decided against that and instead cut left handed and made for the deep cleft in the hills that I've called the Mountain Pass. The descent on the south side of the hill is really tricky, as it's scree on an extremely steep track. Several times my foot rolled on a piece of rock and I nearly went down. I think I'll limit my use of this hazardous mountain pass in the future, at least in this direction. There was one advantage in that it was sheltered from the north-west wind. Thankfully the sun had also come out and it was getting warm. The heat had also brought out hoverflies, and dozens were feeding greedily on the ragwort where the path started to level out a bit nearer the bottom. Though ragwort can be poisonous to horses, it is a great source of nectar and pollen, and a number of insects totally depend on the plant. It can't be all bad!

I entered Creag Bheag Wood, a mature wood of conifers, mostly (I think) Norway spruce that had been thinned to decent spacing at some time in the past. I almost stood on a single chanterelle mushroom, and had a look about for more as they are delicious sautéed, but it was all on its own. I was a bit surprised to see it in any case as they are normally either under beech or birch trees. Further along there was a young puffball toadstool. I've never tried these, but they are meant to be tasty. A roe buck suddenly ran across my path, the only deer I had seen, and just a fleeting glimpse.

At the end of Creag Bheag Wood I came out into the grassy area and sat down; grass is much more comfortable than rocks. This was a good position to see right along the Craigie Face and also down over the woodlands in the centre of the estate. A flock of birds, a green tinge obvious in the sunshine, flew from an old birch tree ahead of me. Their undulating flight and the colour confirmed them as greenfinches. I was surprised when about 10 minutes later a jay flew screeching from the same tree into the wood I had just come from. I could hardly think it had just become aware of my presence. At the same time another jay joined in the screeching from Creag Bheag Wood just behind me. They are one of my favourite birds; it's just a pity that they don't sit still in front of you so you can admire their amazing mix of colour.

After my comfortable seat I made down the hill to the duck pond in the Henhouse Wood, and watched the mallard on the pond. The young drakes' feathers were beginning to get some more colour to them and before long they would be totally different from their drab female counterparts. Their beaks were beginning to show a greenish-yellow colour, contrasting with the brown beaks of the females. Still with few species of birds to show for my day's walking – probably about eight miles so far – I made for the loch back at the shooting lodge. The four swans and a flotilla of mallard were on the loch – though not the white one – as I passed its south shore. The black rabbit scuttled from the reeds and stopped at the edge of the Loch Wood, eyeing me up from 20 yards away. It was a well-grown rabbit from this year, and its coat had an incredible sheen to it. I hope it keeps clear of myxy. I sat down on a log in a clearing in Loch Wood and waited to see if any wee birds would appear. Meantime half a dozen pheasants were dusting at the entrance to rabbit burrows, with a rabbit sitting beside them as a curious but perplexed onlooker. A roe buck gave a loud cough to my right before bounding out of cover towards the edge of the wood. No wee birds were to be seen, and though I had thoroughly enjoyed my day I had no new bird species to add to my list. It is the transition period between summer visitors and winter visitors, and I look forward to new species returning towards the end of September.

New birds identified: none
New mammals identified: red deer

Chapter 8

Monday 5 September. Weather: Dry and sunny.

The red squirrels are busy now gathering and storing food for the winter. I drove very slowly up the estate road and saw two on the ground in the wood to my right. They were industriously searching for suitable morsels to stash away in a variety of nooks and crannies known only to them so that they might have an easily-found bite to eat on the warmer winter days, when they can venture out of their cosy drey. I parked at the shooting lodge, having decided to look at some of the woodlands on the lower ground today before going to the hill. I made my way up to the Larch Wood, noticing when I looked back to the sheep field that its only occupants were sheep and rabbits. The bird life had moved to the recently sown grass field at the other side of the estate road. There was a real mixture: lapwings, starlings (these two species seem to be particularly compatible), rooks, jackdaws, pheasants, red-legged partridges and, right in the top corner near the cottage with the poultry, hens and cockerels. Had these birds been grass-eaters rather than invertebrate-eaters, there would have been no grass left.

I walked along the track through the Larch Wood, rather muddy after the heavy rain during the night and George's to-ing and fro-ing on the quad bike. At first it seemed quiet, but when I got to the far end beside the pheasant release pen I stood quietly for a while. And listened. The autumnal blend of sounds was incredible. Woodpigeons were bubbling their pleasant *hoo-ooo-ooo-ooo-ooo-ooo-hoo-ooo*. I always think that if this is their scanned line of music, which they repeat three or four times, it should end with *ooo*, but it doesn't; they nearly always add on an extra *hoo* at the end. Next time you hear a woodpigeon listen for this. A robin in a bush next to me was trilling its lovely spring and autumn song, and somewhere high above, a buzzard, settled in a tree rather than soaring in circles, was mewing mournfully. A flock of chaffinches feeding high in a larch tree were communicating with each other with a regular *tzweet* and, probably on the top of a dyke near the edge of the wood, a wren was sounding its alarm at a threat unseen by me, with an extremely high pitched *tic, tic, tic.* A flock of jackdaws passed somewhere overhead, chattering to each other with their distinctive and raucous *chak, chak, chak*. Lastly, the wood seemed alive with bees, with a constant buzzing high above my head.

I stood for nearly half an hour in appreciation of this veritable feast of sound, and at the same time trying to identify birds high in the tree tops. This was not easy in a mature wood and my neck was getting sore with the effort. Most were chaffinches, though I could see bigger birds flying into the tops of the same trees from time to time. My first thought was fieldfares, though I discounted these winter visitors as it was too early in the season. I eventually managed a quick look at one as it settled on a branch not obscured by other branches or leaves. It was a song thrush. Whether the rest were song thrushes I've no idea and I never did get a good look at another. I was standing beside the release pen, and a dunnock landed on the top wire not 10 metres from me. This was the first one I had seen on the estate, and I thought I'd be more likely to see them nearer habitation. Anyway I was pleased it had appeared, and realised that it's not always the more common birds that are seen first.

I then followed the release pen fence back and round to near the dyke at the edge of the wood. I was watching chaffinches at the top of a larch again when I spotted a much smaller bird, very similar in colour to a female chaffinch, but with a completely different feeding strategy. While the chaffinches were flying frenetically from tree to tree, hardly staying in the same spot for more than a couple of seconds, this wee bird was very methodically inspecting branches and cones, sometimes on top of the branch; sometimes underneath. It gradually picked its way along a branch until I could see the lovely streak of yellow along the top of its head, as if it had been among a flock of sheep when a shepherd was marking their heads with yellow identification keel (paint) marks and it had been similarly marked for good measure. I watched the goldcrest until I eventually lost sight of it, and when I turned to look at a larch tree behind me a red squirrel was sitting on a branch half way up, with a curious female chaffinch a metre away watching the squirrel intently, probably while the squirrel was watching me with equal curiosity. Mr (or Mrs) squirrel then ran along a branch, its bushy tail glowing almost gold as it passed through a ray of sun, before nimbly jumping to a branch on a neighbouring larch. I was thoroughly enjoying my visit to the Larch Wood, and there was more to come.

As I started off down the track to leave the wood I heard the *kew kew kew kew kew* of a green woodpecker, often nicknamed the Yaffle because of this call resembling a loud laugh. I remember this as the most common woodpecker of my youth, though it seems to have been almost replaced by the great-spotted woodpecker. This is the first time I had heard it for years and I looked forward to *seeing* it, which may be easier on a future visit when the leaves are off of the trees. Before I left the wood I was aware of the buzzing of bees again. I could see them high in a sycamore tree, and had a look through my binoculars. They were not bees at all, but wasps, hundreds of them. Whatever they were interested in it seemed to be on sycamore trees. I looked at other trees and no other type seemed of interest to them. I went back up the wood to where I had heard them earlier, and again the host tree was a sycamore.

Leaving Larch Wood I made for a point where I could sit and have a good view over towards the Craigie Face, and to my right, up Eerie Valley. Even before I reached my favoured rock seat, I saw a red kite off to my left, which gradually came towards me and flew low over my head. This bird had a white tag on the right wing and a red tag on the left wing. I suspect it had been the one I had seen several times – always at a distance – that I thought had two white tags. It joined a couple of circling buzzards and the three wheeled about for a few minutes before the kite peeled off round behind me. I had reached my rock, but couldn't sit on it today. It seemed to have a new use as a rabbit and red-legged partridge toilet, though the less comfortable rock beside it sufficed once I put my rucksack on it, opened the top flap, and sat on it as if on a saddle.

As I ate my piece the track leading to the field ahead of me, full of pheasant poults at a former visit, began to fill up with red-legged partridges. They virtually surrounded a three-quarters-grown rabbit that was sitting near the edge of the track scrupulously washing its face with its front paws. Neither species was concerned about the presence of the other and they went about their own business almost rubbing shoulders. After about 10 minutes the kite returned and had a playful swoop at two carrion crows sitting in the middle of the grass field ahead of me, making them jump, probably in mock alarm. It was interesting that neither the partridges nor the pheasant poults paid the least attention to the kite, clearly not seeing it as a threat. The kite landed on one of a line of beech trees at the edge of Ell Wood, which bordered the field on the east side, shortly after joined on the same branch by the carrion crows. They hopped gradually closer to the kite, one of them eventually sitting just a couple of feet from it. The stoical kite disregarded them, and getting no reaction that they could capitalise on to pester it further, the crows flew off in disgust. Kite: 1, Crows: Nil.

I walked up to the top right of the grass field, wondering if a walk along Eerie Valley would be worthwhile, but I could see through the binoculars that the track came to an end and was only to facilitate the guns on a shooting day to get to their pegs. I decided against it. There were a handful of lone trees on the hill and my interest was taken with what I at first thought was a laburnum. It bore cascades of what appeared to be yellow blossom, but a laburnum is one of the earliest springtime trees to bloom and of course we were now in early autumn. A scan with the binoculars showed that it was simply a birch that was turning, in a rather unique and beautiful way, into its autumn colours. The birch, rowan and chestnut seemed to be the first trees on the estate to anticipate the change to autumnal temperatures and were about to finish the year in a flourish of colour before hibernation. The leaves on one young rowan at the top corner of Ell Wood were already completely red.

I walked along the top of the grass field, past the gate on to Craigie Face for the guns to get to the pegs for The Shudder, and over the stile into the next field, a grass field re-seeded last year. The sun was blazing down and I sat for a while again on a comfortable rock against the hill dyke. Partridges at the other side of the dyke, unaware of my presence, were calling to each other, and the hillside echoed to their *ko-chic* and *chuk-chuk-chukaaar* calls. One flew on to the top of the dyke, so close I felt the draught from its wings on my face. It sat for a minute or so, then carefully walked along the top of the dyke, jumping down on my side, finally running full tilt when realisation of possible danger dawned.

Suitably rested, I walked on towards the far corner of the field, but stopped abruptly in my tracks as I was sure I heard a raven. The sound seemed to be coming from where I'd watched the goshawk fly into Creag Bheag Wood on an earlier visit. I looked with my binoculars and listened, but not a sighting nor further sound. I was annoyed that I couldn't confirm my suspicions, and started to walk diagonally across the field towards the gate at the bottom of Ell Wood. My beliefs were vindicated when I heard the *prukk, prukk, prukk* again. The raven must have circled north-westwards, and though I heard it several more times, and suspected it was probably somewhere over Law Wood, it was not showing itself today.

I made my way back, through a grass field recently vacated by cattle, to the loch at the shooting lodge. I came round the west end of the loch to see a heron rise from the burn running in to the loch and land again on the south shore. It was a young heron, still without the magnificent crest it would have by next year. I'd disturbed its fishing, but, knowing the size of the trout in the loch, I suspected there wouldn't be many it would manage to swallow. It would be better looking elsewhere for a meal of a more realistic size. I skirted the loch, watching my second myxy rabbit of the season stumble its way up the field in the direction of the wood. Despite its blindness it managed to find a burrow; one I'd just seen a rabbit clear of the disease entering. No doubt there would be a transfer of rabbit fleas and the vile man-induced disease would be perpetuated. I'd seen a rabbit earlier with just a touch of scabbing on its nose. This was myxy, but its eyes and ears were free. This would be one of the many with some immunity. It would get no worse than this and, barring predation, would survive to pass on its immunity to its progeny next year.

I relaxed for a while on a chair on the veranda of the shooting lodge (much better than a rock), watching trout rippling the surface of the loch as they sucked in flies, and the white mallard and some of its more ordinary companions resting in the sun on the island. I watched the swallows on the wires, sometimes 40 at a time, interspersed with an odd house martin. One wee swallow, just fledged, sat on the wires, flapping its wings wildly and opening its still-yellow gape every time an adult swallow flew near it. It was being well fed, but with probably less than two weeks to go until they leave en-masse for Africa, I couldn't imagine this wee soul ever reaching its winter residence. Before I left to head out to the hill, a pair of goldfinches flew past, their scarlet face, yellow-striped wings and white rump unmistakable as they disappeared behind me between the wood and the shooting lodge.

Leaving my comfy seat, I walked a couple or so miles out the hill to the bottom of Grey Crags, but the hill was eerily quiet. The Middle Hill buzzards were certainly there, but they must have been resting on rocks. One slipped silently off to the right round the shoulder of a hill, and shortly after I saw the other sneaking low over the skyline to the left. It was as if they had been up to something naughty and didn't want to be caught! The red-legs were quiet on my way out the hill, but there were some on the hill track on my way back, having been disturbed by George and Victor (of Victor's Nightmare), who were putting out pegs at which to place the guns for the first of the partridge shoots on 17 September. I chatted to them for a while before heading back to my car. It had been a delight to be out on such a fine autumn day.

New birds identified: dunnock, green woodpecker; goldcrest; raven; heron; goldfinch
New mammals identified: none

Chapter 9

Saturday 17 September. Weather: Heavy showers.

This was a visit with a difference to the estate, as I'd been invited to shoot at the opening partridge day. The partridge shooting season begins on 1 September, but many estates wait until the birds are a bit older and wiser before shooting. There were nine guns and we all got to know each other over a breakfast of tea, coffee and bacon rolls. The estate owner had not intended to shoot, but as one of the guns had to go home unwell after the second drive, he took his position. For those not acquainted with shooting, peg numbers are drawn at the start, with each gun moving up two places at each drive. I drew number 6.

Some people are completely against the shooting of game, even the culling of deer. If they don't eat chicken then they may have some sort of argument. Chickens are usually kept in intensive rearing sheds and normally killed at 45 days old. Pheasants and partridges are reared and released as poults, with a good proportion surviving through to the next season or beyond. I know which has the better life! Some people don't mind shooting, or are ambivalent in their views, provided the law is complied with. Shooting estates across the board get bad press because of the illegal killing of birds of prey (and sometimes other protected species) on some estates, particularly on driven grouse moors. All estates are not like this, with this estate most certainly being one of the exceptions. In this case it is not just as straightforward as complying with the law: the owner wants to see as wide a biodiversity of species as possible, including birds of prey that can sometimes impact in a negative way on game management. An eagle, which I have not seen yet, is causing havoc with pheasants on the hill ground. It will be killing very few pheasants – or maybe even none; it is just its huge presence that is upsetting them, and shifting pheasants from some of the hill drives on to lower ground. The birds are not being lost, just unevenly distributed. It is a problem the owner and his keeper accept they have to live with.

Before the shoot the owner gave the safety talk. Safety is the most important aspect of shooting. A careless shot could easily be fatal, and the rarity of fatalities – or even serious injuries – is testament to the attention shooting folk pay to safety. The species that could be shot today are red-legged partridges and snipe. Ground game – rabbits – are not shot on game shoots, though if a fox came through the line it could be shot provided the shot was safe.

On the first drive, named Shooting Butts, a red kite was circling to the west of the drive, its forked tail clearly visible each time it banked. My picker-up for the day, on spying it, said, "Buzzards are just everywhere nowadays." He was considerably older than me and has probably lived in the countryside all his life, yet didn't recognise this bird. Snap-shooting was the order of the day in this drive. It meant that some birds had to be shot at close range. For someone who eats what he shoots I couldn't get used to this as many of the shot birds would be so full of pellets as to be inedible. I only had four birds for the drive; those that were passing slightly wider right or left.

The next drive, Middle Hill, was interesting in that one of the Middle Hill buzzards passed over the drive and shifted some of the partridges before the drive started. It was an example of how a bird of prey *can* make a difference to the number of birds shown over the guns. The birds, of course, were not lost: they had simply moved down on to the next drive but one. I was at peg number 8, which was quite quiet, and though I fired half a dozen shots they were all misses. I've twice shot grouse in my early twenties when numbers of grouse at the end of November were too high and the keeper invited the beaters to shoot and beat time about. Though the grouse were difficult, I have found that the partridges on this estate are even more so. On some drives (like Shooting Butts) snap shooting is required. On Middle Hill the birds were low but wide to the left (I couldn't shoot those to my right as I was high above the rest of the line and I would have put my fellow guns at risk).

The next drive was Victor's Nightmare. I was at peg number 2 and was told that I would have a very short skyline. When I got to the peg I had indeed a short skyline, but there was a second, more distant, skyline where I thought I would see the partridges coming. I *did* see them coming, but the devils disappeared into a dip and re-emerged at my 'short skyline', creating extremely difficult snap shooting. I managed a couple in front and, after the horn was blown for no more forward shooting as the beaters were getting close, I took two birds behind over my left shoulder. Birds flying over my right shoulder might have been easier but I was conscious of my picker-up 10 yards behind me and to my right. He was crouched down in the heather and he said he would be safe if I fired over his head. He would have been but his position was off-putting, so I stuck to birds on my left. There were plenty of opportunities and, like the other guns, I was not out to break records.

The next drive was called Dank, being the nearest to Dank Wood, and I was at peg number 4. This was the drive into which the Middle Hill buzzard would have shifted some birds. At the start of the drive the rain came down in torrents. I had no hat (it was in the Land Rover) and the rain was running off my head on to my jacket, then down my trousers and in to my wellies. I felt my feet rapidly getting soaked. Worse, my eyes were full of water and I had difficulty seeing. I maybe shoot more accurately in adverse conditions as I took a right and left out of the first covey of half a dozen that came past, crossing the line from my right to left. Despite the rain I shot well in that drive and finished with a respectable 12, all shot in front.

A lovely steak pie lunch prepared by George's wife Christine gave us all a chance to dry out, and when we got to the first of two drives in the afternoon – Eerie Valley – the sun was shining. The owner asked what peg I was at, and when I told him 'number 6' he said that was his favourite peg in that drive. He referred to it as 'The Hole'. It was indeed a hole. I was down beside a burn with a high bank in front of me. The early afternoon sun in the south was right in my eyes, but even without that I could see bugger all. I wondered how I would ever manage to shoot anything from here. Much of my shooting has been at rabbits bolted by ferrets. This is snap-shooting at its best, and this is what I had to do here. Even though the birds were higher than in any of the drives so far there was only a split second to shoot a bird in front. I managed 10 in front, including another right and left, and, surprisingly, two behind. This was probably shooting at its most difficult and I could see why the owner, probably one of the best shots in the country, liked this peg.

For the last drive, Eerie Return, I had to remain at this peg but turn round to face the other direction. Birds started to come early, even before the picker up – in front of me now since the birds would be coming off the crest of a very high ridge – had finished picking my 12 birds from the previous drive. This time they were flying exceptionally high, with the first of them from left to right down the valley. I shot one, then another one that for whatever reason was flying up the valley from right to left! The birds then started to come straight at me from over the towering ridge ahead. Though these birds would fly even higher as the season progressed, they were still high for me, though I managed to connect with seven of them. It is always good to finish well, and the last bird I took was high and wide to the left, killed stone dead.

I finished with a very respectable 41 birds for the day, by far the most I have shot in a day at a grouse, partridge or pheasant shoot. The variation on shots was exactly what was provided at a police clay pigeon shoot I attended at Gleneagles Hotel one day. I enjoyed that day, which probably helped me cope with these extremely testing drives. The day was completed with more of Christine's fare, this time tea and cakes, the late morning soaking a distant memory.

Chapter 10

Monday 19 September. Weather: Showers.

I had another 'boating day' on the big fishing loch. The weather forecast was dry in the morning and some showers later in the afternoon. The Met Office would get no prizes, as rain drops started to spatter the windscreen at 9.30 when I was still five miles from the estate. The light rain persisted as I turned in the road-end leading to the loch, but the day was brightened up as a roe buck ran across the road just in front of me and cleared the dyke – and the fence above the dyke – with an amazing jump that I've usually only seen at a distance or in the darkness. The buck ran a few yards into the grass field on the left of the loch road and stood and watched me. I stopped and watched it. Stalemate for a minute or two, but the buck gave in first and bounded off across the field.

My boat today was No 9. It was complete with a large landing net, which I wouldn't need, though the thought of dipping it in to the loch to land a sizeable trout tempted me to do just a bit more fishing in future. The loch was flat calm apart from the raindrops interspersed with much larger concentric circles as rising trout sucked in flies, some with a very loud *gloop*. These feeding fish are the ones over which to cast. As the fly lands somewhere within the concentric circles there is often another *gloop*, or a swirl and splash, and the fish is hooked… or not.

Anyway there would be no fish hooked by me as my main interest was in other wildlife, with the fish surfacing around me a pleasant distraction. Seven boats were out and, with no need to find a spot sheltered from wind, were well spaced round the loch. I headed left and passed very slowly through a group of 14 tufted ducks. They were diving regularly and paid scant heed to the silent boat in their midst. With no wind, the two anglers in the boat nearest to me were casting in opposite directions. This is often a recipe for disaster, finishing in a tangle as the two lines cross and collide, but not on this occasion. After a scan with the binoculars I thought the south side of the loch seemed clear of birdlife, so I head towards the top (west) end. An adult great-crested grebe was swimming just out from the reeds on the south shore of the bay, probably one of the parent birds I had watched on my first visit. Interestingly great-crested grebes are similar to birds of prey in that they start to incubate as soon as the first egg is laid. With larger clutches of up to six eggs this means considerable disparity in size between the first chick hatched and the last, with almost a week's difference. No doubt this is a survival strategy so that in years with less food available the smaller chicks will fall by the wayside, leaving the adults to concentrate only on the strongest.

Much further up the loch, I could see a couple of swans in the distance. As I got nearer I could see they were keeping close company with about 50 Canada geese. Canada geese are very smart-looking geese, with a black head and neck, white cheeks, a brown-grey body with white at the front end and at the tail end. I thought the Canadas were acting a bit strangely as they were keeping close to the reeds at the top end and were swimming close together, back and forward. Two or three on the right edge were squabbling and splashing with their wings. Some took off with much loud honking, and circled my boat before landing again in the same place. I was not sure what was going on but the geese seemed to be pestering a bird that was to the left of their flotilla. Initially it looked like a heron, but of course herons don't swim. I realised then it was a young great-crested grebe, most likely one of the two very small chicks I saw with their parents on the last visit, and now independent. I scanned further left, where there were two other birds. They were grey with a dark brown head and a lovely golden eye. They were goldeneye, diving ducks similar in some ways to tufted ducks. I suspected because of their colouring that one, mostly grey with a brown head, was female. The other had much more white on its lower body but still had a brown head. This would be an immature male, which doesn't get its greenish head and the large white spot at the top of its beak until it is an adult. They kept themselves to themselves, swimming off if the bullying Canadas came too close, or diving and coming up a safe distance away.

I relaxed watching this eclectic mix of wildfowl and even managed to take some photos with a small Canon camera with a 14x zoom lens I had just bought. I was pleasantly surprised by the results, as the last time I tried to photograph a live bird – a short-eared owl – it came out moth-sized and barely recognisable as a bird. Unfortunately, through my previous job as the force wildlife crime officer with Tayside Police, I've been much more used to the simple photographing of birds and mammals dead at my feet! I watched two anglers in a boat parallel to mine. They could see my interest was in birds rather than in fishing and respectfully went no closer to the birds than I did.

I moved across the loch towards the bay at the north-west end, giving plenty space to the anglers. I drifted very slowly along the west shore and put my binoculars up to look at what I at first thought was a lone tufted duck. I was not surprised to see that this was an otter, as I knew there was one in this part of the loch. I let the boat drift closer, as the otter raised its hump back out of the water and dived. I followed the line of bubbles in the water, and the otter surfaced again, even closer to me. I was sitting low in the boat, power off, with not even a ripple of water. The otter dived again, and came closer still. I was so enthralled I didn't think of getting my camera out. The otter was a mere 30 yards away and with the zoom, would have been a great shot. I saw that I was nearly in the reeds and didn't want to risk tangling the propeller, so the next time the otter dived I put the motor on to low power and slowly edged out into deeper water. The otter was now in the reeds, still on the surface and watching me. I was amused that a lot of the time its tail, as well as its head, was out of the water, forming a roughly 30 degree angle. It dived again, and this time I couldn't find where it came up, as I couldn't follow its bubble line in the reeds. I sat for 15 minutes or so but it never reappeared. In any event the sighting of a wild otter so close had made my day.

I went slowly down the north shore of the loch, where there were dozens of mallard under the oak and beech trees at the loch side. I was also pleased to see a female goosander near the mallard. It was hugging the shore line and I imagine, as a fish eater, would be getting small fish in the shallows. I sat watching for 15 minutes, then started up and began to head further down towards the moorings. I had only gone 50 yards and I was aware of two cock pheasants *cuck, cuck, cucking* on the shore, and two carrion crows voicing alarm as well. I wondered if a fox, a cat or maybe a stoat was on the go so cut the motor again. I saw nothing and was about to move off when I saw a bird flash into an oak tree behind me. By its speed and colouring I wondered if it was a sparrowhawk, so turned and headed closer to the tree. I stopped about 50 yards from the tree, to find that the bird was a jay. The bird was unconcerned, and sat on a branch for a full two minutes. Jays are normally so wary and so jumpy that it's unusual even to see one sitting still; they always appear to be flying. I had a great view of its pinkish-brown body, its pale streaked crest, almost like a wig, and of course the vivid blue and black barred patch on each wing. I watched the jay, and the two carrion crows which by now were sitting right on the top of the same tree. The jay then hopped around the branches, possibly looking for any remaining acorns and showing its white rump each time it half jumped, half flapped to a new branch, and was at last lost to sight among the higher branches. I marvelled at how close, sitting quietly in a boat, you can get to otherwise extremely wary wildlife. It is as if you are out of context and not recognisable as a human. In the same way, on another continent, safari vehicles full of humans are ignored by lions, cheetahs, gazelles and other African wildlife. I certainly enjoyed my water safari.

New birds identified: Canada goose; goosander; goldeneye
New mammals identified: otter

Chapter 11

Tuesday 11 October. Weather: Dry and sunny in morning, though with cool wind. Failed to realise that the weather forecast can sometimes be wrong and got caught in very heavy rain away out on the hill in the early afternoon!

I've missed being out and about on the estate. Between other commitments, avoiding shooting days, deer stalking days and bad weather, it has been just over four weeks since I had a quiet walk in the woodlands or on the hill. In those four weeks, the purple had gone from the heather and the bracken had changed from a lovely emerald green (if bracken can be lovely) to a rust brown. The hills had been transformed. The swallows and house martins were now in Africa and the first bird life that I saw was a skein of greylag geese flying southwards quite low in a V formation, with one leg of the V much longer than the other. I watched the geese change leader, then split to form two Vs, finally merging again into a rough boomerang shape as they disappeared over the top of the trees. Geese, and to a lesser extent, gulls, have this energy-saving flight formation perfected.

I headed for the Larch Wood, and was immediately aware of the mewing of buzzards up over Dank Wood. I lifted the binoculars and first found a pair of red kites. One was my old favourite, with red and white wing tags (one of the two chicks of this year), and I scanned the other one closely as it lazily banked, and confirmed it was not tagged. The buzzards, three of them, were in the distance, nearer Dank Wood. It was quite early – just after 9 am – and they seemed to be enjoying pitting their flying skills against the brisk and cool wind. It may have been them that disturbed the lapwings off the sheep field above the duck ponds, but 25 to 30 lapwings were circling in the sky, with, incredibly, almost the same number of starlings following exactly the same circling and banking pattern as their larger companions. This is becoming a common sight here, yet I've never seen it elsewhere.

I moved on up to and into the Larch Wood hoping for some small bird life, especially hoping to see or hear the green woodpecker. With the strength of the wind it was raining leaves inside the wood; mostly sycamore. It was a real sign of winter approaching and by their absence maybe the smaller birds thought that as well. We had endured weeks of strong winds and even the spiders' webs that normally abound at head height at this time of the year seemed to have been blown away. My meanderings disturbed a buzzard from the top of a larch tree, and it flew off mewing in complaint. There were plenty pheasants at the feeders, and red-legged partridges lifted in ones and twos at my approach and flew further along the wood. Apart from that, and a robin that ignored me and continued to sing in apparent merriment, the wood was pretty silent. I walked quietly up the quad bike tracks, much less muddy than on my last visit, and hung about for 15 minutes at the empty pheasant pen at the top of the wood. The wee birds seemed to be on holiday, so I gradually made my way back to the open gate at the beginning of the wood again.

From the Larch Wood I went to my favoured rock with a view across to the Craigie Face and up Eerie Valley. Miraculously some elfin cleaners had been out (or had it just been the recent torrential rain and gusting winds) and the rock was now purged of its former unsanitary mess. It was now spotless, with hardly a sign of its recent use as a rabbit and red-legged partridge toilet. It was also dry, making my rucksack redundant as a cushion. As I settled down, a dozen red-legged partridges made their way up the track towards the field then lifted off and flew towards Eerie Valley. Immediately, another dozen did likewise, then another two dozen, then about another five dozen. All flew in convoy and landed at the top corner of the grass field near the gate leading into Eerie Valley. A small brown bird landed on the wire of the fence at the spot the partridges had just vacated. A quick squint with the binoculars showed that it was a dunnock. It then took off almost following the flight path of the partridges. I watched its flight, which was several quick wing beats at a time, then a change of direction downwards, upwards or sideways. It was completely out in the open and vulnerable and I was in no doubt this was a tactic to confuse any avian predator that might have wanted dunnock as a mid-morning snack. It was a tactic in the manner of fleeing springbok on the African plains frequently bounding high into the air rather than following a predictable pattern that would allow a predator to anticipate and use to advantage.

This is a spot where I have regularly seen red kites, and I was not disappointed today. White and red tag came past and I even managed to see that as well as the wing tags, the sun was glinting off a radio antenna sticking out above its tail. As well as the locating of live birds by conservationists, radio antennae and satellite tags were invaluable in my former job in the finding and recovering of golden eagles, white-tailed eagles and red kites that had been poisoned. It is to be hoped that the fact these birds are more easily traced might also provide some deterrent to the criminals who unjustifiably want to kill them.

I walked up the grass field diagonally towards The Shudder partridge drive. As I walked I watched a couple of hundred jackdaws swirling around above the scree and trees of Craigie Face. Like the buzzards and kites earlier, they seemed to be making the most of the wind and I was in no doubt that their activity was playful rather than for any other purpose. When I reached the gate at the far corner of the field they were still enjoying themselves, and I was close enough now for a photograph. Any fright (or frights) they had from the deadly goshawk that had seriously disturbed them during the summer time had been forgotten.

I continued along the dyke-side separating last year's re-seeded grass from Craigie Face, but stopped abruptly when a bird flew up the field and landed on top of a juniper bush. Its flight reminded me of a green woodpecker, which I thought it was at first, though the undulations in its flight when it closed its wings were maybe not so deep. It was quickly joined by a second bird, then a third. That certainly eliminated green woodpeckers and a glance through the binoculars revealed not three but at least seven fieldfares on the bush. They were joined by a male blackbird, which was unusual since fieldfares usually see off other members of the thrush family from a food source, but there must have been plenty for all and they left it in peace. There really must have been a good food supply as three pheasants patrolled under the bush waiting for gravity to give them a share of the spoils. I checked later and this juniper and one or two others were laden with purple berries, though most of the other juniper bushes were bare.

I made my way down the edge of the Pheasant Wood and stopped halfway to have a look in the narrow ride that bisects the wood. As I entered the wood a flurry of finches rose from the wheat that had been scattered on the ride, and a dozen or so pheasant sneaked off into the trees. With some difficulty I managed to locate one or two of the finches high in the trees and confirmed they were chaffinches. Whether there were other species I don't know but it was good to see them taking advantage of the wheat supply. I then went round by the loch in front of the shooting lodge, hoping to get a close-up photograph of one of the black rabbits with my new camera, but they were indoors. I was also surprised that I saw not a single rabbit, live or dead, with myxomatosis. After seeing the beginnings of this vile disease more than a month before, this was really unusual though pleasing. As I passed the dam at the bottom of the loch I at last saw a species that had so far eluded me: a blue tit was busy hopping about in a willow tree looking for insects. It was barely credible that it had taken so long to spot one of the most common of birds!

I lunched in comfort on the veranda of the shooting lodge again, noting that all the rabbits beside the shooting lodge were clear of myxy, this despite the unfortunate rabbit with well advanced myxy eventually stumbling its way into one of the burrows on 6 September which I thought would infect its neighbours. I had the four swans on the loch and a couple of dozen mallard for company, though no white mallard today. I missed the antics of the swallows and the house martins on the wires and wondered how many of them had perished over the sea or Sahara Desert on their marathon migration.

It was still sunny, with a clear blue sky, and I was almost tempted to take off my jacket as I headed up the steep road out towards the hill. Rabbits were taking advantage of the heat and were sunning themselves outside their damp and dark burrows. Most were stretched out on their sides, and some were carrying out ablutions, including… washing behind their ears. My granny always told me that if a cat (and presumably a rabbit) washed behind its ears it was going to rain. She was wrong. The sky was clear of clouds, and the weather forecast said it was to be dry and sunny.

I was about two miles out the hill, and watching the red kites, which were now four in number. Two of them seemed to have been following me about all day, much to my delight. White and red tag was there, and the other kite without any tags. The remaining two were a bit further way and were being harassed by half a dozen carrion crows. Though they were in sharp focus against the cloudless blue sky they were just a bit too far out for me to see if they had any tags. They were originally to the south but heading over my head to the north-west. I followed them round with the binoculars and gradually began to see that the sky in the north-west was not nearly so blue. In fact it was black. Within minutes the first spots of rain appeared, and got heavier. And heavier. I had been travelling light, without my waterproof jacket, leggings or hat and was soon soaked. There was absolutely no shelter, and I had no option but to pack up for the day and head back. My granny had been right after all.

New birds identified: blue tit; greylag goose; fieldfare
New mammals identified: none

Chapter 12

Tuesday 1 November. Weather: Sunny and unseasonably mild; a lovely day to be out and about.

Three weeks since my last estate visit and I was keen to get going again. I had a meeting first thing in the morning in relation to my role with the UK National Wildlife Crime Unit so never made it to the estate till 11.30 am, but with one of the best days we've had for many weeks a shorter-than-usual visit is still well worthwhile. Some of the trees were now completely bare of foliage, such as the ash and rowan. Some had lost half of their leaves – the beech and larch – but the oak trees still had good leaf cover, albeit more brown than green. The bracken had completely died off and, though far from being my favourite plant, I can reluctantly concede to the colour as a lovely rich golden brown. Though the sun was out, it was low in the sky and my view of any birds that may have been to the south – then later in the day, the south-west – was limited.

Today I decided to start off in the junipers of Geordie's Moor, below and to the east of the shooting lodge. This is getting to be one of my favourite parts of the estate as the habitat is superb for wildlife. I'm really looking forward to seeing which birds settle in this part in the spring, as I'm sure I haven't seen a fraction of the species here yet. I picked my way through a muddy track where there was a break in the drystane dyke, the entrance to the junipers I find easiest. Once inside the dyke, the junipers lie to the left, and the mature oak woodland named Lament (that I've still to explore) lies ahead and to the right. My entrance disturbed a lone woodcock that had been feeding under the oaks and it flew towards Lament. I suspect this would be a resident as I doubt the main fall of woodcock ('fall' is the collective term for the large number of migrants that appear here once the weather in the Baltic countries gets colder) has arrived yet. Woodcock just look like medium-sized brown birds as they fly off. In fact when seen close up they are the most beautiful dark brown, light brown, buff and cream-coloured birds, with huge inky-black eyes and a long beak, held downwards when in flight as opposed to the heron's beak which it holds arrow-like in front of it, almost pointing the way ahead. If a woodcock sits tight on a carpet of leaves or bracken it is almost invisible, such is its camouflage.

I made my way through the junipers, disturbing dozens of rabbits that had been lazing in the sun. I watched one old buck rabbit chase a smaller one, probably a younger buck, out of its territory. It was a half-hearted pursuit, but in the early spring, when the rabbits begin to breed, bucks further down the pecking order can sustain severe injuries from bites and even scratches, some in time suffering from septicaemia. The old buck sat awhile, its large round head betraying its gender, as opposed to the slightly slimmer heads and more pointed snouts of does. It seemed to be on guard duty, checking to see if there may be any other intruders, but the most dangerous intruder – me – caused it to scamper off into the juniper bushes as I continued my walk. There were few birds visible in this area today, though I heard birds in the oaks, probably chaffinches, but could see none of them.

I crossed the dyke out of Geordie's Moor and headed up the hill past George's hens, which he keeps in an enclosure at the edge of a small wood. I took a left then right after the hens, which took me into a grass field where I watched a roe deer feeding on the woodland side of the fence. Its back end was towards me, with the anal tush (sometimes mistaken as a tail) clearly identifying it as a doe. The doe walked off a few steps but it had a dull coat and I wasn't convinced it was in the best of condition. It took another two or three steps, taking it out of sight, so I tried to catch up with it. This cat and mouse game went on for five minutes, with me gradually getting closer, but before I got a really good look at it the doe winded me and ran off. Hopefully I had been wrong about its state, but it just seemed to lack a healthy sheen to its coat.

I moved uphill to my left making for the wood known as Wericky, which lies above the duck ponds. Three wee rabbits scampered into a burrow and I had to remind myself it was 1 November. They looked less than eight weeks old and would be lucky to survive the winter. A thrush-like bird landed on a small tree 100 yards away and I was almost sure it was a redwing, but there were too many branches obscuring my vision and before I made a positive sighting it had gone. Damn! I crossed a fence into the next field and sat on some rocks at the fence-side to have my sandwiches of boiled ham. I had a great view down over the ponds, though they were devoid of ducks today, just as the sheep field was empty of sheep, lapwings and starlings. I was surprised at the absence of lapwings as there had been no frost and I doubted the food supply would have reduced that quickly after the sheep had been moved. The absence of sheep gave me a better view of the rabbits in the field: one outside nearly every burrow. They were smallish burrows but I wondered why there were no pairs. I was sure there would be at least one other rabbit in each burrow, but they had obviously decided to stay in the dark rather than sunbathe.

Having dined, I moved on up the fence on the west side of Wericky. This wood runs uphill from south to north, has oaks at the bottom end, spruces in the east and larches and Douglas firs on the west and at the top. This is a wood I had never been in as earlier it held a large number of pheasant poults which I didn't want to disturb. They were now adults and had been released from the pen for well over two months. They were scattered throughout the wood and beyond so my entry and quiet walk would cause no problems. I walked along the grassy ride inside the wood till I came to a crossroads. A bird landed on a spruce tree near to me and I saw it was a coal tit. This spruce had a dozen or so cones, hanging upside down, and the bird was pecking at the seeds inside. It was joined by a mate and the two were having a good feed in the way typical of coal tits in that they take a morsel, fly off to eat or to hide it, and come back for more. Coal tits are dainty wee birds, smaller than blue tits and with a similar yellow breast, but with grey rather than blue wings. Their head is black, with white cheeks and a broad white stripe running lengthways on the back of its head. They certainly had a good feed over the 10 minutes I watched them. I was impressed with this new wood, and wondered if it might hold some crossbill. I could see none just now but when they are much more vocal in spring I might have a better chance.

As I came out of the wood I saw a pair of buzzards and a pair of red kites circling over Dank Wood to the west. This was the direction I was heading and yet again the kites circled nearer to me as if to have a better look, one being the usual white and red wing-tagged bird with the radio tag. Only one of the birds had been radio-tagged, the main purpose being, as kites roost communally, that the tagged bird might identify their night-time roost. As I passed a pile of boulders near the edge of the field below Dank Wood I saw a rabbit sitting there in the advanced stages of myxy. It really is a horrible disease. Cream-coloured pus was running from its unseeing eyes and there was swelling at the base of both ears. It looked absolutely miserable and was probably in extreme pain. It flicked its head as a fly landed on its eyes, just before my stick found its mark and ended its suffering. I left it on the grass where it would be food for the kites.

I walked down the road in the direction of the shooting lodge, then cut through the recently-sown grass field. I was surprised how wet the field was, but it would dry considerably as the grass matured and soaked up the moisture. The field is full of hillocks covered in bracken, and I kept clear of these not to disturb any partridges that were likely to be there as George had said this area would be part of the partridge shoot the following day. I was heading for the Larch Wood which, so far, has to be my favourite wood. I was surprised at the amount of blackbirds in the wood, and I looked to see what food source there might be for them. There was plenty of wheat scattered on the track through the wood but they are not seed eaters. I was looking for bushes with berries, which is their favoured autumn diet, but could see none. Something must have attracted them in such numbers and I'll bear this in mind for future visits.

Since I had been looking at so many blackbirds I was not surprised when a thrush-like bird landed on a tree beside the now-empty pheasant pen. I again thought 'redwing' and since it was much closer than the earlier one, and much more settled, I got a great view through the binoculars of… a redwing. Apart from rust red on its flanks and under its wings, the main identifying mark of a redwing is a bold creamy-yellow stripe above its eye. This bird had that, but it seemed also to have a yellow stripe below its eye. I looked and looked through the binoculars, but finally saw that the lower stripe was in fact a ray of sunlight. For much of the time its breast was facing me and it seemed that the dark brown spots on the breast faded as they reached nearer the tail. I tried to get closer and eventually managed a photograph (of sorts) and the lack of spots further down the breast was also evident in the photo. I wonder if this might have been a young bird. I eventually got too close for its comfort and it flew down into some bracken, where I left it in peace.

I walked up the side of the pheasant pen and spied into some open woodland – mainly birches with an odd coniferous tree – just outside the main Larch Wood. A number of wee birds were feeding high in a mature birch. They turned out to be bullfinches: two males and a female. They were feeding on what I could only think were either seeds or new buds, though I thought buds unlikely in November. My new 14x zoom camera even managed a photograph despite the distance, and when I blew it up a bit, I was quite amazed at the clarity. Hardly 'Wildlife Photographer of the Year' stuff, but more than sufficient to keep me happy. The bullfinches were shortly joined by a great tit, then a flock of half a dozen chaffinches; a great mix on one tree.

All the time I had been in the wood I could hear a fallow buck grunting some distance to the east. I had missed the main rut, but it obviously wasn't over yet. I headed towards the sound through Boggy Bottom, the flat boggy area running from the Larch Wood to the Henhouse Wood. As I walked along the track at the top end of Law Wood I saw a dead rabbit under an ancient juniper bush (this estate is fantastic for juniper!) I wondered if it had been killed by a stoat and managed to retrieve it with my stick. There were no tell-tale stoat or weasel bite marks at the back of its neck, nor was there any sign of myxy. The rabbit was in poor condition and with a dull, lacklustre, coat. I guessed at coccidiosis, which can kill many rabbits, and was a real problem disease at a time in my teens when a school friend and I bred New Zealand white rabbits. I checked this disease out on the internet and the treatment is sulphaquinoxalene given in the drinking water. It was the same remedy in 1962, but unfortunately not very successful. It would be impossible to administer to wild rabbits.

As I examined the ex-rabbit, I saw a dark coloured fallow doe with a dark calf slip quietly across the track from Law Wood into the grass field that runs up the side of Ell Wood to the Craigie Face. I then saw that I was being watched from deep within Law Wood. A dappled fallow doe stood facing me, and I wondered if I could manage a photo. Slowly I went to my pocket for the camera but the shy beast was having none of it, and turned and trotted off, followed by a dark coloured calf. With all this going on I failed to notice that the grunting of the fallow buck had stopped. It may have seen me or got my wind, or it may have given up rutting for the time being. I never did see it.

I headed back towards the loch at the shooting lodge, down the south side of Law Wood, and watched three pheasants dusting in ground so dry it was almost fine sand under a larch tree. They really were enjoying it, and getting the best of the sun at the same time. I could see there was a dead pheasant outside the fence and headed down to examine it. Reluctantly the pheasants forsook their pleasurable dusting at my approach. A freshly dead hen pheasant lay in full view of them, only separated by a fence. It had been well plucked, then predated, by a bird (mammals don't pluck their prey), and I wondered if it had been killed by the goshawk, since it was in the same area of the estate. It could, of course, have accidentally hit the fence *then* been predated, but I thought that less likely.

Round at the dam at the loch I had an interesting experience with a trout. I heard the sound, not so much as splashing but of rippling and gurgling on the water, and as I got closer I could see that it was being caused by a very substantial trout. I crept to the dam wall and peeked over, to see a trout surfacing with great regularity, then diving like a hump-backed whale, with its tail right out of the water. This went on for a good 10 minutes and I was puzzled as to what was happening. The fish must have surfaced and dived at least 40 times. I wondered if it was tangled on something but it was at distances from me varying between three yards and 15 yards, so that was unlikely. Suddenly the fish was gone and I was left with the enigma as to why it was carrying out this strange behaviour. I managed to take some photos – mainly of rippled water after it had disappeared – but in several photos chunks of the fish were clear enough to show it was a rainbow trout of maybe four or five pounds.

Now in possession of a camera, I was keen to get a photo of the Loch Wood black rabbit that lived just beyond the boathouse. I walked quietly forward, camera at the ready. Half a dozen cock pheasants ran from the lochside into the wood and I thought my chances of seeing the rabbit would be slim. I edged forward, peeping round the bracken on my left. The rabbit was in its usual spot, but well aware of me and ready to bolt into the wood. We had met under these conditions three or four times now and maybe it sensed I meant no harm. Its trust – or naivety – allowed me two photos before it hopped to a burrow and disappeared. As I crossed the bridge over the burn running into the loch I looked at some of its pals up in the adjacent grass field. This field has some of the largest warrens on the estate and there must have been 50 rabbits sitting sunning themselves, including another black one. Their day was clearly as enjoyable as mine.

New birds identified: woodcock; redwing
New mammals identified: none

Chapter 13

Monday 14 November. Weather: Mild, light wind and light drizzle. A dreich November day!

With the pheasant shooting on the estate now started it is more difficult to get a day when no shooting and dry weather combine to make seeing birds possible. There was more likelihood of seeing birds on the big fishing loch, since wet weather makes little difference to water birds. Apart from some pike fishing competitions on the loch, fishing was finished for the season. I knew there would not be a boat with an electric outboard motor available as the electric points at which to charge the motors had been vandalised. The owner said he had left one boat with oars available for me so that would have to do. The boats are very light and rowing them is no problem in any case. I was just a bit concerned, though, that the movement of the oars might limit how close I could get to any birds.

The loch was flat calm at the restaurant end, which is the east end. The wind, not surprisingly since it was wet, was from the east and was causing some rippling of the water further up the loch but nothing too turbulent. A raft of 40 or so tufted ducks was busy just out from the flotilla of anchored boats. Only about two-thirds were ever on the surface at one time and whatever they were getting off the bottom of the loch during their dives it was keeping them occupied. Halfway up the loch I could see a black shape, low in the water. It was a cormorant, and beyond it a whitish bird that proved when I put the binoculars on it to be a male goosander.

I set off rowing, noting the sign, words of the late King George VI, between the boats' anchorage and the loch proper to read, *'The wildlife of today is not ours to dispose of as we please. We have it in trust. We must account for it to those who come after'.* The sign encouraged anglers to appreciate the wildlife on the loch and to dispose of litter safely, in particular nylon line. Compared with those who participate in most other sports, most anglers are by nature very quiet, out to enjoy the tranquillity of the countryside whether or not they take home a trout. The risk of them disturbing wildlife is remote.

I realised in the first hundred yards of rowing that, in the normal rowing position, anything I wanted to see was behind me. I persevered for a wee while, turning the boat slightly every so often to scan the water ahead of me. I soon got fed up of that and sat on the next seat back in the boat (*aft* would be the nautical term) so that I could push the oars rather than pull them. It was not a great hardship and the benefit of course was that I was looking in the direction in which I was travelling. The downside was that I'd already dried and warmed up one seat, and here I was on a wet and cold one again! I rowed round the loch in a clockwise direction, remaining about 200 yards out from the shore. A group of mallard were resting on the shore, many standing on one leg and with head tucked under wing. After scanning them with the binoculars, I was happy there was nothing unusual about them or any more unusual species hiding amongst them. I continued up the south side of the loch, seeing a small flock of goldeneye some distance ahead. Even though my rowing was smooth and quiet they appeared rather concerned about a boat with two oars flapping at either side and, when still about 200 yards ahead, took off over my head to land at the end of the loch from which I'd just come. Oars were not a good idea.

Ahead of the goldeneye I'd spotted four goosanders, lovely looking birds with their salmon pink serrated bill, white throat and russet brown head contrasting with their grey back. They kept paddling just ahead of me into the small bay at the west end of the loch, with nowhere to go from there. I was now 150 yards from them and suspected if I closed the distance any further they'd join the goldeneye at the other end of the loch. Two were female and two were sub-adult males, with a white bar along the side of each wing that differentiated between the two sexes. All were keeping a close eye on the 'boat with wings'. They began to swim back down the side of the loch again and I managed one or two photographs as they filed past in line astern. They swam past a lone coot, foraging happily just out from the reeds and much less alert to danger than the goosanders. I had heard a coot several times at this end of the loch but had never seen one until now, as they seemed more at home in the reeds.

Leaving the goosanders in peace, I turned the boat and headed out of the bay, past a pair of mute swans (there were only two pairs and a single swan on the loch today though, if they breed, three pairs is maybe about right for the size of the loch). The swans completely ignored the boat, despite the oars, and had their heads underwater more often than above. Their vulnerability in this position, with bums in the air, does not seem to concern them. They have few avian predators, probably just the white-tailed eagle. These are still scarce in the east of Scotland but those that are here regularly take geese, particularly in Montrose Basin, so I suspect they would manage a mute swan as well. I've no doubt that white-tailed eagles are occasional visitors to the estate and I hope to see one here in due course.

I had hoped, this being my first time on the loch with no other boats present, that I might see the otter, but no such luck. The absence of boats did not seem to increase water bird numbers as, apart from another pair of swans, there were only a few mallard down the north side of the loch. I rowed, in the strange manner of facing forwards, down most of the north side then cut across the centre as I could see a large number of birds had gathered on the south shore again. A jet black cormorant flew over my head. Cormorants are remarkably big birds, with their full size being appreciated when they take to the air. When they are swimming a higher percentage of the bird is underwater compared with duck and goose species, so they look deceptively small. I was surprised at how close the bird came to me, especially considering that they can be held as pests by fisheries and anglers and licences are granted by

Scottish Natural Heritage to shoot a small number every year. This one surely hadn't heard of this!

As I got closer to the birds on the south side of the loch I could see that many of them were common gulls. Behind the gulls, a cormorant stood upright on a rock that jutted out of the loch like an iceberg, wings open to dry them. This bird, unlike the last one I saw, had a grey breast, which made it rather penguin-like. To the right of the common gulls were my goosanders from earlier, having made their way back down the loch. They were now eight in number, with one of them an adult male, which looked almost pink rather than white. As the group preened themselves, sometimes lying on one side to do so, I could see there were at least two sub-adult males now in the group. They still had the brown head, like the females, rather than the black head they would have as adults. As they were preening much more white was visible on the young males compared to the females, and as they rose in the water and flapped their wings again it was obvious they had more white on the wings than their female siblings. Since goosanders lay somewhere between eight and 10 eggs this would probably be a family group, in The Broons terms, of ma, pa and the survivors of the weans. As I got closer to the birds they swam ahead of me towards the shoreline, then in line astern again, with dad in the centre, up the loch heading westwards. I took some rather long range photos and left them to it.

To the left of the goosander family as I'd been rowing across the loch were the goldeneye. They had moved down the loch to just beside the restaurant. It's a pity it was closed for the winter as anyone there would have had a great view of them; far better than I was getting. I watched them at a distance, like the goosanders, preening and splashing about on the surface. There were three males and three females, and one of the males was having a great time, with water splashing in the air like a fountain. This was the only adult male in the group, its green rather than brown head and the large white spot at the top of its beak differentiating it from the slightly drabber females and sub-adult males, all with brown heads. The females seemed more intent on feeding, and they were diving much more than the males. A very dark coloured buzzard flew quite low over them, but they did not see it as a threat as they knew they could soon disappear underwater.

I sat for a while in the flat calm waters, watching the many trout mouthing the water's surface, sometimes breaching the water slightly with a little swirl, and occasionally jumping right out of the water. Most seemed sizeable trout, but one smaller one of maybe half a pound came clean out of the water twice in quick succession in the manner of a porpoise or penguin. I wondered if it was being chased by a large trout or maybe a pike. It certainly gave the impression of trying to escape the jaws of some terrifying underwater creature.

I cut across the loch again, heading for the harbour and meaning to give the goldeneye plenty of space. They didn't like the oars, though, and three males and two females took off, circling the boat ahead of me and making towards the other end of the loch. The third female must have been underwater when the others took to the air, and when she came up she probably wondered where they had gone. She then took off towards the other end, but circled round the back of the boat rather than following her companions.

I edged in between boats 12 and 14, and tied up my boat. I had enjoyed the rowing, but had the oars really been a drawback in trying to approach birds without disturbing them, or was it because I was in boat 13?

New birds identified: coot
New mammals identified: none

Chapter 14

Monday 12 December. Weather: Cold but bright. Little or no wind for a change.

It was almost a month since my last visit, and six weeks since I had been walking on the estate rather than rowing on the loch. The weather over the past few weeks had been terrible and on the days when I was free, or when it wasn't blowing a gale or teeming down with rain, there was a pheasant shoot on. If any of the shoots coincided with the very windy days I'm sure the cartridge to kill ratio would be very high, since fast and high flying pheasants curling on the wind are extremely testing shots. I did have a visit a couple of days earlier, being asked by the owner to stand in on a syndicate shoot for one of the members who was poorly. There were only six guns and we were shooting odd corners of the estate rather than the main drives, and had a nice mixed bag of pheasant, red-legged partridge and one or two duck. Since I've already given a report of a day's shooting I'll not detail this one, but I mention the day because of an interesting sighting in the late afternoon.

We had finished for the day and were having a cup of tea in the shooting lodge when I was asked to come out and have a look at some birds in the distant sky. It was about an hour before dark, with the sun sinking low, the light just beginning to fade. The birds of interest, which were thankfully to the east, were wheeling about in a large group probably three quarters of a mile away. I suspected them to be red kites but ran to my car for the binoculars. Indeed they were mostly kites; nine of them plus one buzzard. They wheeled about in the same area for a good half hour and I was sure they were about to roost. I have seen kites several times now gathering in the last hour of daylight above a roost not too far from where I stay. On the evenings I watched, numbers gradually built up until there were between 30 and 40 in the air. After their social interaction (which I'm sure it was), they gradually started to land for the night in the oak wood over which they were circling. I was sure with the nine kites I was watching that this was another communal roost, and I was pleased it was on this estate. The owner passed the information to the red kite monitoring officer from the RSPB but the really odd thing is that they were never seen there again. Might it have been a one-off roost? That's a mystery which may not be solved.

I was pleased that the first bird I saw this morning as I got out of the car was a male kestrel. It was perched on the top of a young ash tree at the edge of the farm buildings at the shooting lodge and not 50 yards from me. I had only seen a female kestrel on the estate so far so it's good she now has the chance of a mate. They'll need to produce a decent brood this coming spring to make up for losses of kestrels (and owls) last year due to the deep and prolonged snow. The kestrel eyed me up for a few minutes then flew off to prospect elsewhere. Though kestrels are not rare birds, their numbers have been falling steadily in the last few years. Consider how common it used to be seeing a kestrel hovering at the side of a motorway, then try to think when you last saw one. It was a really nice start to the day.

I headed up the hill towards the cottage with the hens, which is really the 'gateway' to the hill. I could see that the duck ponds were frozen, and in the sheep field there was not a lapwing (or even their pals, starlings) to be seen. Starlings are a bit more omnivorous in their diet but lapwings need invertebrates and can't survive on frozen ground. I'm really looking forward to their return in the spring, not just to see their aerial acrobatics as they attract or impress a mate and lay claim to a nesting site, but because the weather will be a damn sight warmer than it is now! A buzzard lazily flapped over the frozen ponds and made me think that seeing pairs of buzzards in springtime on different parts of the estate will give me a better idea of how many breeding pairs there are. It will be interesting to try to identify nest sites as well. I've never had time to do that since I was at school in the 1950s, though not in relation to buzzards as they were as scarce as hens' teeth at that time due to the unchecked poisoning campaign by the majority of gamekeepers.

As I passed the cottage, a dunnock hopped about among the hens and cockerels. I've seen very few dunnocks on this estate, though as it turned out I probably saw more today than I've seen since I began this survey: four in all. I could probably see four most days in my garden, but they have an easier life there than on hill ground. As I rounded the corner past Dank Wood and the hill proper came into view, I could see that the bracken had completely died down. It had a good covering of snow the previous week and nothing puts bracken down quicker than wearing a heavy snow overcoat. Remnants of the snow remained, as I had found to my cost trying to walk up the track thus far, but as I got on to the hill it was really tricky. Trying to walk on a slope with snow that had been tracked by vehicles, frozen, partially thawed, frozen again and had a shower of rain (which I had just missed) on top of that, was not pleasant. I found that I was looking down more than looking up, which was not conducive to seeing what was going on around me.

I continued out the hill road, not looking forward to the downhill journey as I'd already slipped several times, though still managed to remain upright. The day was a complete contrast to the windy weather we'd recently been having. It was just above freezing but the sun was out and the wind was completely gone. A red kite was flying above the far horizon, nearly a mile away to the north, but dipped down out of sight before I could see if it had any identifying marks. Cock pheasants and red-legged partridges were calling all round the hill. Their three-pronged tracks were frozen into the ice on the hill road like fossilised dinosaur footprints on sandstone. I looked closely at the ice and the snow for evidence of any mammal I knew lived on the hill but which I'd yet to confirm – stoat, weasel, field vole, shrew, probably pine marten – but the closest I came was the dainty cloven hoof footprint of a roe deer.

I'm always amazed at forest-dwelling animals like roe deer living and breeding successfully in an almost treeless landscape, but they seem to survive well, and may only make their way to arable or forested land in the very worst of weather. As I studied the roe deer marks I heard the loud *cucking* sounds of cock pheasants further up the hill and looked up quickly to see what had alarmed them, hoping to see a fox. I was disappointed (though George won't be) as there was no fox: it had simply been rivalry between two males, and one seeing off the other. They flew towards me in tandem, only seeing me at the last minute and less than 20 yards away, veering off with tail feathers spread wide to accomplish a sharp left turn, their competitiveness temporarily abandoned.

About a mile and a half out the hill the track was getting decidedly worse, and a view ahead with the binoculars assured no improvement. I'd no wish to limp (or be carried) off the hill so decided against continuing. There being no dry places to sit, I stood for a while arguing with myself against the decision, and at the same time ate the first course of my piece. I watched a carrion crow sitting on a corner of one of the partridge feeding stations, possibly wondering if it was safe to pass through one of the gaps meant to limit entry to partridge and pheasants rather than deer. The crow was still contemplating when I heard, then saw, a single raven soar high over the hill, its bulk and wedge-shaped tail along with the *prukk, prukk* calls being the clear identification signs. It was a lovely silhouette against the cloudless blue sky. It knew where it was going and did not deviate. My decision was finalised over a drink of red grape juice and I turned and headed back to lower ground.

I walked down towards the shooting lodge using the fields rather than the steep and icy road, then cut right-handed up towards the Larch Wood. There is a small roundel of spruce and larch trees just short of this wood and I could see some tits feeding on the branches of the top part of a spruce tree that had been snapped off in last week's storm. I spotted a stone that looked dry and sat to watch. There was a good collection of tits. Most were coal tits, frenetically grabbing a morsel of whatever was taking their fancy and flying with it to the safety of a higher branch, returning seconds later for more. Taking a more sedate approach to lunch were two blue tits and a single great tit. They were enjoying their snack and didn't seem bothered that it was at ground level rather than 40 or 50 feet in the air.

This was a fortuitous (though hardly comfortable) vantage point so I quietly took the rest of my food out of my rucksack. It was one o'clock and everyone seemed to be at lunch. I watched a pair of mistle thrushes, on a track of well shorn grass, feeding on worms that had been incautious enough to have come above ground overnight and had probably been frozen. They seemed to have plenty to choose from and each gulped down three or four in the time it took me to eat my sandwich. I was distracted by the *prukk, prukk* of a raven again. This time when I looked up there were two. They circled like vultures and may have been waiting for me to keel over so that they could also dine, making me think of the first two verses of the poem, 'The Twa Corbies' –

> As I was walking all alane,
> I heard twa corbies makin' a mane;
> The tane unto the t'other did say,
> "Where sall we gang an' dine the day?"
> "In ahint yon auld fail dyke,
> I wot there lies a new-slain knight;
> An' naebody kens that he lies there
> But his hawk, his hound an' his lady fair."

The corbies stayed with me, though circling higher, for a good five minutes, before eventually giving up thoughts of a potential corpse and heading off to the north-east. I had been so engrossed with them that I'd forgotten about the mistle thrushes, which had now gone. All the time I sat there I was aware of the smell of wood smoke from the various estate cottages. I could detect this despite the nearest house being nearly half a mile away. Imagine how much further away this and other scents can be detected by the considerably more developed olfactory senses of mammals.

George had said that his pheasants were rather jumpy, so rather than go up through the track in the Larch Wood I continued down in the direction of one of my favoured rock seats looking out to the Craigie Face and Eerie Valley (the rabbit toilet one). Surprisingly it had been a good choice not going into the Larch Wood. When I'm in the trees there I can always hear buzzards, but they're not easy to see through the canopy. By being on the *outside* of the wood I could see three buzzards circling over the trees. Like the ravens, they spiralled higher and soon three became five, then six. They were joined in their aerial waltz by two red kites, one of which was the ubiquitous red/white tagged bird. There was no animosity or competition between the two species and their acrobatics, diving and wheeling, were a joy to witness.

Having a sporting estate should not only be about game birds and deer. This estate, along with one or two other estates that I know, has such a fantastic variety of wildlife. Surely all estates should consider the value of having diversity rather than cursing – or worse, killing – every bird of prey that is seen. I've just finished reading a news article about the grouse season that finished a couple of days earlier. The article stated that 2011 was the best grouse season in recent living memory. Two of the estates named in the report are Glenogil and Millden in Angus. In the past five years more poisoned baits and victims have been found on these two estates than in all the rest of Tayside put together. The estates have repeatedly claimed they do not kill birds of prey. If they can have such a fantastic season *without* killing birds of prey then why are birds of prey demonised… or am I just a cynic?

I made my way down to the rock favoured both by me and rabbits, though for different reasons. It was soaking wet today so I made do by standing beside it. The flock of jackdaws from the Craigie Face were out in force, with a couple of hundred *chak-chaking* loudly and wheeling about above me. As I watched them I thought they were doing this for nothing more than pleasure, but something else caught my eye. Any birds that temporarily broke away from the main flock were in pairs. Looking more closely at the flock, the main bunch was surrounded by at least a dozen satellite *pairs* of jackdaws. I watched for some time and this was not coincidence. It made me wonder if this flocking was a means of finding a partner, and do they keep their partner from one year to the next. I'll watch flocks of crows and jackdaws with more interest in the future.

The buzzard and kite skydance was ending and the participants were making their way elsewhere. Two buzzards were now perched atop a larch tree on the south slope of Eerie Valley. One kite was circling low over rocks where guns one to three stand on the drive named The Shudder. I knew there had been a shoot on 10 December and wondered if there might be a missed carcass lying there. Another buzzard flew east along the Craigie Face ridge. It disturbed what I initially thought was a peregrine but was in fact a kestrel, which then mobbed it, though rather half-heartedly. Because of the distance (probably two-thirds of a mile) I couldn't see if it was male or female, but at least it was another kestrel, and maybe establishing or even defending a potential territory. I'll look out for a pair there in the spring.

I headed along Boggy Bottom, the bog area that runs between the top of the Law Wood and the bottom of the Ell Wood, then walked clockwise round the Henhouse Wood, noting a couple of dozen sitka spruce trees toppled by the wind and lying into the field. I climbed up the hill to the west of the Pheasant Wood, noting more trees toppled and part of the fence now 20 feet in the air, lifted by the tree roots. As I entered the track running through Creag Bheag Wood I spotted a dark coloured fallow doe watching me from behind a tree. Its tail was straight up in the air; a sign of danger. We watched each other for a while, then the doe bounced off, springbok style with all four feet off the ground at the same time and tail still in the air, towards the top of the Pheasant Wood. I walked along the track through Creag Bheag Wood and watched a small flock of birds feeding, flitting between the lower branches of a bush and some nearby heather and blaeberry. I could see they were finches but a magnified view through the binoculars identified them as bullfinches. There were between 10 and 12 in the group and slightly more females than males. The heather seemed of most interest to them and, being seed and bud eaters, I imagine they were eating heather seeds. They flew ahead of me as I walked on, then curled back to resume their feeding as I passed.

At the other end of Creag Bheag I came down onto the track that runs through the large wood referred to as West End from the Hill Loch to the public road. The loch was partly frozen but the four domestic swans had kept an area clear and had been joined by a dozen or so mallard. I could barely see the mallard, though heard them quite plainly. I took a couple of distant photos with my camera on 14x zoom. Looking through the viewfinder I could only see the swans, but remarkably when I looked at the image the ducks were quite clear; in fact in the second photo some of them were taking off. The last time I was in this wood I was amazed at the different mature trees, which (in August) were still in full leaf. This time the deciduous trees were bare, but this made the aging pine trees even more outstanding. There is a huge stand of juniper just down from the loch, part of the Boat House pheasant drive and called Colin's Wardrobe, named after a now deceased friend of the owner who sometimes shot on the estate and came each time in a different array of gaudy clothing. I walked down the mile or so to the public road, admiring the bare oaks and ash trees with the sun glinting through them, and listening to the gurgle of the trackside burn, running almost at capacity as it carried away the overflow from the loch.

I walked up past the huge estate house still owned by the original estate owners. Though one or two trees in the policies were down and the tops off others, the huge and ancient Wellingtonia trees near the tennis court, towering above all of the other trees, were still standing proudly. They will have weathered storms worse than the 80 mph gales of last week during the many centuries of their life.

Arriving back at the shooting lodge, the tree on which I saw the kestrel on my arrival now held a small flock of fieldfares. For birds that seem constantly on the move they sat a remarkably long time and may have been resting after a feast of berries elsewhere. As my gaze panned from northwest to northeast I glimpsed a bird of prey at a low level flying away from me over the fields. I still hadn't seen a sparrowhawk on my travels (though I've seen them regularly on the estate in past years) and this bird's height off the ground was consistent with the sparrowhawk's low-level attack strategy. I scanned the area with the binoculars and saw in fact that it was a male kestrel, now perched on a distant fencepost. My day had started with a kestrel, and finished with probably the same one.

New birds identified: mistle thrush
New mammals identified: none

Chapter 15

Monday 16 January 2012. Weather: Sunny with some blue sky and some cloud. Temperature varied between -7 and -2 degrees centigrade. Thankfully no wind!

I had no great hopes of seeing much due to the very low temperature, but I was keen for a walk anyway. I set off out to the hill, surrounded by white hoar frost, yet not feeling cold. The whole countryside was sparkling in the morning sun, and I watched a rabbit munching the frozen grass in the sheep field (minus any sheep now of course) above the shooting lodge. This seemed to be the same rabbit as I saw there on the last visit. I had looked at it through the binoculars that time thinking it might have myxy, but its eyes were clear. I checked again as the rabbit just didn't look right. Its eyes were still clear, so no myxy, but as it hopped away towards a fence-side burrow its back was hunched more than usual and I could see its coat was duller than it should have been. It was suffering from some disease – possibly coccidiosis or enteritis, which are very often fatal.

About half a mile out the hill road the frosted remains of a duck was lying on the track. The head end and the tail end were missing but the centre chunk, still with plenty meat and with the wings attached, remained. The wings initially looked a bit short for a mallard but wiping the frost off them with my glove exposed the vivid blue wing bar and confirmed identification. Some mammalian predator had filled its belly on the duck, most likely a fox. In mid-January foxes are mating and will have more on their minds than a good feed, possibly the reason the carcass was abandoned rather than buried. Red-legged partridges rose in front of me from time to time, and I had never seen so many cock pheasants on the hill.

One rose from the highest part of the hill on my right and flew over the hill road at an amazing height, far out of range of a shotgun. It had maybe learned from experience. On two or three occasions cock pheasants at different parts of the hill voiced their loud *kor-ok ok-ok-ok* in synchrony. This is usually done when they hear a loud noise such as blasting or thunder. Their hearing must be better than mine as I heard nothing. This was repeated several times when I came down to the lower ground later on, though with many more cock pheasants participating in the chorus because of the higher numbers there.

Fallow deer seemed scarce on the hill, probably because the bracken had died down and with it, their cover. Three roe deer, probably mother and twin offspring from the previous year ran along a ridge on my right, running eastwards in the direction of a wood over the march fence on the neighbouring estate. Before they disappeared over the ridge they all stopped to look back at me. I'm always amazed at how they know exactly where to stop before they lose sight of the cause of their flight. After studying me for a couple of minutes, two more bounds and they were behind the ridge.

I continued on past Middle Hill and turned right at the fork, taking me up Grey Crags. A dozen or so small birds flew from a stunted larch tree ahead of me and on my left and landed in the heather. I suspected they were the bullfinches I saw near there on the last visit, but I never managed to confirm this as they had disappeared before I came abreast of the last sighting. Birds seemed scarce on the hill and apart from these, a pair of buzzards and some carrion crows, every other avian resident seemed still to be in bed.

At the top of Grey Crags I crossed the ridge and cut straight down the hill towards the march fence with the estate to the west. I wanted to walk almost parallel with this march fence and in a northward then eastward direction, where I would meet the hill track that would eventually take me back to the shooting lodge in a complete clockwise loop. I knew there was a narrow track where the heather had been swiped and that's where I made for as it would make the going, even downhill, a bit easier. I found the swiped track and followed it to its end, which neatly brought me on to a part of the hill where the heather had been burned in the 2011 fire. I had come *up* this route on an earlier visit and it was an absolute bugger, not just walking up the steep hill, but walking against the lie of the burned heather stems. Going downhill was a dawdle and I'll not be doing this route again anti-clockwise!

I heard voices coming from the neighbour's side of the fence (on a still, frosty day sound carries for miles) and saw a man, woman and a dog coming down the hill about half a mile away. They disturbed three roe deer, which jumped the fence and ran along the hill below me. I had crossed the Chapel Burn and was gradually moving right in any case. As I came to the top of a ridge the deer were running past on the other side. It was a doe with its 2011 fawns again and in true tradition, having seen me, stopped to look back before they disappeared over the next ridge. I was still gradually sweeping right-handed and when I stopped to sit on a large rock to have my piece (and to take off my outer jacket, bonnet and gloves as despite the below-zero temperature I was hot) the three deer appeared above me, slowly making their way back towards the place from which they had been disturbed. They were interesting to observe while I had my sandwich.

The remainder of my circuit, passing a line of ancient stone grouse butts that ran almost from the eastmost neighbour's march well up towards the top of Connell Hill, was without incident and I left the hill in the direction of the Larch Wood. I was still avoiding going into any of the woods until the end of the shooting season (1 February) but could see sufficient for now to keep me going from the outsides. A buzzard and a red kite were flying through the trees heading into the Larch Wood, with the kite landing on a tree and the buzzard disappearing further into the depths of the wood. I looked for a second red kite but there was no sign today. It would be great if *two* pairs breed on the estate this year.

I made for my favourite rock seat looking out to the Craigie Face and Eerie Valley, disturbing a black rabbit that I'd seen there before and which hopped off to the safety of some rhododendron bushes.

I sat on my rucksack and had my second sandwich, with a view over a lovely part of the estate. I never fail to see buzzards from this point and today was no different, though only two rather than the usual six or seven. I was hoping two red kites would materialise, but not to be. The owner had told me earlier that the radio-tagged red kite with the red and white wing tags had recently been identified by RSPB at a roost site near Crieff. This coincided with two of this estate's kites, probably the young from 2011, having disappeared. Both may still be together and one may well return here with a mate, though usually kites are at least two years old before they begin to breed.

Leaving my rock, I put on my gloves again as the temperature was dropping due to the sun now being covered by cloud. I headed through the gate into the grass field, cutting diagonally up towards the drive known as The Shudder. I passed a large rabbit warren en route and saw that, earlier in the day when the sun had been out, some of the warren's population had come out for some fresh air; the small oval-shaped areas in strategic places near the burrow entrances where the heat of the rabbits' bodies had melted the frost being evidence of their earlier sunbathing. I skirted the top of the Ell Wood and came down the far side. About 30 medium sized birds were in search of something to eat on the frosty grass, though on a frozen surface I couldn't think what this might be. I looked at them through the binoculars and thought they were blackbirds… but they were all males! This couldn't be right, as my initial thoughts were that this was a flock of fieldfares. Two things put me off plumping for fieldfares: they looked to be black, whereas fieldfares are brown and grey on top, with a speckled breast, and – normally flighty birds – they were letting me get quite close. In fact it had been a trick of the light; darkish birds on a white surface looking much darker than they really were. Indeed they were fieldfares and as I came closer they lifted and flew back up the field, landing behind me. They were certainly finding food in the frozen field, but as birds that eat invertebrates and berries I was stumped as to what it could be.

I crossed over the track at the end of the grass field and as I entered the grass field opposite, which is bounded on one side by Law Wood and at the other by the Henhouse Wood, I caught a whiff of fox. Fox urine is strong at any time but seems even stronger during their breeding season. This is hardly surprising as they need to advertise their presence to find a mate. The weather conditions were also perfect for picking up a scent and I could imagine *Vulpes vulpes,* sometime over the past couple of nights, squatting over a tuft of grass to make other foxes aware that he or she had passed. Further down that field, nearer to the loch at the shooting lodge, a dozen or so rabbits were out in the field having a late breakfast of unappetising frozen grass. As I approached they scurried into the wood, but even had I not seen them, their scrapings in the frost and plenty of fresh, round, droppings were evidence of very recent lagomorph presence.

I made towards the west end of the mainly-frozen loch and was surprised when two of the swans took off from the unfrozen west margins and flapped and pattered across the ice to study me from the surface of the ice near the far end. The swans on the loch are tame, like those on the Hill Loch, and much more inclined to swim towards someone than fly off. I looked at the swans still at the edge of the loch and there were four – the correct number. The wary pair was in fact a pair of wild mute swans that had come in to visit, probably because their home loch or pond was completely frozen. Comparing those two with the domestic ones, their beaks were very much brighter and more orange, and they looked altogether bigger than the tame residents of Polish origin. They'll be unlikely to stay, but it was nice of them to call in!

I skirted the west end of the loch and as I crossed the wooden bridge over the burn that runs into it, saw another of the four black rabbits that I know of on the estate. It was sitting near its burrow beside the drystane dyke that, on a shooting day, bisects the line of guns waiting on pheasants being driven from the Larch Wood. I'll keep an eye on all these 'ministers', as black rabbits are often termed, in the coming months to see if black offspring appear.

With the recent mild weather (apart from today) I'd be surprised if some of the doe rabbits on the lower ground are not already pregnant. The gestation period is 28-30 days and it is not unusual in mid-February to see evidence of a doe rabbit having pulled out some of her belly fur (which it does above ground) to mix with dry grass and line a nest chamber immediately before the kits are born.

As I climbed the short hill through the grass field that leads from the loch up to the shooting lodge I was aware of some small brown birds on the grass. At first I thought they were house sparrows but even without the binoculars I could see they were much more industrious wee birds than sparrows. They walked (and ran) about the grass rather than hopping, and were slightly smaller and much more streaked than sparrows. The giveaway, confirming they were twite, was the small yellow beak – hardly a beak at all compared with other finches – and an almost imperceptible white edge to the wing in the bird that I was studying closely. There were five in the group, maybe a family group, and they busied themselves hunting the grass in their search for seeds. Though I've possibly seen twite before, I've never recognised them as such. Like the otter, I was so engrossed with the encounter that I never thought about the camera in my pocket. Damn!

New birds identified: twite
New mammals identified: none

Chapter 16

Saturday 28 January 2012. Weather: Cold (-2 degrees) with white frost, but sunny and mostly blue sky. Very light wind.

I started with a quick visit to the big fishing loch. I thought it would have been completely frozen after two nights below freezing, but it seemed unaffected by ice. Upwards of a dozen goldeneye were swimming in the bay near to the restaurant. The large, round, white patch above the beak of the males was easily visible even before I got out of the car, but I wished I had stayed in the car as they were very jumpy and took off up the loch as soon as they saw me, even though I was more than 100 yards away. The tufted ducks that had been near them, much less concerned about human presence, were unfazed and remained where they were (or below the surface, feeding). I scanned the loch with the binoculars, recognising a pinky-white bird away at the far end of the loch as a male goosander. A few mallard were at the edge of a reed bed between me and the public road, and, apart from the usual pairs of swans, that was my lot. The adjacent loch has a far bigger variety of waterfowl than this, and I am quite sure they regularly visit the fishing loch, though maybe just on the days that I'm not there!

I moved on and parked at the shooting lodge, thinking on my way up the estate road about the diseased rabbit I saw in the sheep field on my last two visits. I scanned the field with the binoculars and saw a rabbit carcass not far from where I had last seen it feeding. Heading up the field I examined the carcass; the crows had picked out the eye that had been facing skywards and it was well predated, probably also by crows, though maybe with some help from buzzards and red kites. When I turned the rabbit over, the other eye was clear and eliminated myxy as the cause of death. I suspect it would be the one I thought either had coccidiosis or enteritis and wasn't at all surprised that it had died.

I headed up through the middle of the sheep field and the one above it, making for the corner of Dank Wood. A buzzard was sitting on the fence near the corner and seemed huge in the binoculars. Even without the magnification it was a large bird, probably a female, which in the manner of birds of prey is considerably bigger than the male. When I walked round Dank Wood I was surprised at the number of spruce trees round the edge of the wood that had the tops completely taken off them by the wind. If this was the damage in one small wood, the recent storm-force winds must have damaged or toppled thousands of trees across Scotland.

After having circled the wood anti-clockwise, I came out on to the hill road just at the top side of the wood, and continued out to the hill. I was pleasantly surprised to rise nine mallard off the wee pond that is on the right just a quarter mile or so out the hill. Despite the pond having hides for duck shooting (which must indicate that ducks at least *used* to come in to it) I had never seen ducks on it. They curled back over my head, probably heading for the ponds near the shooting lodge. With my attention on the ducks, I just got a fleeting glimpse of a bird of prey that came from left to right and disappeared over the crest of the hill. I immediately thought 'hen harrier,' even having seen it for just a second. It was too light-bodied for a buzzard, was slim like a kite, had a longish tail though the tail was not forked. All this pointed to hen harrier and I was frustrated I hadn't had enough time to confirm the sighting. I continued up the road, hoping to see it once I was round the next bend.

The next bend unfortunately gave no view to the right of the road, as there was still a crest. Annoyed, I marched on and took a right fork off the main hill road on to the track that goes round the march of the estate to the east. I noticed four roe deer on the skyline ahead but ignored them for the time being and concentrated on looking for the unconfirmed hen harrier. Luckily it appeared again, though still only a quick view before it disappeared over the near horizon. This time there was no mistake, with the clearly visible white rump and long tail with dark coloured bars across it letting me confidently identify it as either a female or immature hen harrier. Though male hen harriers are a beautiful grey-white colour with black wing tips, they don't metamorphose into this completely different-looking bird until around two years old. If it is a female I hope it remains here to nest in late April.

My attention returned to the four roe, which were still on the skyline in almost exactly the place I saw three on my last visit. They looked in great condition and have had an easy winter so far, though February can sometimes bring heavy snowfalls. It seemed to be a day for roe deer as further along the hill, west of Middle Hill, three roe were making their way up the hill, gradually curling right-handed to the area of the two stunted holly trees. So there were maybe *three* topiary artists rather than just one. Maybe the doe I had been watching since the summer time *did* have twin fawns after all. They certainly seemed to regard this patch as their territory.

One of the Middle Hill buzzards was circling above as I came to the next Y fork. I headed right up Grey Crags again, meaning to try a different route round the hill for a change, and – again for variety – walking on a swiped track that ran parallel to and 30 or so yards to the right of the hill road. Halfway up Grey Crags I was thinking that I hadn't seen a mature roe buck on the hill for a while, and that the last one I saw had been just at this point. Roe are unusual in that they shed their antlers in winter rather than in summer when food is more plentiful. In January antlers will either be absent or beginning to grow and in velvet. I was still thinking about the Grey Crags buck when I looked across to the west side of the hill road and saw what I was sure was a dead roe deer half way down the face. I confirmed this with the binoculars, and also realised that it was directly under a vertical crag about 40 feet high. I wondered if the deer had fallen over the crag, and, of course, if it was the buck that had barked at me in August.

I crossed over to the hill road and looked up towards the crag. The face of the hill was extremely steep, beginning with about 12 feet of scree at the bottom. I hate walking up scree and as soon as I put a foot on it I liked this version even less. It was covered in frost and ice and if the scree did not give way and start to avalanche then my foot slid over the stones, upward progress was reversed and I finished up at the bottom again. Buggeration! After several attempts I eventually managed to get far enough up the scree to get a hold of some heather, but before I managed to pull myself up my feet slid away again, though I stoically retained hold of the heather. There's not much you can do, even with a handhold if you are stretched straight out, and I'd to start again. This time I managed to grip the heather and keep my footholds. I gradually went up the remaining part of the scree rather like a caterpillar; drawing my feet up almost to my hands, then reaching out again for another strong chunk of heather. It was an effort, and once past the scree even the steep climb to the crag seemed a dawdle.

The deer was a doe, probably a young doe. Though it was quite fresh, three quarters of the carcass had been predated. A fox had definitely been a diner at the banquet as one of the deer's back legs was turned almost inside out, something even a golden eagle couldn't do. There were white splashes of bird droppings around the deer, so birds, possibly crows, ravens and buzzards, maybe even a golden eagle or a red kite, had been there. I looked around for any fox scats and was surprised that there were none as they often 'mark' a carcass in this way. From the considerable tufts of deer hair and some blood under the overhang of the crag the feast had begun tight into the rock underneath the overhang. The deer couldn't have fallen to that position; I doubted even if it could have fallen to the position it was in now as it was still slightly under the overhang and would certainly have bounced or slithered further down the slope had it fallen. I felt the deer's legs but none appeared broken. The two forelegs felt as though they were dislocated, but that was just because the muscle joining them to the shoulder and breastbone had been eaten away. I doubted it could fall 40 feet without breaking at least one leg and had to conclude that it had been unwell or even injured and had simply died under the overhang. It was a pity, but at least it wasn't the buck.

I walked right to the very top of the Grey Crags track to see if there was a better way round the back of Connell Hill since I was at quite a high point anyway, rather than going downhill and round the west march. I sat on a rock at the very top of the hill road, having my piece and admiring the view. With the day being so clear I could see in the distance to the west the snow-covered Schiehallion at Kinloch Rannoch. To the south-west I could see the turning blades of one of the 68 huge wind turbines at Griffin Forest in Strathbraan. At 400 feet high, these turbines are twice the height of most. Apart from a small plane that passed overhead, there was not a sound to be heard. Apart from an occasional munch as a boiled ham sandwich was masticated!

The hill road I was on degenerated into an unmade track, then a quad bike track, which eventually looped in a direction I did not want to go. I imagined it would be a very short hike through the long heather to the fire-burnt area at the back of the hill. It turned out to be longer than I thought, but not particularly onerous as it was mostly downhill. I passed a rock face on my left, with the midday sun shining on it. I was thinking it would be a great place for a fox to lie up when I spotted a fresh fox scat. Despite the sunshine, there was still frost on the ground where it was shaded by heather and I noticed round and dainty footprints on the frost on a track; Reynard had slipped away downhill ahead of me. I scanned the empty hill and suspected that, in the way of a fox, it had deviated either left or right around crags ahead where it would be out of view. I saw its tracks in the frost several times but after I passed these crags they disappeared.

The other side of the hill was more shaded from the sun and I was surprised to put up a cock pheasant just before I reached the burnt heather. It *cuck-cuck-cucked* in alarm as it swung back over my head to the sunny side of the hill where it would have much more food available in the feeders, but would still need to survive the beaters' shoot before the season ended on 1 February. Walking was easier on the burnt heather though there was little sign of wildlife. Despite it being almost barren, in some parts thousands of blaeberries had germinated, and these would be followed in a year or so by regenerated heather growth. From desert now, it could turn into one of the most productive parts of the hill within a few years.

I had hoped to see the hen harrier again, but no such luck. I could hear the Middle Hill pair of buzzards mewing, though couldn't see them. I marched on and re-joined the hill road just up from the pond where I'd disturbed the mallard, then kept heading downhill past Dank Wood and cut across towards Larch Wood. A buzzard lifted from the wood and headed silently across to Eerie Valley as I made for my rabbit toilet rock, noticing the black rabbit hopping from under an ancient juniper bush at my approach and across to the rhododendrons. The buzzard settled on a larch tree in Eerie Valley and watched me eat my second sandwich. The Craigie Face jackdaw clan seemed to be busy behind me and to my right above the big scree face at Eerie Return. They lifted noisily several times before circling and landing in the same place and I wondered if they were taking advantage of grain from the partridge feeders. As I was finishing my piece they came back en masse to their home scree above The Shudder almost directly ahead of me on Craigie Face.

I walked along the bog between Law Wood and the Ell Wood, then crossed the fence on my left to go along the side of Law Wood. This field is a favourite with rabbits and I could see several in the distance, and one closer to me that hopped round a dog leg in the fence. The *chip-chipping* of birds drew my attention to a flock at the very top of one of two small-leaved lime trees in the same place. I suppose I expected them to be chaffinches, but when I looked at one through the binoculars I was momentarily startled, thinking I was looking at a green parrot. This initial thought changed to green woodpecker, but because there were several of them I considered the unlikely possibility of a family of woodpeckers. This thought process only took seconds, until I realised I was looking at birds I had never seen before – crossbills. I was surprised how large they looked; even though they were only slightly larger than a greenfinch they somehow looked a lot bigger. The males were orangey-red, with brown wings and a forked tail, while the females were a streaked greeny-yellow with dark wings. The unique feature about them was their large heavy-looking bill with the ends crossed, giving the birds their name of course. They were quite noisy, much more acrobatic than most finches and seemed to climb the branches rather like a parrot or budgie.

Having given me three or four minutes to observe them, they suddenly lifted as a group and flew to my right across to the Henhouse Wood. They *chipped* away as they flew, with the typical undulating flight of most finches. There were over 20 in the group. I was surprised at seeing crossbills there at all, and amazed there were so many. I am aware there are three separate species of crossbill in Scotland: the common, the Scottish and the parrot. Which species they were I was not sure, though I didn't think their beaks were big enough to put them in the parrot category. Having researched the distribution in Scotland of the three species, it is most likely that these were the common crossbill. I had thought some time ago when I was in Wericky Wood that it was an ideal place for crossbill to breed. I'll give it some extra attention now as crossbills are often early nesters.

So yet again on the home run I encountered a bird I had not seen before. The sightings of the hen harrier and crossbill now bring the bird species tally to 64. Can I make the 100?

New birds identified: hen harrier; crossbill
New mammals identified: none

Chapter 17

Monday 13 February 2012. Weather: Mild for the time of year (around 11 degrees). Some sunny spells but the north-west wind picked up during the day, unfortunately becoming quite strong by 1.00 pm.

The spring-like weather is trying to lull me into a false sense that winter has passed. I doubt it. February and March can often bring heavy snow, but I am prepared to enjoy the moment and take advantage of the welcome but unseasonable mildness of the day. I intend to have a walk in a large oak wood named Lament, one where I have only skirted the edges so far. Lament runs on the west side from the public road to just over halfway up the estate drive, and extends eastwards to the march fence. An extension of the same wood continues over the march.

I parked at the shooting lodge and began walking back down the estate road to begin my walk at the bottom of Lament. After 300 yards I reached the dam and I could hear a great tit singing in some willows on the banks of the burn running from the loch. Its song, resembling *tea-cher, tea-cher, tea-cher*, has been etched in my mind ever since we were given as a present a china great tit replica which we put in the conservatory. Every time the invisible beam coming from the bird was activated by someone passing it, it voiced this very presentable imitation of its song. Alas it has since become mute after its battery ran out and now sits observing passers-by without comment. The (live) great tit's song was joined by that of a more distant mistle thrush. This song was similar to that of a blackbird but with shorter bursts of song and longer pauses between the phrases (or in musical terms, between bars). I often have to listen carefully when I hear a mistle thrush to ensure the sound is not emanating from my wheezing after exertion, easily eliminated if I can still hear the sound and I am holding my breath!

I entered Lament just short of the fence dividing the wood from the narrow field between it and the public road. Most of the trees are mature oaks, though tall and slim because of close planting. Some, for whatever reason, had a much thinner trunk originating from the same root. Some of these weakling secondary trunks had died and the rotting wood was clearly a great source of insects for woodland birds. This became evident very quickly as blue tits, coal tits and great tits seemed to be everywhere. Though it took me a long time to see such a common bird as a blue tit on the estate there were certainly plenty here. The birds were feeding on the ground amongst the ferns, on the tree trunks and also on the branches. One wee coat tit was visiting a number of young buds on a thin outer oak branch and picking at the ends. I'd no idea whether its target might have been insects or something in or from the bud but it had found a niche that it was exploiting to the full.

It was depressing to see that quite a number of oaks had been blown down; some in this winter's severe storms, and some during earlier years. Taking a very short term view this was a disaster. Taking a medium term view, the broken branches and uprooted trees would rot providing even more invertebrates as food, and additional nesting places in the upturned roots and the extra ground cover. Trees broken but still standing had now many more nesting hollows and splits, especially for birds such as tree creepers, which often creep (as their name suggests) up under cracked bark. In the longer term, the fact that chunks of the canopy have been removed will permit more light into these clearings to allow natural (or even human-assisted) regeneration. Having thought about this I felt a bit better.

This was the wood in which the red kites successfully nested the previous year. In total I saw three large nests high in the oaks but nothing to indicate any of them had been the red kite's nest. Usually red kites decorate their nest with something plastic and often colourful, but these looked plain, unadorned nests, and unless any decoration had blown away, were probably those of buzzards. Buzzards were almost continually overhead while I was in the wood, probably two different pairs, though there was neither sign nor sound of kites (indeed for the whole of the day). Hopefully they *will* return to nest here this spring.

At the end of the wood I cut uphill, skirting to the left of a sheer rock face, and began the walk back along the top half of the wood. I passed a couple of roe deer 'couches'. These are scrapes on the ground where the oak litter had been pawed away by cloven cervine hooves, resulting in a cleared oval patch which must be thought more comfortable by the deer for their daytime resting place than on top of the leaves it had removed. I see my dog doing the same circling and scraping 'nest building' just after it gets into its basket. A robin began to sing from its perch in a holly tree, so I thought this would be a good place to have the first piece of the day. I sat on a mossy rock, without any preparatory scraping, and enjoyed my musical lunch. The robin has a high pitched and quite melodious song, in a way like the mistle thrush with fits and starts, but with shorter breaks between phrases. I was really appreciative of its company.

Parting with Mr Redbreast, I continued along the wood, a movement half-way up an oak tree catching my attention. Binoculars revealed not one but two great-spotted woodpeckers. They were engaged in flirtatious frolic rather than food-finding, one following the other to the adjacent tree, then to the next, and finally into a corner of the wood that was coniferous, mainly spruce trees with a mix of ash and possibly wild cherry creating a narrow buffer between the two different habitats. Even had I not seen them, the single *'chik'* one of them made on the flight to the conifers would have made me aware of their presence.

As my line of sight followed the woodpeckers, I saw another wee bird near the base of an oak and jerkily making its way upwards, and gradually spiralling round the trunk. The wee tree creeper would find plenty of insect food in Lament, in fact the wood could probably support dozens of them. I was reasonably close to it and its white eye stripe was easily visible even without the binoculars. It was using the stiff tail feathers to help support it in its climb, as do the previous birds I saw, the woodpeckers. As I was getting my camera out it flew to the bottom of another tree and started its ascent again, this time disappearing round the back. I moved forward to get a photo opportunity when it came back round, but yet another shape caught my eye further up the tree behind it, this time a red squirrel.

There was too much going on at the same time and, since the squirrel was in view anyway, I followed its course. Its arboreal skills were incredible, using the thinner branches half way up the trees as an aerial highway. It seemed to know where it was going, verification of this being when the terminus was seen to be a hole in the tree into which it poked its head. It came out to check for danger, and in went the head again. I wasn't sure whether this might have been a source for a small pool of water or was one of its nut stores. Business complete, the squirrel made its way back to the conifers on what appeared to be the very same aerial route. The tree creeper, of course, was gone by now.

I walked up the east edge of the block of conifers and cut back again next to the dyke at the top of Lament, crossing the dyke further along into Geordie's Moor. I made my way up towards the release pen in the junipers and spotted a rabbit snoozing among some flattened bracken inside the pen. I crept slowly closer, taking a series of photos of snoozy rabbit, until I was less than 20 yards away. He (I'm sure by the broader head it was a buck) heard the click of what was to be the final photo as I was now against the netting fence, and quickly bolted into the standing bracken behind. To achieve old age rabbits need to be more observant than this!

I walked round the pen and as I approached a large oak tree ahead of me a female sparrowhawk darted across my path from right to left close to the ground. It was most certainly on a hunting foray, hoping to ambush a small bird by suddenly appearing from behind a tree or a clump of junipers like a fighter aircraft. Being a female (it was much larger than a male, with a brown back as opposed to the blue back of a male) it could easily tackle a pigeon sized bird, but smaller birds were more likely victims among the junipers. Had I been able to see the underside of the sparrowhawk, the barring on the white underside would have been brown rather than the orangey-red barring of a male. The owner and keeper did say that they seemed scarce this year and there had been almost no partridge kills that could be attributed to sparrowhawks.

I continued through the Geordie's Moor and up past the duck ponds to Wericky, but by now the wind had strengthened, bending the tops of the huge Douglas firs at the top end of Wericky and at one point blowing my bunnet off my head. Apart from an odd pheasant the wood seemed empty, as did my next wood, the Larch Wood, the next again, the Ell Wood, the Pheasant Wood, the Henhouse Wood and the Loch Wood. The circuit of the woods was good exercise, but nothing seems to make birds disappear like a strong wind. It is a temporary absence and I'm sure they'll be back for my next visit.

New birds identified: long-tailed tit; sparrowhawk
New mammals identified: none

Chapter 18

Sunday 19 February 2012. Weather: one or two inches of snow on the ground, having fallen the previous evening. Temperature -3 degrees, gradually reaching 4 degrees as the sun came out about 9.30 am. Thankfully no wind.

There was only a dusting of snow at home, though I suspected there would be slightly more on the estate. The forecast was good so I thought I might take advantage of an opportunity to track birds and mammals that may have passed earlier. If snow has lain overnight without freezing it is an open book as to what has taken place during the night. I hoped that would be the case. A light snowfall, in line with yesterday evening's weather forecast, makes little difference to the nocturnal activities of mammals, thought a heavy snowfall severely limits the movements of the smaller ones. I could see as I drove up the A9 that the hills were white; in fact after leaving the dual carriageway the narrower roads were white as well, and demanded careful driving to avoid landing in the ditch.

There was a good omen soon after I left the dual carriageway. As I passed a sawmill 10 or a dozen fallow deer were ambling from one side of the bellmouth to the other, and about 10 yards from my car. They took no notice of the vehicle, though I was unable to stop or even slow down before I had passed the entrance and lost them to sight. Most were the dark variety, with a single dappled one among them. A good start!

I left my car at the shooting lodge. There was an inch or so of snow there, more where it had been drifting in yesterday evening's wind. It was crunchy underfoot, but thankfully that was only on any field or hill tracks. If I walked to the side of any tracks the snow was quite soft, and allowed me to walk quietly rather than alert every beastie within quarter of a mile. Rabbit tracks were everywhere, and as I headed up towards the Larch Wood a fox had crossed my route. Its passage must have been during early evening as drifting snow had partly filled in its tracks, but the neat straight line of paw prints, with toe marks still visible in an occasional one, confirmed who had left the tracks. Fallow deer had also been down very close to the shooting lodge. Their cleat marks were mostly filled in with snow as well, but where they dragged each foot forward, barely off the ground, they left two virtually parallel lines, punctuated every time they put a foot down. Roe are much more dainty when walking and, unless the snow is deep, are less inclined to drag their cleats through the snow.

I cut into the small roundel of mainly larch trees immediately before the Larch Wood. A rabbit ahead of me thumped the ground with a back foot (the sound carrying quite clearly in the absence of wind) and another rabbit came out of a nearby burrow to assess the danger for itself. The two looked at me, 20 yards away, trying to work out – in almost monochrome vision – what this apparition was. It's strange that birds see in colour yet most mammals, with the exception of primates and some marsupials, only appear to see shaded versions of colours. Most mammals in Scotland are nocturnal so I suppose improved night vision might be the reason, and certainly an advantage. As I was watching the two rabbits I was aware of a chaffinch half-heartedly trying to sing. I've heard chaffinches singing at home over the last few mornings, but these mornings were milder with no snow. The one above me sounded a bit downcast that the route to spring had faltered spectacularly and eventually gave up its musical efforts.

The rabbits' patience was wearing better than mine, and I finally moved forward, causing both of them to take off through the wood. Most observers might wonder why they did not bolt down the adjacent burrow, especially considering one had not long emerged from the it. When I walked forward I could see that the burrow was quite small with only three entrances. Taking refuge in what appeared to be a small, shallow, burrow might put them at great risk if the 'predator' had seen where they had gone. Making for a bigger burrow, or even an equally small burrow but out of sight of the predator, was a much safer option.

I was torn between looking down at tracks and looking up for birds, but when I did eventually tear my gaze away from the myriad of tracks in the snow I could see a buzzard's nest high in a larch tree. It looked in good repair and was probably from the previous year. The chances are they'll be back to the roundel, or even the same nest, this year. As I came out of the roundel, two dunnocks were feeding on the tip of a blown fir tree, apparently the only two avian companions for the despondent chaffinch.

I crossed a narrow, damp area to reach the entrance to the Larch Wood. On the left of the entrance there is a huge area of wild rhododendrons. Red-legged partridges started to explode out of there at my approach. I was amazed as they continued to come out, making a total of at least 70. I saw from the footprints in the snow as I went in through the open gate to the wood that other partridges had run across to the right; tracks with three toes forward, one back and with a small furrow in the snow made by the middle toe scraping the snow, thereby joining the footprints together. This was an incredible pack of partridges for mid-February, especially after an excellent shooting season. I'll be interested to see if they pair up; whether they'll nest on the lower ground rather than on the hill; if red-legged partridges are good parents, and if there is a good enough food supply to sustain chicks. I suspect there will be plenty food, as no chemicals are used on the estate so insects, essential for many young birds, should thrive.

The Larch Wood was quiet. There were plenty tracks of fallow and some of roe, but the only bird I saw was a robin. A primary school pupil once wrote in a nature diary during a project I ran that '*robins only come out when there is snow.*' There was certainly snow today; maybe she was right! I walked to the top of the wood to where larch and sycamore trees give way to sitka spruce, and wondered if I might see a red squirrel. The red squirrel habitat had degenerated with so many recently-fallen trees, but hopefully there may be sufficient remaining to sustain a few of the scarce and lovable beasties. At the top of one of the trees, though out of my view, a mistle thrush was singing. Even he, like the earlier chaffinch was putting little effort into the song and gave up after a few bars. It was nearly 10.00 o'clock and the sun had come out, but not enough to convince birds that their musical endeavours – which are really about communication and territory – would be wasted. Did they know of a spell of wintry weather ahead?

I left the wood and had a look round the corner at one of my favourite rock-seats (too wet to sit on today) to see if there was any sign of the black rabbit. En route I crossed fox tracks heading in that direction and hoped black bun had not been on last night's menu. There was no sign of the black rabbit, but I'll not give up hope just yet… The fox tracks continued down over the burn and up the small incline to the gate leading to the grass field that leads up to Eerie Valley. The tracks were nice and clear, probably made around dawn, so I decided to follow to see what *Vulpes vulpes* had been up to. When the fox walked in a straight line it was easy to confirm the habit they have of placing the hind foot almost on top of the imprint of the front foot. Unlike some other mammals where there are usually two parallel lines of tracks the fox normally leaves a single line of tracks. This single line led to a rabbit burrow, where the fox had investigated two of the entrances before moving on and turning right to head down to the dyke separating the field from the hill. It followed the line of the dyke to near the top of the field and was joined (or at least its tracks were joined) there by the tracks of another fox coming in from the centre of the field. The two sets of tracks continued, without any signs of one fox greeting the other (which made me think the tracks were made at different times and that the two foxes had not, in fact, met), through the gate at the top of the field and through the next gate 20 yards along that led to the hill and Eerie Valley.

Once on the hill one set of tracks veered sharp left, but the other – my original fox – continued along the track through the hill that leads to the pegs for the partridge drives. A couple of hundred yards along the track it deviated sharply to the left to the bracken, flattened by the winter frosts, and almost immediately came out onto the track again in two bounds. At that point there was a small red bloodstained patch of snow where the fox had crunched and eaten the morsel it had caught, probably a long-tailed field mouse or a field vole. I could even see in the snow where the fox had briefly sat on its haunches while it dined, with the impression in the snow of the lower part of its back legs, from toe to hock, forming an open 'V', almost surrounded by the semi-circular impression of its backside. Any countryside walk in fresh snow can reveal these secrets to anyone who can interpret them. The fox walked on a bit further, investigating – though not eating – a fallow deer gralloch, before cutting right-handed again down towards the burn running through Eerie Valley. Just after the fox left the path, the tracks of a small mammal, probably a field vole, crossed the path from left to right. Surprisingly I've never seen a live vole on the estate, but they were certainly here. Maybe this year will be a good vole year, and consequently lead to better breeding success of species such as stoats, weasels, owls, kestrels, hen harriers and merlins. The vole doesn't have many friends!

As I walked up Eerie Valley, small groups of red-legged partridges rose from the scree on my right, most flying up over the high ridge behind them. Further up the valley a large flock of what I thought were fieldfares rose on the right and flew over the crest of the hill on my left. They were a good distance away and unfortunately had disappeared before I got the binoculars up to get a better view. By this time I was at No 6 peg, the spot where, as I described earlier, I had the most exciting half-hour's shooting of my life. Memories came flooding back as I looked at the peg down in the hollow and wondered if I would ever be lucky enough to stand there again.

I decided at this point to turn back and to make for the Ell Wood. I followed the dyke at the top of the grass field I had already been in and crossed fox tracks again half way along, just at the point where some junipers, rough heather and bracken encroach from Craigie Face onto the field and where rabbits abound. The fox will know every inch of this area. I entered the Ell Wood at a gate half way down the fence and followed the track made by George's quad bike (now replaced with a Polaris with a roof – much warmer, drier and of course, very much more posh!). Ell Wood has been a bare wood so far for birds, yet has everything that birds need. It is primarily young birch with a good sprinkling of other mature hardwood trees, particularly beech, and one or two conifers round the outside. There seems no reason that birds should not be here in decent numbers in springtime. Finches form large flocks in cold weather; safety in numbers as a flock rising together confuses a bird of prey such as a sparrowhawk. Large flocks mean a lot of birds in one place, but an absence of birds elsewhere. Once the flocks disperse and the birds form pairs they'll colonise every available wood on the estate.

In fact a surprise was in store: as I came round a corner I could see some birds under a pheasant hopper. Through the binoculars I saw that they were chaffinches, taking advantage of the wheat spilled by pheasants as they picked at the conical spring under the feeder that dispensed the grain. Among the chaffinches was a bird that looked almost identical, but wasn't a chaffinch; it was a male brambling. I scanned the group again to see if there might have been a female but they flew up into the birches before I could check every bird. Bramblings have a rust coloured upper breast compared with the salmon pink colour of the chaffinch. The belly and the chin are white, which may be the easiest identifying features, since chaffinches have no white apart from on wing feathers. Bramblings are winter visitors from Northern Europe. From time to time in winter I see them at home, mostly in small numbers, feeding with chaffinches, though they have only ever been there, like today, in snowy weather.

I left the Ell Wood by the bottom gate and crossed over to the grass field between the Henhouse Wood and Law Wood. As I turned left on entering the field I looked back to the Ell Wood… to see two roe deer crossing the path I had just left, then muzzling at the wheat under the hopper just vacated by the brambling and its chaffinch pals. The first roe was quickly obscured by trees, but the second was a buck with antlers beginning to grow back and of course in velvet. I had rattled the conical spring under the barrel as I passed, releasing some wheat, so there was certainly a decent feed of grain left for them.

I walked down the outside of Law Wood and crossed to the Loch Wood, also following it down the outside. I then made for a wooden bridge that would take me across the burn which runs from the dam at the shooting lodge loch. A tree had fallen, partly blocking the bridge, and I had to squeeze past. I was not the first to cross the bridge: a cat had crossed earlier, its rounded paw marks, with no claws visible, showed that it had crossed in the opposite direction to me. It had jumped a branch impeding its route (as it did mine) then, like a tightrope walker, completed its crossing on the narrow piece of wood running lengthwise at the outer edge. No-one near there owns a cat, so it is likely to be a feral moggie. These are the cats that in the northern half of Scotland hybridise with pure wildcats, depleting the already threatened gene pool. If it was a male, hopefully it was neutered before going feral. If not, it would be much better for wildlife, especially the Scottish wildcat, if it is tempted into one of the live-catch cat traps that George is currently operating. With only 400 of our native Scottish 'tigers' remaining that are believed pure wildcats, they need all the help they can get.

Leaving 'Cat's Bridge', I turned right down the estate road heading for Lament. I walked slowly down the road checking the gorge wherever I could hoping to see dippers. I'll be really interested to see where they nest in the spring, as it will be in this gorge somewhere. No dippers, but a lone woodcock rose and flew out the far side heading towards the Loch Wood. As I've said before they're magical and mysterious wee birds and I'm always pleased to see one. Even more than the brambling, that made my day. I went into the top corner of Lament, causing half a dozen pheasants to scurry off and the same amount of partridges to fly over my head. My entrance had not gone unnoticed by the jays, and two started to screech at my presence.

I continued on, still cutting the corner to a degree, till I was near the bottom of the wood, then followed parallel to and about 50 yards up from the bottom fence. At least two great-spotted woodpeckers were drumming; a tremendous method of communication as it carries a long way on a quiet day such as this was, only being interrupted by the mewing of three buzzards overhead. Halfway along the wood a flock of birds rose from among some oak leaves where the snow had all but melted. They landed near the top of one of the trees on the edge of the wood. I suspected they were fieldfares and I had some difficulty finding them for identification; every time one moved it was to land in a tree further away. I eventually found one in the binoculars and was surprised to see it was a redwing. I know that redwings are often along with fieldfares so I was keen to see what species the remainder of the birds were. I edged forward, but unfortunately so did the birds, now being three or four trees distant.

Giving the birds best for the time being I made my way up onto a path that very gradually took me further away from the wood edge. I was hoping that they would fly back round me, giving another chance at ID. Meantime I could hear the *chik* of a great spotted woodpecker ahead of me. Before I could locate it, it flew over my head at tree-top level and landed four or five trees behind me, where it started drumming. Simultaneously I heard the *kew kew kew kew kew* of a green woodpecker. The sound came from the top side of the wood and probably a bit ahead of me. I scanned with the binoculars but still no sighting; it was probably too far away in any case, though I hoped I would fall in with it when I came back along the top edge of the wood. It was all happening at once! The flock of birds (redwings or fieldfares?) began to filter back over the trees at the bottom edge of the wood. As they landed behind me I managed to confirm two as redwings, so I thought it reasonable to assume redwings comprised the whole flock. There had recently been some extremely cold weather in north-eastern Europe that could cause a late migration, though I always thought that the redwings that wintered in Scotland were Icelandic birds.

White fallow calf, Creag Bheag Wood.

Dead roe deer beneath the crag at Grey Crags.

Roebuck at the Hill Road.

The loch below the shooting lodge.

Grey Crags.

Goosanders and nesting swan on the fishing loch.

Cygnets on the fishing loch.

Swallows near the shooting lodge.

The snoozy rabbit, Geordie's Moor.

Craigie Face.

Garden warbler singing on Craigie Face.

Coal tit in Wericky Wood.

Pearl-bordered fritillary on Eerie Valley.

The nest from which the author disturbed the mallard.

Mallard with ducklings.

The hill road on a cold day.

Fox tracks in Eerie Valley.

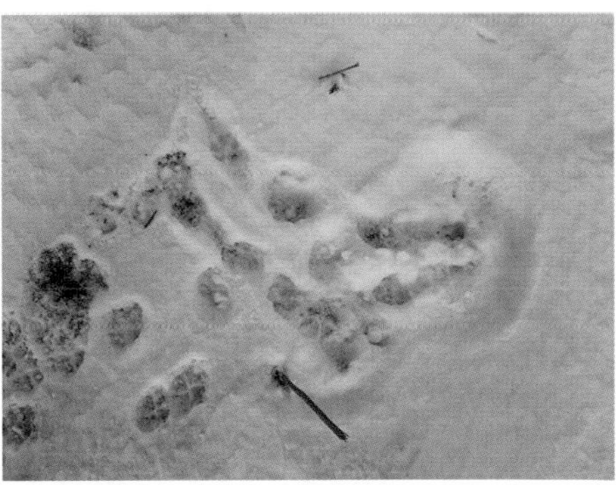

Evidence of vole killed by fox in Eerie Valley.

Hooded crow in crow cage trap.

Roosting tawny owl near the shooting lodge.

Red squirrel.

I followed the fence line at the far end of Lament (which I should maybe ask the owner to re-name *Woodpecker Wood*) and began to return along the top. I had to climb the edge of a rock face that came right to the top fence line, and as I did so I spotted an immature dark-coloured fallow 10 yards away at the other side of the fence. I slowly reached into my pocket for my camera, every delicate movement being watched closely by the young deer, with ears facing forward straining to hear the least sound. I brought the camera ever so slowly up to face level, but the click as I switched it on was enough for the deer already on the starting blocks, and it was off. I gradually stood up and peered over the rock face, to see three fallow looking in puzzlement in my direction. I lifted the camera and took a couple of photos, but only got ears. The ears heard the clicks and now 20 fallow, all dark, were bounding into the trees, where they stopped for another look, still unsure of the danger. This time, with considerable luck more than any stalking or photographic skills, I managed to get a photo as the last three began to melt into the trees.

I followed the fence line along – the boundary with the estate to the east – and climbed over once I came to Geordie's Moor. I cut through the junipers and at the end crossed a boggy patch, again sticking to the rabbit hops to ensure I didn't sink in the bog. The rabbits had developed this safe route over many years and I'd have been daft not to trust to it. I could see two blue tits on top of a blackthorn bush at the side of the drystane dyke separating Geordie's Moor from the grass field beyond. They were flicking their wings and clearly alarmed. I couldn't hear them at that point but as I got closer I could hear their *tsee tsee tsee* alarm calls. Their calls attracted another blue tit and there were now three on top of the bush warning fellow birds and mammals of danger. I had a good idea what the danger was and made a squeaking sound, sucking with my lips, somewhat (hopefully) resembling a rabbit squealing in distress. Within a few seconds a small brown triangular face, with two dark eyes and an equally dark and shiny nose, poked out of the dyke. Knowing how inquisitive stoats and weasels are, I continued squeaking and he (or she) came out a bit further, resting his front paws on one of the stones to get a better look at me. He was a smart wee chap, with a light brown coat and white belly. He went back into the dyke and re-appeared two or three stones further up, repeating this twice more before giving up on identifying the cause of the squeaking. Whatever the weasel had been up to – or was going to be up to – the blue tits had given everyone around an early warning.

I headed back through the sheep field (still with no sheep) to the car, disturbing several rabbits en route that had been basking in the midday sun. Flattened snow, dirtied brown from earth on their paws or with urine stains ranging from yellow to orange, showed where they had been resting, and resonant thumps below ground conveyed their alarm and annoyance. My day in the countryside in the snow had been rewarding beyond all expectations.

New birds identified: brambling
New mammals identified: weasel

Chapter 19

Thursday 1 March 2012. Weather: Very mild (13 degrees), sunny with very little wind.

Spring was definitely in the air today, confirmed at almost first light by the sight of a rook breaking a twig from the top of one of my larch trees and carrying it off to the nearby rookery. This will be the first of many visits by this rook and its hundred or so cronies to prune the tops of my maturing larch trees.

The big fishing loch was my first destination today. It opens with a pike fishing competition on 3 and 4 March, for rainbow trout just after that since rainbow trout are not given an official close season, and for brown trout after the end of their close season, which is 14 March. On my arrival just before 8 am the new fishery manager, Craig, had a boat ready for me with a fully-charged electric outboard motor, though as it hadn't been tested he put in a set of oars 'just in case'. The loch was flat calm, and a couple of rafts of goldeneye were bobbing on the surface 100 yards offshore, but they were very jumpy and took off to the south east corner even before I got into the boat.

It was great to get back on to the loch again, especially on such a beautiful spring morning. The quiet purr of the electric motor and the swish of the silvery water being parted by the bow of the boat were joined by a chorus of birdsong. Mistle thrushes sang a stilted and slightly repetitive – but nevertheless wonderful – stereophonic duet from the north and south shores; a pair of oystercatchers flew from the north shore in a semi-circle over the boat, voicing their rapid *peep-peep, peep-peep, peep-peep* call, and an unseen moorhen made its single *kurr-uk* call from deep within the reedbed near the boat anchorage, answered by another skulking out of sight further round the reeds. This was a great start, and I'd only just got onto the loch.

I scanned round the loch with the binoculars, as I was keen to see what was there with as little disturbance as possible. The raft of goldeneye in the south-east corner numbered about 30. The goldeneye normally nests off the ground, in tree holes or nest boxes in woodland near to a loch. Some already seemed to have paired, though I've no idea if there will be suitable sites round this loch. Since there are such high numbers of goldeneye here maybe the owner could get some nest boxes up for next year. Some mallard were behind the goldeneye, mostly resting on the shore. Several took off in fright as a heron pitched in over their heads to land at the lochside in the hope of a fish small enough to swallow. It was a mature bird, and I could see the long plumes of its crest as it stood with neck bent forward ready to strike any unwary fish.

I veered right, up the loch and away from the goldeneye. A lone great-crested grebe was in the middle of the loch and I wondered if its partner was another lone grebe I had glimpsed from the car as I passed the adjacent loch earlier. Three pairs of swans seemed to have established territories now, with one pair at a reed bed right at the top (west) end of the loch, and the other two at reed beds on the north shore. I wondered why there were no young reared last year. Maybe I'll get the answer this year. As I headed up the loch a small flock of about 15 lapwings flew over. From underneath they looked like a flock of male hen harriers (not that any harriers would flock) with their white underparts and black wing tips. That's the lapwings and the oyster catchers beginning to come back now from their winter coastal haunts, though with the mild winter we've had they could easily have been back much earlier. I always thought weather was the trigger, but another trigger may well be the time of year; maybe mid-February, even with mild weather, is too early.

Another bird that spends its winter on tidal mudflats and salt marshes was now also back. I was thrilled to hear what is probably the most magical of bird sounds: the bubbling *coooor-lee, coooor-lee, coooor-lee* call of the curlew came from just behind the trees on the south shore. The first sight (or sound in this case) of a curlew is yet another true reminder that we have left the worst of the winter weather behind and that we are now entering what is – at least for me – the best season of the year: springtime. Somewhere between me and the curlew a great-spotted woodpecker drummed on a tree in support of the curlew's promise of spring. I cut the electric motor so that not even the slightest sound interfered with this delectation.

Having savoured the moment, I started off up the loch again, disturbing one of the most wary of birds, a cormorant, which was a good 200 yards away in the centre of the loch. It is the most persecuted of the sawbill ducks, hence its reticence to be anywhere near humans. It flew off towards the adjacent loch to resume its fishing there. Beyond the cormorant there were another three pairs of goldeneye and three females in the bay at the top of the loch, so rather than disturb them I moved right again towards the 'otter' bay. With the flat calm surface any otter movement would be easy to spot and I fervently hoped it would emerge from its holt for a spot of fishing or exercise. I'm much more aware now than when I last saw it of the camera in my pocket, but it didn't oblige today. I had sat with the motor off for 15 or so minutes, and was entertained by a large trout that kept rising between the boat and the shore. It broke the surface four times, each time moving about 10 yards further along the shoreline. Though it never came right out of the water it seemed a substantial fish, but I couldn't determine whether it was a brown trout or a rainbow.

With no show from the otter, I headed down the loch again, noting another raft of goldeneye – maybe 30 or so again – near the north shore. I kept my distance from them and swung further right to avoid the great-crested grebe, which had now moved further down the loch not far from the anchorage. I steered between the grebe and the flotilla of goldeneye still at the south-east corner. There would be at least 60 goldeneye on the loch, probably as high a number as on any of the Scottish lochs. I edged the boat into its berth and chained it up, having thoroughly enjoyed my outing.

Leaving the loch, I parked my car at the shooting lodge and walked down to the bottom of Lament, rapidly gaining favour as a favourite wood. I passed a frog, squashed on the road. It seemed a pity that this poor wee amphibian managed to survive the winter in hibernation only to be killed as the breeding season is about to start. It was fresh and would make a snack for a buzzard or a red kite. As I entered the wood near the bottom of the estate road I sat to eat my piece, some roast chicken. I sat on the trunk of an oak tree that had fallen some years earlier and was now covered in moss, which gave me a comfortable cushion. Rabbits also favoured this perch, their droppings the length of the trunk evidence of their regular use of it as a thoroughfare or look-out post. Sitting quietly in the sunny glade I was aware of two chaffinches singing. Both had the very same version of a song which has regional variations, normally in the last few notes, and I could hear that the ending was slightly different from the chaffinches at home. I was also being regaled by a song thrush and a robin. This was only the second song thrush I had heard this year. They are lovely songsters, repeating each line of their song three, four or even five times. The song thrush has a loud 'voice', and this one seemed to be at least 100 yards up the wood yet I could hear every note clearly. The robin, meantime, was in a holly bush just behind me, singing vigorously to proclaim its territory. It would not allow any other robin, except for its chosen mate, inside the invisible territorial boundaries, and might even fight to the death with any interloper. For such delicate birds they're certainly feisty and aggressive.

Having munched my way through my roast chicken, I continued quietly along the wood, noting the high number of blue tits and great tits. I passed a line of freshly excavated mole hills with a dead mole lying near them. The mole had been dead for some time and certainly hadn't been the busy subterranean worker that had been pushing all this rich and crumbly soil above ground. Moles seem not to be particularly palatable and are sometimes killed by a fox but not eaten, which might have been the fate of this fat wee chap in the black velvet jacket. As I looked up another small flock of lapwings flew over the wood heading towards the fishing loch I had just left; maybe the same flock as I had seen earlier still making their mind up where to settle for the rest of the year. In the distance I could also hear a swan flapping along the surface of the loch, maybe the male of one of the north shore pairs seeing off the male from the other pair. Their territories *are* fairly close and this might be a regular display of ownership and defence during the next few months.

Three-quarters of the way along the wood I cut uphill to avoid the rocky outcrop near the end of the wood as foxes sometimes cub in a den there. They'll be cubbing shortly and I didn't want to incur George's wrath by leaving my scent near the area and moving away any fox that might be considering *that* den rather than another den that might not be known. I like foxes but I have to respect the fact that part of the use of this estate is as a sporting estate and that foxes are controlled to protect game birds and wild birds alike, though will never be eliminated. At the top of the wood I cut back towards the estate road again, thinking, in contrast to my last visit to Lament, I had not seen or heard any woodpeckers. Concomitant to these thoughts I heard the *kew kew kew kew kew* of a green woodpecker behind me. Since I'd not had much luck seeing this bird I found a comfortable seat on a moss-covered rock and sat for a while to see if the bird might come to me. Fifteen minutes into my wait I saw a group of fallow deer making their way, quietly and unconcernedly, up the wood towards where I thought the woodpecker might be. They were all dark coloured; in fact I'd never seen any of the light dappled variety at this end of the estate. They gradually picked their way up through the trees till they were lost to sight. Like the otter, the green woodpecker failed to show and I moved on up to Geordie's Moor.

I picked my way up the west side of the junipers on Geordie's Moor, heading away from Lament at almost right angles, and was surprised to hear the familiar mocking call of the green woodpecker again. Assuming it was the same bird, it had left the oaks in Lament and cut the corner to issue its laughing cry from ahead of me. Though green woodpeckers feed quite a lot on the ground, I considered it wouldn't be vocal while it was in that more vulnerable position. There were four or five old birch trees ahead and I suspected that's where it was. I didn't doubt it could see me, but even though I scanned the trees with the binoculars there was no sign of it. I walked slowly forward, hoping even if I couldn't see it in a tree I would see it flying off; a flash of green and red with deeply undulating flight, closing its wings after every four or five flaps of its wings – much like some of the finches. Even before I finished my stalk I could hear it behind me in the Lament oaks again.

Determined not to let this bird beat me, I turned to go back towards Lament… in time to see a huge bird, some distance away, soar at considerable height in the sky but quickly lost to my view as it disappeared behind a large birch tree. I was convinced it was not a buzzard but I needed a second look to gauge the distance that the bird was from me and thus get a better idea of its size. I ran forward and had to completely pass the birch tree before I saw the bird again, now almost a mile away and probably over the top of the fishing loch. Even at this distance there was no mistaking a white-tailed eagle, with its huge size and disproportionately short tail. I could see no white on the tail, meaning it was an immature bird. It banked at one point, giving me a great view of its broad wings, with long fingering on the ends. It was the underside of its wings I was seeing; the top side would have been much more interesting since all the young white-tailed eagles released as part of the East of Scotland reintroduction programme have different coloured tags. I fervently hoped it would bank again and show me the top of its wings but it now glided further and further away until it was just a speck in the sky. White-tailed eagles are much less wary of humans than golden eagles and it's not unusual to see them comparatively close to human habitation. This is now the third live one I've seen in Tayside (unfortunately I've seen an almost equal number of dead ones, victims of deliberate poisoning) and can't wait till they start to breed in this area.

The excitement had taken my mind off the green woodpecker, which I could now hear pecking at a tree. Green woodpeckers are less inclined to drum than their great-spotted cousins and the sound of this one tapping was as if a person was slowly and methodically hitting a tree with a small hammer. There was a hollow, resonant sound to its tapping and I suspected it was looking for insects on one of the many dead or dying trees. I also realised the tapping was coming from the place in Lament where I had earlier sat hoping the woodpecker would come to me! I sat on a banking with a rabbit burrow beneath me and waited and watched again. A song thrush sang very close behind me and another some distance away, making my wait much more pleasant. A rabbit thumped a warning underneath me, anxious at my presence on its doorstep, but the sounds of the woodpecker had finished and I had to concede it to be the victor – for today at least.

I left Geordie's Moor and made towards Wericky. A red kite flew quite low over my head, coming from the direction of Wericky and heading towards Lament. That was a good sign. I hadn't seen a kite for several visits, and now that I had seen one it was heading towards where they bred successfully last year. It didn't have wing tags, but of course the one with the white and red tags and the radio tag was on one of the 2011 chicks and it had left the estate to prospect in the Crieff area, though it probably wouldn't breed anyway until the following year. I walked through Wericky, going for the first time into the steeper section at the very top with mature larch and spruce trees. My attention was immediately taken with a red squirrel searching the ground for nuts or some other delicacy. It scampered round behind a fallen tree and as I closed in, camera at the ready, it climbed a short distance up a larch tree and sat on a larch branch holding some item of food to its mouth with its dextrous front paws. It would have been a great profile photograph, but it heard the 'ping' of the camera being switched on and jumped to the larch tree behind. I managed to get closer, keeping a tree between us as cover, and watched it finish off its morsel before gradually making its way further up the larch, run out along a branch and jump to a neighbouring spuce. It had seen me by that time and flicked its golden bushy tail several times in agitation before disappearing into the topmost branches.

As I emerged from Wericky a red kite was circling over Dank Wood. I'd no idea whether this was the same one I'd seen earlier but hoped that it was the second one of a pair. I continued on from Dank Wood across to the top side of the Larch Wood, seeing three or four coveys of red-legged partridges on my journey, probably a hundred birds among the coveys, which is a remarkable amount for this small area and which might hopefully breed successfully later in the spring. They have settled down since the end of the shooting season and in each case only flew a short distance before landing again. I could see, through the bare branches of an old birch tree, two white dots bobbing away. At first I thought they were birds, then realised of course that they were the back-ends of roe deer. In their predictable way they stopped to look back at me before finally jumping the dyke into Larch Wood.

As I circled the wood I could see that George had been busy with a trapping programme. I passed three fox snares, one of which I reset as it had been knocked, a tunnel trap for stoats and a cage trap for a feral cat. Crow trapping would also begin soon, all reminders that on an estate that depends on forestry, farming and shooting as well as valuing its wildlife, some species are controlled to protect others. The species that George is legitimately reducing in number prey not only on pheasants and partridges, but on ground nesting birds such as lapwings, oystercatchers, curlew and mallard.

My day finished with an unexpected bonus. I was loading my car with some blown timber, cut into manageable pieces, near to the shooting lodge. At the other side of the steading there is a small wood of conifers and I was surprised to hear a tawny owl. I've heard tawny owls in daylight before, though it is quite unusual. This was not a full blooded *hooo-hoo-hoooo* of the male's call, but rather a hoarse, gurgling, almost half-strangled *hoooo-oooooo*. This call is usually associated with a female tawny, whose main call is *kee-wick*. The owner had told me he heard plenty tawny owls at night and I had been thinking during my walk that I would need to come out to the estate some morning before first light to confirm their presence for myself. I was quite pleased that such an early morning start is no longer required.

New birds identified: moorhen; curlew; white-tailed eagle; tawny owl
New mammals identified: mole

Chapter 20

Monday 5 March 2012. Weather: Cold wind first thing but the day warmed up in the sunshine and the wind became weaker by 10 am. Clouded slightly at midday, then quickly returned to full sun. Peaked at 11 degrees.

My attention was immediately taken by two new inhabitants of the shooting lodge loch on my arrival at the estate. With the brief glance I had I was sure that new arrivals were Canada geese, and I went on to the veranda of the shooting lodge overlooking the loch to confirm. Sure enough a Canada goose and gander were proudly resting on the island, the gander considerably larger and slightly paler in colour. The four resident mute swans were close by and there seemed to be no animosity with their recently-arrived wildfowl cousins. As I watched them I became aware of a blackbird chattering behind me in the small conifer wood adjacent to the lodge. I couldn't see the blackbird, but knew its tone meant an avian predator, probably an owl. Blackbirds in particular are great at letting any observer know what is about – provided of course the observer can read the signs. In contrast to the high pitched chattering, the blackbird gives a single note *pink* if it spots a predator such as a cat, stoat or weasel on the ground, with this warning repeated for as long as the danger persists. I could now see two chaffinches joining in the warning, emitting a similar *pinking* note, though pitched higher than that of the blackbird. They were nervously flitting about the branches half-way up a sitka spruce tree near the corner of the wood.

I went round the lodge to get to the edge of the wood and looked up into the trees. Barely visible, and blending perfectly with the trunk and branches, was a tawny owl. It was tight against the trunk of the tree, and had I not been peering up with some confidence of what would be there I probably wouldn't have seen it. With my presence the small birds had gone, their whistle-blowing job done. Having brown feathers streaked down the breast with white, the owl merged perfectly with the dappled shade of the woodland. Its head looked almost as wide as its body, with a creamy white semi-circle on each side and a brown stripe down the centre, ending in its beak. Its eyes were firmly shut, and it seemed to be enjoying its siesta despite its raucous and inconsiderate neighbours. This could well have been the owl that I heard on my visit a mere five days before. I went to the car for my camera and managed to get a few decent photos that rather surprisingly looked as if I were opposite the bird rather than underneath it.

I came back to the veranda and sat for a few minutes. Observing the Canada goose earlier, I heard a bird that always brings back many childhood memories, but had been briefly forgotten because of the owl. I looked across to the marshy part of Geordie's Moor between George's house and the junipers, where there was a lapwing displaying: rising in the air, then diving back towards the ground again twisting and turning as it did so, all the while rendering its lovely *peeee-weep, weep-weep, peeee-weep* call, evocative of the months of March and April, and which of course gives the bird its countryside name of peeweep or peewit. When these birds were much more common on arable land, we farm boys always stopped the small grey Fergie tractor to move and replace the nest, or harrowed or rolled round it rather than flatten the four olive spotted eggs with the pointed ends all facing the centre of the rudimentary straw and stone nest so that the bird could more easily incubate them. Now with much larger tractors, all with cabs, it would be doubtful if their driver would be able to see any nest. This coupled with an increase in insecticides that wipe out the essential food supply for so many young birds, the late rolling of fields for silage or with grain long-since sown and already through the ground (briered, in farming terms) plus the very late cultivation for a pea crop of fields ploughed much earlier in the year, all result in eggs and chicks being flattened and have combined to all but banish lapwings from arable land. They are now mostly consigned to moorland edges and marshland such as Geordie's Moor. Even on moorland, with less predator control nowadays, a high proportion of chicks and eggs are still hoovered up by crows, gulls and foxes.

Getting clear of the shooting lodge at last, I headed up the road towards Dank Wood. A small flock of greylag geese briefly flew parallel with me, spread out in the loose formation more related to seeking out a feeding place rather than the disciplined V formation more usual when moving from point A to point B. They curled back over the duck ponds as if showing an interest, but if they had an interest it quickly waned and they flew on in the direction of the big fishing loch. On the other side of the track a pair of oystercatchers were feeding, and between them and me a single starling pecked greedily at the ground – maybe an emissary of the larger group there in the autumn and scouting to assess the suitability for the flock's return – then flew to the company of the oystercatchers as I came closer.

I cut anti-clockwise round two sides of Dank Wood then headed uphill alongside the eastern march dyke to visit a small pond well off the hill track. I'd never been close to it before and wondered if it held any interesting secrets. The shallow water was frozen after the sharp overnight frost and since it was crystal clear I could see the rich weed life under the thin ice, which would be great for amphibians such as frogs and newts. A pair of mallard, probably prospecting for a nest site, rose from the heather just beyond the pond. I regularly saw drake mallard at home intently watching their mate choosing a suitable nesting site, the drake sitting near the chosen site early each morning as the female laid her daily egg; a clear indication of the nest location to the knowledgeable observer.

I returned to a minor fork of the hill road, cutting a corner past the pegs of the Shooting Butts partridge drive to join the main hill road, where I found a suitable flat-topped rock for a seat. I scanned the hill to the north-west and saw two roe deer quietly feeding on the area of last year's big fire. Further up the hill were three more roe, but they were alert, with their heads up, and bunched together as I watched. I could see nothing to alarm them but something clearly was, since they started to walk down the hill towards me, the walk turning into a trot. Looking up to the north-east I could now see two figures coming into view: a young man wearing a green top and a young woman with a brilliant white top and with a small greyish terrier-type dog on a flexi-lead. They seemed incongruous with their surroundings, having none of the more usual hill walkers' clothing, rucksack or, so far as I could see, binoculars. They were still quarter of a mile distant, but then disappeared round the back of the hill. I thought little of it and took advantage of photographing the roe deer, now only 60 yards away.

I continued along past Middle Hill, with the pair of Middle Hill buzzards in attendance overhead. I heard the *prukk* of a raven, though trying to see the bird meant looking straight into a blinding sun, and I saw nothing. It must have been some distance away as it was a good few minutes before it eventually passed behind me, curled round the Middle Hill and flew up over the Shooting Butts drive towards where I had last seen the couple with the dog. I watched to see if there was a reaction from the raven which might give me an idea where the folks had gone. The raven continued straight on, heading north-east, which I took to mean that the couple had *not* gone that way, and had probably continued on a route pretty much parallel to mine, round the back of Middle Hill.

I took the left fork on the hill road ahead, taking me up the side of North Eerie. I continued over North Eerie and met George in his posh Polaris at the other side. I chatted to him and casually mentioned that the couple I had seen were the very first folks I had seen walking on this estate since I started the survey last August.

Leaving George, I walked down the steep (and exceedingly greasy with the frost coming out) hill track leading down towards the western march. The track veered to the left and became more level, which was a relief as I hadn't enjoyed my earlier slipping and slithering, with clay building up on my boots, making the going even more difficult. A herd of 10 fallow deer, all dark coloured, trotted over the track ahead of me and made towards the Hill Loch. Dark is definitely the predominant colour of the fallow here. A single dark adolescent fallow grazed unconcernedly right down at the march deer fence. Several large sitka spruce were lying over the deer fence since the winter's high winds, making its purpose of keeping deer in – or out – redundant.

It was now 12 noon and I had a welcome stop on a rock in a sheltered sun-trap gully overlooking the Hill Loch. On each side of the gully were a few dozen larch trees, interspersed with an occasional spruce and pine. It was a lovely tranquil setting. As I ate my lunch I watched the mallard on the loch. Two lots seemed happily paired but a single duck had the close attention of two drakes that chased her around the loch with much quacking and splashing, and occasional aerial sorties culminating in much more splashing as the three landed on the water almost in a heap, such was the intent of the drakes to mate with the harassed duck. A flash of red from my left brought my head round to see a red squirrel bound across the ground and climb a few yards up a larch tree. It regarded me suspiciously for only a second or two, and climbed higher for a better – and potentially safer – look. I reached into my pocket for my camera but the squirrel was not in a photogenic mood and raced along a branch to allow it to the next tree, a spruce, where it climbed to the top out of sight. I've had 'roe deer days' here, 'fallow deer days', 'buzzard days', 'red kite days', 'woodpecker days', but never 'red squirrel days'. This was to turn out to be such a day as there was much more to come.

I walked in a clockwise semi-circle round the Hill Loch, thus avoiding a potential fox den I would pass – and possibly disturb – if I went anti-clockwise. I entered Creag Bheag Wood at the pheasant pen at the west end, disturbing a roe buck that rose from among some juniper bushes just a few yards from me. The advantage in walking slowly and quietly is that you can usually get much closer to birds and animals before they become aware of your presence. There was possibly another reason that this buck was caught off guard: he was ailing in some way. He did not spring up off the ground in the manner of a healthy buck; to use a good Scots word, he 'sprachled' up. Although I just got a quick look I could see his back-end was thin and weak and I fully expected him to be lying collapsed at the back of a large square rock he stumbled around. I was amazed when I got past the rock that there was no gasping, shivering deer. The fence of the pheasant pen continued on for some 50 yards so he could not have gone left, and he certainly didn't cross the track that bisected the wood. It just seemed incredible that such a weak beast could have vanished into thin air.

I was checking all around for any sight of the buck as I walked, but before long my attention was diverted… by red squirrels, a pair of them this time. The squirrels were just ahead of me in adjacent larch trees. I took very slow and steady steps towards the trees. The squirrels were much less wary than the one I had seen earlier and seemed quite content to study me from the top half of their respective trees until I was 20 yards away. Even then they just moved to the next tree back. I sat and watched them for a while. After a few minutes they came together and there was a slight skirmish, ending in one chasing the other from tree to tree, probably in a pre-mating ritual, until they again settled close to each other and their minds turned to food rather than procreation.

I returned to the track and managed to slip past them without undue disturbance, but I had hardly gone 100 yards when I had another red squirrel encounter. This time I didn't see the squirrel at first but I heard the scratching of its sharp claws as it scurried round the base of a mature trackside conifer. I knew the squirrel would be hiding behind the tree but suspected its curiosity would eventually get the better of it and it would need to have a look to see where I was. I stood stock-still and eventually saw a pair of golden tufted ears emerge from the right hand side of the tree just about head height. The ears were slowly followed by a pair of ink-black eyes that gazed in my direction. I remained still and quiet and the inquisitive wee beastie climbed onto a branch, still gazing intently at me. I had difficulty not laughing at the squirrel's incredulous expression; I was no doubt the first human it had seen at such close quarters. As it stared at me it was making a quiet sound somewhere between a squeak and a light exhalation of breath, which it did at least a dozen times. I slowly lifted the camera up, and incredibly the squirrel continued to pose. It moved up to the next branch… and posed again. It got better. From somewhere it managed to lay its dextrous paws on a morsel of food and began to munch. Ten feet away from me! After nearly five minutes, and without the least fear, the squirrel eventually started to make its way up the tree and I left it to contemplate its adventure whilst I did likewise. Only after taking a couple of steps did I notice that a second squirrel, possibly its mate, was watching the episode from a tree 30 yards away. A real red squirrel day!

A few more steps and I glimpsed movement from the edge of the wood. This time it was a fallow deer, but not just any fallow deer, a pure white fallow calf, a beautiful animal not dissimilar in looks to the calf of a Charollais cow. I wondered if this was the creamy coloured calf I had seen in the autumn with its pure white mother. The calf had walked behind a tree, which gave me some cover to get closer. At 30 yards away I sat down with my back to a tree to watch it. It grazed for a while on some very short grass then lifted its head to stare at me. Like the squirrel it stared for some time, but unlike the squirrel it opted for discretion rather than curiosity. It gave a snort, turned on its heels and bounded, stiff legged and with all four feet hitting the ground simultaneously, down the outside of the wood. I sat for a few minutes to ensure it was out of sight before emerging from the wood. All the time I had been in the wood there was a pair of buzzards overhead. This is probably the second nesting territory identified.

I walked past the top of the Ell Wood, where a field vole ran across my path, the first one I had seen. It was a wee brown fattie with a snub nose, minute ears and a short tail. Let's hope they have a good breeding season ahead and feed the many species that depend on their proliferation. I headed to the Larch Wood. This is a wood that seems to have a high density of the thrush family, with the only member I haven't seen there so far being the fieldfare. Today a mistle thrush was singing from the top of a larch tree. I sat down on a tree stump to enjoy the aria. It's not easy to scan some of the more complex bird song, but I had a go at it as I sat listening. The bird sang a line at a time, with a pause for breath in between. It was repeating something like *weee choo weee; weee choo weee choo; chooo weee; weee choo weee*. Every version had a very slight variation and I revelled in its exaltations.

I headed back to the car and had a brief word with George before setting off for home. He'd been checking his traps and found that since the previous afternoon a live-catch cat trap he had set in the Middle Hill had been flattened by someone jumping on it. He found fresh tracks of two people and a small dog…

New birds identified: pink-footed goose
New mammals identified: field vole

Chapter 21

Saturday 17 March 2012. Weather: Mostly sunny and warm, though quite cold when it clouded over. Wind varying light to moderate.

I checked first of all in the small conifer wood beside the shooting lodge to see if the tawny owl from the previous visit was still in the same tree. It was in exactly the same position on the same branch, so it seems that if they are not disturbed, tawny owls may well roost in exactly the same place every day. I took a few more photos and left it to its daytime slumber before heading down the road to the tranquil Lament oak wood. As I passed the shooting lodge loch three lapwings silently flew over my head from Geordie's Moor and landed on a spit of land that runs into the loch. I was sure I had seen two pairs on the previous visit, and was pleased to see a fourth lapwing join them a few minutes later. The swans had split into two pairs. I'm not sure if they are two males and two females, but one was adopting a possessive and dominant posture, carrying its wings out and slightly up from its body, giving it the appearance of being larger than what it was. It was certainly a male (or cob, to give it its proper name) and keeping close to its mate (the pen, not a particularly attractive or even descriptive name for a female swan). They're very young and I doubt they'll be at breeding age yet. The two Canada geese seemed to be lord and lady of the island, and a dozen or so mallard completed the complement of wildfowl.

I entered Lament half-way down, following a track through a clear-felled area to begin with and bypassing two of George's almost invisible fox snares. A mistle thrush was singing from the top of a conifer and I sat on a tree stump to listen. Its song was different to the one I had listened to in the Larch Wood, and I looked at the notes I had made at the time (notes, in fact, of its notes). While the basics were the same, they were in a different order, this one singing *choo chi choo; chi chi choo; chooo; whee chi whee choo; wi chi weeeoo.* It was an altogether more complex song and I wondered if it was an older and more experienced songster than the Larch Wood one or, like chaffinches, do they have their local 'dialects'. Whatever the answer, it was a lovely singer and I appreciated its melody as I sat in the sun. Completing the choir, a pair of buzzards soared overhead, the male with a feather missing in the middle of his tail. I had seen him several times during the winter, usually between Lament and the Loch Wood. This was his territory and it looked like the chosen nesting place for the pair was the west end of Lament.

As I walked quietly through the oaks a flash of black and white alerted me to the presence of a pair of great-spotted woodpeckers. There was no sound of drumming and I assumed that the woodpeckers had paired up and no longer had any need for drumming. I'd seen a pair – maybe this pair – in this part of the wood before, and I wondered how many pairs there might be in Lament, which I would guess extends to around 200 acres. I'm sure the habitat would easily support four or five pairs. They'll be nesting shortly so there may be more clues at that time as to their numbers. The pair gradually moved away, replaced by three roe deer which had probably caught my scent and were moving slowly and warily up through the wood, stopping and glancing in my direction every so often as if not quite sure where the danger lay. They group was a doe and two almost yearling offspring. For the yearlings their time with their mother was almost over as she most likely would have two new fawns to take her full attention in May, now only a few weeks away.

When I was about three-quarters way along the wood I gradually headed uphill to return along the top near the march dyke. This was into green woodpecker territory and I had regular stops and seats on mossy logs (much more comfortable than the rocks on the hill) to watch and listen for them, but without success. I watched two roe deer make scrapes for themselves near the far end of the wood, a good 300 yards away. They pawed and scraped with front hooves, circling as they did so, before eventually settling down for probably the remainder of the day, and to ruminate in the biological sense of the term. Whether or not deer, or any animals, can ruminate mentally I've no idea. I imagine they can and it would certainly be nice to think so.

I crossed the dyke into Geordie's Moor, cutting through the myriad of junipers, with rabbits scuttling everywhere. This is great cover for rabbits, and also for red-legged partridges, which seem to have completely forgotten the shooting season and no longer fly off but instead use their wee red legs to trot to a respectable distance. A cock pheasant lay under a piece of broken juniper, thinking it was undetected, but in reality its brilliant red and purple feathers and its crimson cheeks, flushed with blood during the breeding season, made its imagined invisibility slightly ludicrous. I took a quick photo and walked on; one person, walking slowly and quietly, causes comparatively little disturbance to wildlife.

I left Geordie's Moor and walked beside the march dyke up the grass field beyond. Jays on the neighbour's side of the dyke made their presence known and a woodpigeon clattered out of a young conifer just above my head, maybe coming off an early nest. Two birds flew from a small stand of trees on this estate to the edge of woodland at the march. I put my binoculars on one as it landed: it was a green woodpecker at last! I'd no idea whether the second bird was its mate or a different species; I was content watching the bird I had in my sights. It sat in the fork of a tree, continually looking round. The sun enhanced its olive green colour, and the top of its head seemed every bit as crimson as the pheasant I had just left. Its black and red head constantly swivelled, heavy beak mostly pointed skywards and giving me a good view of its black 'moustache', confirming it as a female (the male has a dull red 'moustache'). It sat for a surprisingly long time – at least five minutes – then hopped up on to a higher branch before taking off and disappearing into the distance. It would be really interesting to find a nest hole later in the spring as I've never witnessed any of the nesting activity of the green woodpecker.

I continued past George's hens, wondering if he shuts them in their henhouse every night to keep them safe from foxes. Maybe he doesn't, as there used to be seven or eight, plus a cockerel and I could only see two now. He had chain-sawed a blown oak tree into rounds for splitting, and had kindly invited me to fill my car before leaving. They looked perfect for firewood and I was thankful my car is not a showpiece. I cut along the top of Clarissa's Cover, an area with a pond and where a game crop is planted each year benefiting wild birds as well as game birds, and skirted the top of a marsh above the duck ponds, taking advantage of a wooden walkway built for the convenience of the guns at the Wericky pheasant drive. As I came off the walkway and through the small gate to the next grass field the remains of a recently-killed rabbit lay beside a dyke. It wasn't clear what had killed the rabbit but it most certainly had been fed on at some stage by a feral cat, with the ribs eaten through and the skin pulled back, almost inside out, over the back legs in typical feline fashion. Usually cats in the wild try to hide the remains of their food by scraping some grass or leaves over it, but not in this case.

As I climbed the hill towards Wericky a young rabbit, the first I had seen this season, bolted into a burrow – and almost immediately peeked out again. This was a dangerous thing to do and revealed its immaturity and naivety. Young rabbits leave the nest burrow around four weeks, and this one would be seven or eight weeks old. Further up the hill another young rabbit – a bit bigger and probably around 10 weeks old – scurried along outside the Wericky deer fence. This one would be part of a litter born about New Year; unusual but certainly not a rarity, especially with the mild winter.

I walked up through Wericky without encountering anything out of the ordinary, then cut over the grass field lying to the south of Dank Wood. I am always amazed at the number of rabbits that suddenly emerge in early spring. Of course they had been here all winter but stay much more underground. In spring pairs of rabbits appear at every burrow and under every hedgerow, and this estate was no exception. White cotton tails bobbed everywhere, with nearly a dozen running from the field into Dank Wood. The rabbits knew each gap in the dyke through which they disappeared, seconds later re-emerging running up the bank on the other side and vanishing into the trees. I next walked through the reseeded grass field between Dank and the Larch Wood, equally alive with rabbits. There is certainly plenty food here for foxes, stoats, weasels, buzzards and even scavenging red kites. I sat on a flat stone on a rough bracken-covered ridge in the centre of the reseeded field with a view over the Larch Wood. The sun was shining and I enjoyed my piece and juice while watching a pair of buzzards over the wood. No sign of red kites and I was a bit concerned that they might not breed here this year, but it was still early days.

I circled round to get to the top end of the Larch Wood, passing a new tunnel trap that George had set and which already held its first newly-dead weasel. Though I've no grudge at weasels or stoats it's an important part of a gamekeeper's job to keep their numbers under control, though many more evade capture than those that have an instant death in the jaws of a Fenn tunnel trap. I came through the wood from the top end to the bottom, hoping to see a red squirrel as I'd never seen one there since the autumn. No luck today, but hopefully there might still be a pair here, despite the ravaging the trees got in the high winds of winter.

I made for the hill dyke that runs along the bottom of the Craigie Face, where 100 or so jackdaws and a buzzard were wheeling round above the scree and the few stunted larch and birch that the face supported. Despite the proximity of the buzzard, the jackdaws paid scant attention, drowning out the *mew* of the buzzard with their concerted *chak chakking*. Ahead of me, three dark coloured fallow made their way through some birch trees towards a thick stand of junipers at the foot of the hill, where they would find shelter. I was making for a track up through the junipers to walk to the west end of Creag Bheag and wondered if I would meet up with them again. Five rabbits ahead of me near the corner of the grass field bolted through the open gate into the corner of a marshy area before crossing a gap in the dyke to the Craigie Face. When I reached the gate the rabbit run on the bare earth had been made smooth and shiny by the passage of hundreds of furry paws, with the occasional pinhole claw mark the only blemish on the polished earth.

I went through the gate, carefully stepping over the rabbit motorway, walked to the far end of the marsh, then through the gate to the hill and the juniper bushes. As I made my way up the track made by George's Polaris the three dark fallow walked across in front of me, making for Creag Bheag wood. As I looked up to the wood to follow their progress, a red squirrel ran along a narrow larch branch and sat watching me from where the branch joined the tree, ready for a quick vertical escape if the need arose. As I made my way along the outside edge of the wood two rabbits came running towards me, clearly on a scent trail. They were shortly joined by a third, all of which I'm sure were bucks and, oblivious of my presence, continued their search for an elusive doe. After running almost to my feet they retraced their steps and, using a new tactic, split up. One hopped into the heather; one came back towards me; and one jumped the dyke into the wood where I watched it quartering like a spaniel. It was an interesting encounter and rather unusual in the fact that there seemed no animosity among the trio of lovelorn bucks.

At the far end of the wood I sat on a rock with a view of the west end of the hill and had a second sandwich, again in lovely spring sunshine. I wondered about the ailing buck that I had recently seen at this spot and of its fate. I couldn't imagine it recovering and would be surprised if it were not now dead. I made my way back through the centre of Creag Bheag and halfway down the side of the Pheasant Wood without any further wildlife encounters apart from the *prukk, prukk* of a pair of ravens passing over. I was delighted to see the white fallow yearling again, this time feeding in the marshland that runs between the Craigie Face and the Henhouse Wood. It was some distance away, near the Ell Wood and slowly getting nearer to the Henhouse Wood. I cut through the Henhouse

Wood near the pond to come out at the far end, where I might get a better view of it. This tactic worked well, and when I came out of the wood at the gap between the Henhouse Wood and the Ell Wood I could see it sitting resting at the fence-side. I would get no closer without disturbing it so left it in peace. Odd that it's on its own, though hopefully there is no negative or worrying reason for its current solitude. It will be an easy deer to monitor in any case.

Seeing the white fallow again was a great end to the day, and it had been a real bonus seeing a green woodpecker at last. If my last visit was a 'red squirrel day' this had most certainly been a 'rabbit day'.

New birds identified: none
New mammals identified: none

Chapter 22

Saturday 31 March 2012. Weather: Mostly sunny and warm, though, contrary to the forecast, there was a light shower around 10 am. Wind quite light.

As I drove north up the A9 an osprey flew over the road from right to left. It was coming from an area where there have been two nests in woodland over the past few years. It was great to see it back from its West African visit, though this was not the first sighting of the year; I'd spotted one that was sitting on the top of a tree in north Perthshire during my train journey to Inverness for a wildlife crime trial three days earlier. Anyway my sighting this morning seemed a good omen.

My first task on parking at the shooting lodge was to see if the tawny owl was still in the same place, which it was. It was on the same branch, facing the same direction, and it barely opened its eyes while I captured its digital image once more. I expected the Canada geese to have been nesting, but both were still on the loch below the 'Tawny Owl Wood'. They were accompanied by about 15 mallard drakes, though the female mallard were absent. Mallard are early nesters: I once had wild mallard ducklings on my own pond on St Valentine's Day. With a normal clutch of eight to 10 eggs and an incubation period of around 28–30 days that early duck must have laid its first egg during the first week in January. Invariably these early clutches are unsuccessful, and in fact I finished up hand-rearing the Valentine's Day ducklings after the mother deserted them because of a heavy snowfall.

I hadn't been out on the hill for a while and that was my first destination today. As I climbed the track towards the cottage with the hens a flock of nine Canada geese, possibly parents with a previous year's brood, flew south over the duck ponds. They swung round the loch at the shooting lodge and I thought they might settle there, but they turned and came up low over the duck ponds, heading northwards again, and maintaining that height as they flew up over the sheep field and disappeared over the Wericky skyline. The sheep field was still empty apart from the ever-present rabbits and a single oystercatcher, busily probing the ground now exceptionally dry due to a long unseasonably hot and dry spell.

On the hill meadow pipits were back in force. Many of these skylark-like birds sat atop heather lookout posts as they claimed territory; others flitted with deep undulating flight on a mission to which only they were privy. One landed near me and I got a good look at it through the binoculars. It even stayed still long enough for a photo. What looks a plain brown bird is in reality something a wee bit grander than that. In a way it resembles a miniature song thrush with its pale yellowish breast streaked with chocolate brown. It has a white eye stripe, white underparts, white outer tail feathers and pale yellow legs. I thought the males might have been singing, which they do as they rise off the ground, then parachute down again with wings fluttering half-open. Maybe it was just a bit too early, or maybe they were just having a rest…

Six roe deer watched me from above the shooting pegs of Shooting Butts partridge drive. I sat for a few minutes to watch them, but they seemed quite content to watch me. As I sat there cock pheasants seemed to be everywhere, strutting their stuff and giving voice to their testosterone-laden *cuck, cuck,* followed by a rapid whirr of flapping wings and raising of their head into the air, showing off their iridescent neck feathers and beetroot-red face topped with small feathery 'horns'. By now the deer and I had reached a stalemate, to which I was first to capitulate. I walked on along the hill road, with six pairs of cervine eyes following my every move.

The red-legged partridges also had breeding in mind, and any that rose at my approach were either in pairs or an occasional single bird still seeking a mate. Unlike the polygamous pheasant, where one male will gather a harem of as many hens as he can manage, then leave them to their own devices once they start nesting, partridges remain with the one mate. The male, in fact may also incubate a second clutch that the female has laid, with both hatching around the same time. Pheasants usually start laying around the middle of April, though with the mild winter and early spring they may be thinking of laying very shortly. Partridges will lay sometime in May.

It was a 'deer day', and I watched three dark-coloured fallow deer walk slowly into a hollow, where they watched me with heads just above the heather. With only their rather long necks and large ears visible, they could easily have been mistaken for three hyenas. I noticed as they walked into the hollow that one was shedding its winter coat, and looked rather scruffy around the back end. Further along the track, as I was about to take the right fork up Grey Crags, I spotted a roe deer sitting in the open. It was aware of me, but had simply turned its head to watch rather than rise and run off. I put the binoculars on it and wasn't convinced that it was too healthy. It was less than 100 yards away and seemed to have a lump in the area of the left shoulder. Or was it the way it was sitting and turning round? It certainly looked a bit scabby around the neck area, but that was probably the change from winter to summer coat. After a few minutes it rose and trotted off… along with another deer I had not seen but which must also have been in the open. I was pleased. Since there were two deer, the chances are my initial fears of ill-health were probably unfounded.

I walked up Grey Crags, photographing a fresh fox scat near the top of the track. With the weather having been hot and dry, this must only have been a couple of days old. George has been catching quite a lot of foxes in snares, but he hasn't got them all. He never will! Another 50 yards on, at the bend at the top of the road, I flushed a pair of red grouse. They flew off with the male telling me to *go-back, go-back*. Good to see them paired up, and I hope they have success in rearing a decent brood, though they have a few weeks to go yet till they lay.

At the top of the Grey Crags hill road I cut left through the heather and up on to the ridge, where I could look down over the Chapel Burn. The estate owner is keen to have a pair of hen harriers nesting, and I thought the long heather rising from the east side of this burn was a likely place. I found a large flat rock on the ridge and sat down for an hour or so to watch. I was looking for a male harrier displaying, with its beautiful sky-dancing display over the chosen nest site where he repeatedly flies almost vertically into the air and flips over backwards to come down again almost as steeply. It is one of the most amazing displays of all the birds in the UK and I never fail to be thrilled by it. As I sat quietly I became aware of a roe deer lying in the heather on the other side of the burn, maybe 300 yards away. Just over a quarter of a mile down the burn, again on the other side but this time in the open on burnt heather, three roe were relaxing contentedly. A light shower had been and gone and the day was warming up. It was quite pleasant sitting on the rock, and could have been *really* pleasant if I'd had a cushion!

I watched a bird in the binoculars flying over a small pool a mile away over the boundary to the north. I suspected what it was but continued following it. It seemed about to land in a tree, which gave me some doubts as to its identity, but it bypassed the tree, then seemed about to land in a small lochan, which gave me further doubts. Eventually it crossed over the boundary fence and landed on burnt heather giving a short bubbling call – just audible at the distance and no more – as it did so. Curlews neither perch in trees nor swim. Returning my thoughts to harriers I suspected it was still at least a week early for them displaying and moved on. I used to watch hen harriers regularly and my wife, Jan, was keen to come out with me one day when I told her it was just a case of sitting and watching. Question – how long do you sit? Answer – between three and four hours. No further questions. No further interest in watching harriers.

I retraced my steps along the ridge, then took a quad bike track that took me past some partridge release pens and down a gorge that ended near the bottom of Grey Crags; in fact just about where the roe I though was unwell had been sitting earlier. I thought I might see the fallow deer again as I could now see into the metamorphic hollow that turns deer into hyenas, but there was no trace; the hollow maybe has other still-undiscovered powers. I crossed the hill road and walked along another quad bike track that runs past where the beehives were (still to appear for the summer), then cut right handed into the top of Eerie Valley. I found and photographed an interesting holly tree manicured into the shape of a giant teardrop by the munching of deer over the years. I crossed the burn that bisects Eerie Valley and walked up the south slope till I found a pleasant grassy area on which to have a rest and survey the scene. It was indeed a deer day, as 10 dark fallow had materialised below me and were nonchalantly walking up the dyke side towards the Larch Wood. I waited till they were out of sight round the corner before moving off, then followed a quad bike track along the lower slopes of the Craigie Face, before descending to the young grass field beside Ell Wood.

After trekking along the dyke-side below Craigie Face, I turned right into the junipers that skirt the north east end of Creag Bheag Wood. This is a lovely corner with a couple of acres or so of junipers edged by the wood on one side and by 50 or 60 birch trees and a single very old larch on the other side. The sun was still shining and there was lots of bird life among the trees. I sat for 15 minutes to try to establish what birds were there, either by sight or sound. Easiest were the woodpigeons, with their loud *coo coo coo cooo cooo, cooo coo coo.* As I was looking almost due south into the sun, one pigeon was ahead of me in a birch tree and one behind in the wood. Stereophonic sound indeed, just like the mistle thrushes on the fishing loch nearly a month earlier. Pheasants were still defending their territory, with their *cuck cucks* and wing whirring. A pair of red-legged partridges crept through the junipers, putting on a bit of speed as they noticed me. Jackdaws flew over from The Shudder, *chack-chacking* to each other as they passed, and a chaffinch perched on a branch just above me, warning other birds of my presence with a continual *pink, pink, pink.* A blackbird was just audible in the distance; in fact I'd to listen closely to make sure it was a blackbird and not a song thrush, which of course repeats its notes. This was the first singing blackbird I had heard on the estate, even though I'd been hearing them at home for three weeks now. I had seen blackbirds from time to time along at The Shudder, and this was maybe where it was.

As I sat I heard a bird I had not yet seen here, though the owner said he recently had one below his feeders: a yellowhammer. Its song is unmistakable and is often described as sounding like a *little bit of bread with no cheese*, though it was not its song I heard but a sharp *zit, zit*, maybe echoing the warning of the chaffinch. I followed the sound and saw it perched momentarily on top of a juniper before it flew off. The bird was a male, very canary-like with its bright yellow head and chest, with brown wings and an orangey-brown rump. They are usually associated with nesting in gorse bushes, of which there are none here that I have seen. Maybe it was just passing through, though they are late nesters, not usually laying until at least May. Yellowhammers, already red-listed because of the rapid decline in their numbers, seem to becoming less common every year.

A robin was next to feature, landing in a birch tree near me. Almost simultaneously a dunnock gave a very quick rendition of its song. It was a short, fast warble which was unmistakable. I have heard them singing several bars of their song, but like this one, often it is just a quick burst before appearing to lose concentration and do something else. I was just starting to move off when I heard the *tic* of a wren, which I saw on the root of the old larch tree. As I watched it, it kept waggling its tail from side to side, something I've never seen before. Many birds bob their tail up and down but this was a variation on the tail-wagging theme. I was in full view of it so maybe it was a warning signal; maybe I was supposed to be frightened by the tail-wagging and back off. I lost concentration for a minute, having noticed a run snaking down through the dead bracken and going under a branch of the old larch. It crossed my mind that this would be an ideal spot for a snare and looked along the run. George had obviously been on the same wavelength and I spotted a fox snare, almost invisible, on the run, ready for its passing victim. As I moved on I thought that I had just witnessed a remarkable variety of bird species in a very small area. Missing were the jays that normally show their annoyance at human intrusion, but more of jays later.

At a gap in the dyke I cut through to the wood and continued westwards on the track that leads to the Hill Loch. I then turned left down the track that leads from the loch to the public road. As I've said before, the West End is an incredibly beautiful woodland of juniper, oak, ash and ancient pine. I walked on, or rather limped, as I'd somehow twisted my knee a bit, the pain manifesting itself much more on a downhill gradient rather than on the level or uphill. The *kew kew kew kew* sound of a green woodpecker coming from high on the hill on my left stopped me in my tracks. I found a moss-covered boulder and sat down to see if it might come closer. I'd eaten part of my piece on the flat rock on the ridge while awaiting a hen harrier, now it was time for the remainder. After quarter of a (rather large) sandwich there it was again, the mocking *kew kew kew kew*. After half a sandwich a further rendition, then again after three quarters. But still no closer. As I finished my sandwich I had a distraction: a tree creeper landed on the tree in front of me, 10 yards away, and started pecking at the bark for insects. I got my camera from my pocket, switched it on, put it to full zoom, but I couldn't find the tiny tree creeper in the lens. I checked round the side of the camera and it was still there. I found it at last and was about to press the button… when it flew off. A cock pheasant *cuck, cucked* and flapped its wings. The green woodpecker cackled again in derision. The tree creeper had moved to a tree to my left, but quickly went round the back of the tree. I reached into my rucksack for my juice, distracted while I fumbled. *Kew kew kew kew* again, this time from behind me. How the hell it got there I don't know!

I gave up in disgust, stomping down the track to the road, then walking along the road and in the estate entrance. A tawny owl hooted from the wood on my left; a half-hearted attempt –

hooooooo; a pause, then *hoo-hoooo*, which I was sure was a male's call. Unusual in daylight, and now I'd heard it twice within a month.

I cut along the bottom of Lament, a jay flying across the drive as I entered. It clearly hadn't seen me and it panicked as I approached a boulder it had been behind. At close quarters I was almost dazzled by the pink and white and grey and black and blue of its feathers. It is by far the most colourful of the corvids, but its colour belies its corvid tendencies. Further along the wood I thought I saw two jays fighting. In fact it was a mistle thrush trying to see a jay off from a holly tree amongst the oaks in which it was taking an interest. The jay flew into the holly and the mistle thrush perched for a minute on a nearby branch. It flew into the holly and it and the jay came out again in a flurry of feathers. I was sure the jay was after the mistle thrush's eggs and I edged closer. The mistle thrush flew off at my approach but the jay was still in the holly. I came round the top of the holly and heard a clatter of wings as a wood pigeon flew from the holly tree followed by the screech of the jay as it took off. I had a good look at the tree and the only nest I could see was quite far up. Mistle thrushes usually – though not always – nest in a fork, sometimes quite high up. This nest was on a branch. A high branch. I took off my rucksack and started to climb, but though I almost got within touching distance I couldn't see into the nest. From the twiggy construction it was certainly a wood pigeon's nest so maybe that had been the jay's target. Half a century ago I would have managed to reach the nest, and even higher, but age brings either timidity or caution and I clambered back to terra firma. As the jay knows of the nest I have little doubt the eggs are doomed, but after all that's part of its diet, not grass or turnips.

I headed gradually uphill, restricting myself only to the first half of the wood in case the kites were nesting in the furthest half. At the top I sat on a moss-covered rock (again I wished there were comfy rocks on the hill as well), noting rabbit fur that seemed to have been plucked. Behind the rock there was a piece of rabbit gut, part of the small intestine. From the diameter of the intestine it had been a young rabbit, and the plucking meant the predator (or scavenger if the rabbit had been dead already) had been a bird, probably a buzzard or red kite. So, only part of the mystery solved but interesting nevertheless.

At the top of Lament I climbed over to Geordie's Moor and walked up through the junipers there. I kept to the west side, up the edge of a very marshy section. I was keen to see if there were lapwings present as it is an ideal area for them nesting. Only one pair was there, rising silently into the air and quickly landing again as I passed. Hopefully their numbers will increase. There were certainly two pairs in the area on my previous visit. As I approached the shooting lodge I looked back over Lament and was pleased with what I saw. A pair of buzzards circled, but in addition, and mingling with the buzzards was a pair of red kites. They were over their nesting site of previous years and hopefully they will nest again this year.

New birds identified: yellowhammer
New mammals identified: none

Chapter 23

Monday 9 April 2012. Weather: Dull with a few light showers.

Easter Monday, and I decided to have a boat trip round the fishing loch since Mondays are always the quietest so far as the presence of anglers is concerned. As I parked in the car park I noticed a plant, whose beauty belied its invasive nature, growing in the marsh beside the car park. The yellow skunk cabbage (*Lysichiton americanus*), sometimes called the swamp lantern, is often grown as a bog garden plant and is available from nurseries and garden centres. It is a large plant, growing up to three feet high, with green waxy leaves and a bright yellow flower. The centre of the flower gives off a strong, unpleasant rotting smell which attracts insects that act as pollinators. Plants in the wild like this one probably originate through the dumping of garden material, as colonies of the plant quickly outgrow their space in most gardens. Some will have been established from seed dispersed from nearby gardens, and of course at the edge of a loch the size of this one the seed may have floated some distance. The skunk cabbage like most foreign invasive species unfortunately out-competes native plants. New legislation in Scotland, taking effect from 2 July 2012, is intended to reduce the release or spread of non-native species of both plants and animals and considerably bolsters the Wildlife and Countryside Act.

As I walked towards the boats I met Craig, the fisheries manager, who is lucky enough to live beside the loch. He told me he had seen the great-crested grebes displaying a couple of weeks earlier. These birds have an elaborate courtship display, which involves a lot of beak-to-beak head-shaking, often holding a beakful of weed, and culminates in the birds raising themselves out of the water, side by side, and paddling rapidly on the surface parallel to each other before eventually settling back on the water again. He also had a story of watching an osprey that had gripped a fish too large for it and, after much splashing and flapping to get airborne again, had to abandon its oversized catch. An osprey was circling the loch as I got into the boat, and I watched with interest hoping it would spot a fish, but there was no tempting trout for it and it gradually drifted westwards towards the adjacent loch.

I edged the boat out into the loch and turned left (I should really use the terms port and starboard on a boat) to go round the loch clockwise. There was a strong ripple on the water, though not quite enough to be called a wave, but as the wind was from the west I could see it was a lot calmer at the opposite end. I gradually headed up the loch, keeping about 100 yards out from the south shore so as not to disturb any birds on the shoreline. Only drake mallard were present, with the females no doubt incubating nests of eggs in the woodland. The pair of great-crested grebes was ahead of me, about 20 yards from each other but intent on feeding as they kept diving. I stopped the motor to watch, hoping for some courtship activity, even though it was getting late in the season for this. Unfortunately I had no luck, but what I did see, some distance away on the other side of the loch, was a second pair. Might there be two broods of chicks on the loch this year?

Between the two pairs of grebes a solitary cormorant swam low in the water keeping a close eye on me. It seemed it was trying to hide by sitting as low in the water as possible, but this is their normal swimming posture: the body barely visible, the neck emerging from the water and the head and beak pointing upwards, all rather serpentine and even Jurassic-looking. As I studied the birds on the water I was aware of birds above the water, the first of the season's hirundines back from Africa. I had already listed two last year on the estate: swallows and house martins, but here was a small flock of sand martins. So far as I know these earliest of the swallow-like birds to return to our shores don't breed anywhere on the estate;

at least I've never seen a sandy bank with their tell-tale elliptical nesting burrows. The wee chocolate brown and white birds darted to and fro above me, filling themselves with insects. Though I was sure they were sand martins and not really early house martins, I checked with the binoculars for the white rump easily visible on house martins. No white rump apparent, and my identification satisfied, I watched as their insect-catching activity gradually drifted towards the north shore, then disappeared altogether. I suspected they were still on their travels to a destination slightly further north, but was pleased to have seen them. They and other summer visitors will shortly replace the geese, fieldfares, redwing and other visitors that winter with us.

I slowly edged the boat between the first pair of grebes and one of only three boats of anglers on the loch, heading for the bay at the west end. Several goldeneye were in the bay and, as I kept to the north side, they gradually swam round the south side. They had quickly become accustomed to boats and I even managed a photograph of some of them. I doubt if they'll nest here but if we get some nest boxes up for next year maybe then some will stay. There were only two pairs of mute swans on the loch today, with one nesting on a spit of land on the north side of the bay while its mate kept watch from the south side. The female had its neck curled round under its wing sound asleep, not in the least concerned about the presence of my boat only 10 yards away. It looked the picture of contentment and I wondered how many eggs it was incubating. I also wondered – not for the first time – why there were no cygnets last summer. Maybe the answer lies with the number of pike in the loch, so I'll watch developments with interest.

I gradually headed down the loch near the north shore, seeing the other swan on a nest in reeds half-way down the loch, with her mate much more attentive and only a few yards from the nest. A small flock of tufted ducks swam on the other side of my boat. They should nest round the loch-side yet I never did see any young tufties last year, nor mallard ducklings come to that. Are pike really the villains of the piece? They are certainly voracious predators and can have a significant impact on their prey species. Though their main diet is smaller fish, they regularly supplement it with frogs, waterfowl or any other species that might enter the water. A week-old ducking would be a snack to a large pike, and it could easily manage one half-grown.

As I tied up the boat at the harbour I heard a moorhen *kurr-uk* from the reeds near the yellow skunk cabbage. I'd heard it several times on my visits but had never seen it – until today. As I put my rucksack in the boot of the car it was skulking through the reeds, slowly and carefully placing one large olive-green foot in front of the other in typical moorhen style, flicking its tail as it went, and with its red forehead and red beak tipped with yellow in complete and flamboyant contrast with its dull olive-brown plumage. They're lovely wee birds. I had one for a while visit the burn in our garden and hoped it would bring a mate and remain there, but unfortunately there must have been more suitable habitat elsewhere.

I'd only a short time available that morning but returned to the estate on Thursday 12 April to continue with a walk on some of the lower ground. The weather forecast was good, and despite rain when I first went out the door at 6 am the sky had cleared by just after 7. My first job was to check on the tawny owl. I was disappointed it was not on its usual perch, and I made a check of the rest of the small wood to no avail. That's not to say it wasn't there since they are so difficult to spot, but I certainly couldn't see it. Maybe it had been a female and was now on a clutch of eggs; after all it was a female I had heard in the wood on 1 March. If it was a male maybe it had found a roost nearer the nest hole. I was exultant to see three pairs of lapwings as I walked down the estate road next to Geordie's Moor. They should be on eggs now as I regularly remember clutches of eggs we had to shift and replace, or work round, when we were harrowing or rolling newly-sown grain at the very beginning of April. Let's hope the carrion crows leave the eggs and subsequent chicks in peace as lapwings are getting really scarce.

Nearer the bottom of the estate road I heard a green woodpecker calling off to my right, probably up on the hill somewhere around the Twenty Acre, a clear-felled and replanted wood. It called half a dozen times, with the sound always from the same place. As I entered Lament at the clearing with the high seat used in the control of deer I heard another green woodpecker ahead of me. These birds seem quite common here but why are they so hard to spot? I used to see green woodpeckers regularly when I was young, and that was without even trying! There are three buzzards' nests at this end of Lament, though it was the third one I visited that seemed to be in use this year. A buzzard wheeled above the nest, calling in displeasure at being disturbed. A couple of small branches woven into the nest with leaves still green were indication of current use (apart from a blue tit that cheekily sat on the edge of the nest), and I moved on quickly to let the buzzard back as there may well have been eggs in the nest.

I still wanted to leave the far end of Lament in peace as the red kites could be nesting and they are more inclined to desert a nest than a buzzard. In any case they are Schedule 1 birds and it is an offence to *intentionally or recklessly disturb any wild bird included on Schedule 1 while it is building a nest, or is in, on or near a nest containing eggs or young.* I didn't *know* that they were nesting there, but since I suspected they *might* be, that was a good enough reason to keep my distance. I therefore cut up through the wood about three-quarters way along and started to come back along the eastern march dyke at the top. George has reduced fox numbers over the past six weeks, but a fresh scat on top of a tussock showed that there was still at least one around.

I've had many 'specialist days' here, such as the 'red squirrel days'. This was starting to be a 'day of pairs', which is hardly surprising in spring. Along the wood a further 100 yards I stopped to look at a pair of blackbirds at a willow thicket. I was sure they were nesting – or preparing to nest – in the vicinity. This is rather unusual as I would have thought oak woodland is normally too dry for their favoured diet of earthworms. They *were* close to a part of the wood where a trickle of water running down through the wood has formed a slight bog, with the resultant damp-loving trees such as willow and alder starting to take hold. They are also not too far from Geordie's Moor, so I'll watch with interest to see if they nest in the willow thicket.

The blackbirds had a companion in a wren, which can nest virtually anywhere. I heard its strident song before I saw it. It had been in the centre of a huge oak limb that had snapped off in the gales and now lay on the ground, but it flew to the single strand of barbed wire atop the dyke to give me an even louder version of its song. It was a lovely shot for a camera, but although it sang three or four bars it was off back to the safety of its oak limb before I got the camera switched on. Damn! As I waited to see if might re-emerge I heard the single *chik* of a great-spotted woodpecker. Had this been in different habitat it could be confused with a similar single note often given by a starling. I could hear the soft tapping as the woodpecker probed a tree for insects, but the territorial drumming has finished for the season and the birds are now much more discreet.

I crossed the dyke to Geordie's Moor, and was regaled by the sight of skein after skein of pink-footed geese flying over. They were in V formation high in the sky, beaks all pointing to the north, and no doubt gradually making their way back to their breeding grounds in Greenland and Iceland. As they head north away from us, many other species will shortly be heading north *towards* us, and I look forward to seeing and hearing several that I missed last year. Though the day so far had been OK weather-wise, the sun suddenly shone through, perceptibly heating the air. As if warmed into life like a cold-blooded lizard on a sun-kissed rock, a blue tit on the top of an alder tree above me sang its *tsee-tsee-tsee, tsee-tsee-tsu-tsu, tsee-tsee-tsu, tsee-tsee-tsu*, finishing as if in a flourish with a long trill. At the same time an oystercatcher started to call from the marshy area of the moor beyond the junipers. The call started off with the *pweep-pweep, pweep-pweep, pweep-pweep*, then graduated into a long and rapid *peep-peep-peep-peep-peep*. Though I couldn't see them I could visualise the male – the one calling – flying in a circuit over the marsh in pursuit of the female, possibly the latter part of the call being emitted as they both landed; piebald birds with their plumage colours in complete contrast to their deep orange of their beaks and blood-red of their eyes. Spring and early summer are great seasons for *listening* to birds, which is at least as interesting as *seeing* them.

I crossed to the far side of the junipers, seeing two pairs of dunnocks, at different places, busy round the bottom of the bushes, peck and hop, peck and hop. It's a handy aid to identification that some birds hop, such as the dunnock and blackbird; some walk, such as the starling and the partridge; and others, like the magpie, have a mix of hop and walk. At the end of the moor I heard a tawny owl hoot. It was the real thing this time *hoooooooooo*, then a pause followed by a bubbling *hoo-hoo-hoo-hoo-hoooooo*, not the half-hearted daytime hoots that I'd heard on other occasions. The sound came from coniferous trees just on the boundary with the neighbours to the east. I scanned with the binoculars but saw nothing. I heard another tawny owl later in the morning in the Henhouse Wood. Both appeared to be males and I can only conclude, firstly, that daytime calling by tawny owls is much more common than I realised, and secondly, that it is probably related to keeping in touch with a mate.

Coming out of Geordie's Moor I disturbed a woodpigeon from a nest in the blackthorn bush (used in an earlier visit by three blue tits to pronounce a warning to all who would listen of a weasel nearby). I stood on top of the dyke to try to confirm the presence of the normal clutch of two white eggs but I was still a foot or so short. I walked up round the top of the duck ponds, counting 12 adult rabbits and two half-grown ones outside a large warren in the sheep field. Two pairs of common gulls shared the field with them. I wonder if the gulls have their eye on nesting at the edge of the duck ponds. I'll watch with interest, though the colonial-nesting common gulls I've seen seem to prefer damp, open moorland, pebbly islands in rivers or around stony loch shores. At the far end of the field a red-legged partridge defended his territory from the top of a molehill, before scurrying off as I came closer.

I climbed the hill and went into Wericky Wood about half-way up its length. Another two dunnocks were exploring the ground under spruce trees. I wondered if these rather spiky conifers would make suitable nesting places for dunnocks, but there was little alternative. As I stood with my back to a tree an adult rabbit hopped down the ride, coming quite close before stopping and sitting on its hunkers. A young rabbit hopped from my left and sat a few yards from the adult. Another adult rabbit crossed from right to left, then back again. Dappled sunlight was coming through the trees and I noticed that, whether by coincidence or by intent, the young rabbit and the (very close) relaxing rabbit were each sitting in a shaft of warm sunlight. Much as I was enjoying the rabbit parade I'd to move on, which meant the rabbits had to do likewise.

I left Wericky near the top end, cut across to Dank Wood, where I skirted the bottom edge before heading over towards the Larch Wood. As I passed a small pond on my journey two female goosanders took off, blurs of grey and white with fast and shallow wing beats. Four mallard drakes remained behind, and as I passed close by I was reminded yet again of how relaxed and unafraid many birds become after the end of the shooting season. I walked through the small roundel at the north-east end of the Larch Wood as there had been an old buzzard nest in a larch tree there and I wondered if it was being used this year. Despite the fact that it was quite an obvious nest the last time I was through the roundel, I couldn't find it, maybe because the larches were now greened up with needles. I gave up and became much more interested in any case in a pair of long-tailed tits that were feeding high in a larch tree. I've never seen a long-tailed tit's nest so I'll return to the area later.

My journey was finishing as I passed one of George's crow cage traps. Four carrions crows were inside, their time on the estate just about to come to an end. In the grand scheme of biodiversity their loss, or the loss of the dozens – maybe hundreds – of eggs and chicks that they would guzzle had they not been trapped, would make little difference. On a more local scale – on this estate – there should now be a better success rate of ground-nesting birds.

New birds identified: sand martin
New mammals identified: none

Chapter 24

Monday 23 April 2012. Weather: A mix of cloud, showers and sunshine. Wind moderate.

It had been a fortnight of mostly wet weather since I had been at the estate and I was desperate to get going again. The five-day forecast for the area showed that I might get this morning without rain, but by 1.00 pm that would change. Tuesday, Wednesday and Thursday were to be wet, and though Friday was to be dry, it looked as if it was going to be too windy. I settled for a morning on the hill and an afternoon, possibly at the weekend if the dry weather held over from Friday and the wind dropped (a big ask), on the lower ground.

When I parked at the shooting lodge the first thing I did was to check for the tawny owl. No sign, so I thought my assessment that it was a female and on eggs had been correct. A lapwing ran along the grass field between me and the loch as I came into its view. I've often seen them doing this; coming off their nest and running for 50 yards or so before taking to the air so that their nest location is harder to detect. I spied the ground with the binoculars but there was no sign of a nest. Another lapwing was pee-weeping and tumbling in the air over on Geordie's Moor. Chicks should be well formed in most of the eggs now provided the crows haven't nobbled them. I looked over the shooting lodge loch with the binoculars. No sign of either swans or Canada geese nesting, so I doubt if that will take place this year. I must have a better look at the swans in any case as they may all be of the same sex!

A pied wagtail sat on the branch of a spruce tree beside me at the corner of the Tawny Owl Wood, then flew down to the grass field in front of me and sat on a molehill. I took a few photographs and only when I looked at the photos later did I see that in each one its head was cocked to the side either listening or intently studying the molehill. Its tail was still all this time, which was surprising. Was it concentrating? Its chief diet is insects so maybe more likely – rather than listening – it was looking for any sign of creepy crawlies. Its mate (presumably) was perched on a telephone wire behind me. Its black and grey and white feathers looked a bit dishevelled and not in the pristine condition of the mole hill explorer, so I wondered if it might have eggs, the crush into a nest somewhere in the farm buildings causing its more unkempt appearance.

I headed out the hill, noticing that of three crows George had caught in a crow cage, one was a hooded crow rather than a carrion crow. Even at 300 yards its grey back and breast were clearly different from that of its two captured companions as they jumped from perch to perch. Hoodies are found primarily in the north-west of Scotland, but they and carrions interbreed where their ranges overlap. A hoodie in this area is uncommon, though far from rare. Further up the hill road I got very close to a mallard drake in the pond since its head was underwater and bum in the air. Like the pied flycatcher, it was concentrating on food, but its manner of doing so made it much more vulnerable. It flew off in fright once it surfaced and saw me, but its panic was short-lived: it circled twice and landed on the pond again once I was a few hundred yards further up the hill road. Whatever it had been eating it was keen to resume the feast.

The hill was quiet, and by the time I got to the Middle Hill all I had seen – apart from pheasants and red-legged partridges – was a roe buck. It watched me from half-way up the hill, then bounded away barking at me. It was a rather watered-down *buuuff*, followed by *buuuff-buff-buff*, then silence; not the full-blown long-winded version more common when a buck is disturbed during the rut in late July or August. I sat at the Middle Hill for a while as I was keen to see if there was any sign of the kestrels, which I hoped would be nesting on the crag on the east side. The female should be on eggs, and would only be off for feeding and exercise twice a day, but I thought the male might have been in attendance. I scanned the rocks in case he was on guard somewhere there, but no trace so I gave up after half an hour.

I took the right fork up Grey Crags, stopping to admire a large patch of primroses among the heather. I heard the high-pitched song of a wren near where I had watched a newly-hatched wren family last July, then spotted it on a rock just above me. It flew down Grey Crags 30 or so yards, then resumed its singing from a stunted larch tree. No doubt his lady wren had chosen from the many domed nests of moss and lichen he provides for her, and was sitting cosily on eggs. I wondered if it might have been one of the wrens I saw last year, but there was no way of knowing.

I made for the flat rock where I sat on 31 March with a view down the Chapel Burn. Cloud had been gathering as I walked up through the heather, then as the clouds burst the rain came down in sheets, making me frantically jettison my rucksack and pull out my waterproof jacket and bunnet. When I reached the rock 10 minutes later the rain had just gone off, but the rock was soaked, which meant I had to stand rather than take the weight off my feet for a wee while. Twenty minutes standing around was enough, especially when I saw nothing larger than a meadow pipit. I still think this would be the part of the estate favoured by hen harriers but they have been persecuted so much and are now so uncommon on the east side of Scotland that the chance of a pair reaching this safe haven would be slim indeed.

I had now three different routes in my head to continue the morning's walk. One meant a clockwise round-the-hill trek; the next meant a partial retracing of my steps and crossing North Eerie to get to the Hill Loch; while the third meant going down the hill directly towards the western march then turning left along the flat towards the hill loch. This entailed a 200 yards steep decline through rank heather to a swiped path, then a march along the swiped path to meet the track coming over North Eerie and heading to the loch. So I thought! The reality was decidedly different.

The decline was easy, as was the march along the swiped path… until the path came to an end. The terrain ahead didn't look too bad, but I thought the western boundary at that time should have consisted of a stand of sitka spruce with half a dozen lying over the fence as a result of the winter winds. There was no sitka spruce in sight, only a stand of larch the best part of a mile ahead. Anyway I was now on a long patch of white grass where the going was half reasonable. A patch of dead bracken lay ahead, which didn't look too bad either. Both areas were only 100 yards or so in length, then I was on to a boggy area cut into sections by a series of deep and narrow ditches. One of the ditches had cut really deeply into the land and must have been five feet down. If I'd fallen into there I might never have got out. I saw a walker with a spaniel on the path that runs round one of the lochs just over the boundary. He came from behind me and, because he was on a path, in no time seemed miles ahead of me, making my trek even more frustrating. I splashed and squelched through the bog, which degenerated into large – and not so large – mounds of white grass. The going here was really difficult, with the potential of a twisted ankle every time my foot slipped off one of the mounds. This was a part of the estate I hadn't walked on and I'd no intention of being back on it. It was a real trudge, with the larches now just ahead of me.

I stopped to get my breath (I'd still not managed to sit down since Middle Hill) and heard a buzzard mewing on my left. I looked at the sky, but saw nothing, and eventually located it sitting on a rock 500 yards up the hill. Almost concurrent to my placing it, the buzzard took off, glided downhill and started to circle me, still mewing loudly. It clearly had a nest nearby, which could only have been in the larches. I found the nest on an outside larch, but really hard to spot with the tree now in almost full leaf. It was a smallish nest, almost certainly brand new this year. The buzzard was one which was almost pure white on the underside, and she certainly didn't like my presence there. I wondered if she would have attacked me, had it been later in the year and she'd had grown chicks. So far my experience of buzzards with chicks attacking has only been towards joggers or cyclists, but she did seem quite a bold bird, though not quite in the league of most feisty nesting female hen harriers.

I left the buzzard in peace and continued the slog at almost a snail's pace, passing a hawthorn bush on which deer had carried out an exquisite exercise in topiary art, the lower half thick and tight, while the top half out of reach of the deer – sprouted thin branches upwards and slightly outwards, making the whole bush now almost thistle-shaped. Once over the crest of the hill just past the hawthorn I could now see the sitka plantation, though still a further half mile ahead, and with still no sign of the track coming over North Eerie. Even had it been there it would have been little use to me as it would have been 300 or 400 yards up the hill and I'd decided to keep as close as I could to the contour I was on. I managed to follow a deer track from time to time, which made walking slightly easier, but unfortunately the destination of the deer seldom coincided with mine, mostly heading uphill away from the march fence rather than along parallel to it. In due course I got to the Hill Loch, but what I thought might have been half a mile of relatively easy walking in actual fact had been at least two miles of heavy slog. Apart from the buzzard, all I'd seen were a couple of roe deer that had been as daft as I was to be in that most inhospitable part of the estate.

Like on my previous visit, I'd only a relatively short time available and had to make for home. I returned to have a look at the lower ground on Saturday 28 April. It was a fine sunny day with no wind, and I was pleased to see when I parked at the shooting lodge that nine or 10 house martins were showing significant interest in the nests of the previous year under the eaves of the owner's house. They swooped in to the nests, some landing briefly, clinging on to their outer shell, before returning to join their airborne companions. They must have just arrived and by next week I'd expect them to have begun repairs and refurbishment to their chosen nests. I looked carefully among the swirling birds for sight of a swallow. Though there was not a swallow among the group, a swallow flew over my head as I started to go down the road heading for Lament. It came low and close to me, showing off its russet-coloured throat and long tail streamers. It was good to see these migrants again, and amazing to think that a few days earlier they would have been south of the Sahara Desert.

I stopped opposite the marsh on Geordie's Moor, watching the lapwings and oystercatchers. None were exhibiting warning calls at my presence, so no eggs would yet be hatched. They had been joined by new marsh inhabitants, which I recognised by their call before I saw them. The *too-oodle, too-oodle; too-oodle* drew me to a dark brown bird flying across the marsh, before landing on one of the wettest areas at the far side. Apart from the sound, the most obvious identification of the redshank was its long red legs stretched out behind it in flight, and the white rear edges to its wings. I saw through the binoculars that a second redshank was on the ground near to it, so, like the oystercatchers and lapwings, it would be terrific if they breed here. I'd spoken on the phone with George earlier and he had caught 40 carrion crows and two hooded crows so far this spring, so the chances of breeding success of these waders must be enhanced.

Half-way down the road to the bottom of Lament I stopped to watch a tree creeper. It had been feeding quite low down on a tree near me, and when it hopped round the back of the tree I moved closer, camera at the ready. Only a fraction of wild birds and animals comply with the wishes of photographers (I'm not really a photographer but I have a camera) and instead of hopping to my side of the tree again I saw it flying to the next tree, only much higher up. Further down the road I saw an oak tree that was virtually split down the middle, showing a two inch-wide crack. I wondered if that safe place might be the bird's chosen nesting site. A jay flew from George's pheasant feeders as I passed, taking advantage of an easy breakfast of grain. Omnivorous birds have a definite advantage over specialist feeders, and hardly have to move far to maintain their food supply, unlike the house martins and swallow I had just seen.

Once into Lament I quietly passed near the buzzard nest again. There was neither sight nor sound of the bird in the sky above, but I could see that slightly more greenery had been added to the nest. I wondered if the bird had remained on the nest as I passed. I cut up through the wood halfway along, having heard a green woodpecker's *kew kew kew kew* coming from that direction. Almost simultaneously I heard a great-spotted woodpecker somewhere close on my right. It was not the normal single *tick* given by the bird, but a series of *ticks*, making me wonder if it was a warning call given by the male to warn the female on the nest of my presence. I never did see the bird, which demonstrates the value of being able to make identification from sound. At the top of the wood a coal tit was feeding on the branches in a small birch tree. I was underneath the tree, and three times the bird came down and landed only three or four feet from me at the base. It was definitely keen on something there but wary of my close proximity. There looked to be a small hole in the trunk not far above ground level, and at first I wondered if this was where it was nesting, as coat tits nest quite happily at almost ground level, but when I looked more closely at the hole it was only a couple of inches deep. I moved off in any case to let the bird do what it needed to do, though its persistence to be at the base of the tree still puzzled me.

I made my way back along the top of the wood and stopped at a comfortable moss-covered rock to have a sandwich. My companions as I sat there were a buzzard circling and mournfully mewing above me (I wondered if this was one of the pair from a nest not too far from me half-way down the wood, though I'd never seen any evidence of the nest being used this year); a wren, which was trilling loudly in a juniper bush just behind me; and a bumble bee, which was busily buzzing about and landing in the manner of a helicopter every few feet to examine something that interested it. It was a sound I usually associate with summer, but bees had an early start this year with the exceptionally warm weather during March. Thinking particularly of the coal tit and the bumble bee, how much do we really know of the everyday business of most creatures?

I had noticed as I sat down on the mossy rock that a rabbit had been plucked there. No bones or gut remained but there was clear evidence a bird of prey had been busy, and using the rock as a plucking post. I could see that a rock 10 yards in front was similarly festooned with rabbit fur. These two rocks were only 30 or so yards from the one where on 31 March I'd noticed the same evidence of plucking. Buzzards take young rabbits, and sometimes pluck them near – especially uphill of – their nest. This in fact was the case here, with the buzzard nest slightly downhill from me. Sparrowhawks use a plucking post but their diet is restricted to birds. I may have been close to a goshawk nest, though I'm surprised I hadn't seen any birds displaying earlier in spring. I'll need to be a bit more observant when I'm in Lament to try to get to the bottom of this.

I crossed the dyke onto Geordie's Moor, making for the large stand of junipers. A great tit was sounding its *che che che che* alarm call at me. The old birch trees around me were full of holes, really suitable places for tits to nest, and undoubtedly its chosen nesting site was nearby, though I thought it a bit early for there to be eggs just yet. I was studying some of the suitable nesting holes when a red patch on a birch tree caught my attention. A look through the binoculars revealed a red squirrel sitting on a branch, which I managed to get closer to by taking a step sideways till there was a tree between it and me, and slowly walking forward. When I reached the tree the squirrel was just 10 yards away. It watched me with interest, then went sideways behind the branch it had been sitting on. The branch was quite thin, and the squirrel was hiding lengthways, which must have been a bit of a strain for it. I went forward another few yards, keeping another tree between us, and awaited the squirrel's patience (or endurance at its awkward posture) to run out and for it to come back into view. It had the last laugh: after nearly 10 minutes of fruitless waiting I noticed a small red patch in a fork of the tree just slightly higher than where the squirrel had been. Somehow it had managed to get there without me noticing, and was watching my daft human antics, just its ears and the top of its head in view.

Further through the junipers I found further proof that summer is on the way, in the shape of one of the warbler family. It landed on the ground ahead of me just long enough for me to get the binoculars on to it but not enough to make a study and identification. From the glimpse I had I would put it down to one of three: garden warbler, chiffchaff or willow warbler. My guess would be the willow warbler. I'm still not expert on these wee brown birds, though getting a lot better, but I always need a minute or two to study them.

From the end of Geordie's Moor I headed across the sheep field (now with sheep and lambs, each with bright yellow numbers sprayed on their sides linking lambs with mothers) and up past the small pond near the edge of the Larch Wood. No goosanders there today, but an adult black rabbit ran down the side of the pond and through the fence into the roundel. It was either one I hadn't seen before or one that had moved. Some bucks do tend to move in spring if they are ousted from their home territory by a stronger rival, but there is obviously a strong melanistic gene in this area. Of the different variations in colour of wild rabbits, black is the most common, though I have seen albino, ginger, light grey, 'Dutch' type rabbits with a white band round the ribs and white blaze on the nose, and rabbits with a steel-grey coat, which is a mix of black and white hairs, always without the white belly fur, this steel-grey covering the whole body. No doubt these genetic 'sports' were the origin of many of today's domestic rabbits.

I cut through Ell Wood, noticing a small herd of fallow deer grazing to the north-east of Creag Bheag Wood. It was the pure white fallow doe, Penelope, I saw first. She was in the company of five dark coloured fallow and one slightly dappled. I was still thinking about the deer as I walked past the edge of the Henhouse Wood, where I noticed a cream coloured fallow yearling lying under an old elderberry tree. At first I thought the deer was dead, but realised it had its head laid flat on the ground, hiding, as it would have done as a very young calf the previous spring. As I stopped and turned it realised it had been spotted and bounded through the wood. I was puzzled. I had seen Penelope with a cream coloured calf last summer, and had made the assumption that it was the one that I photographed at very close quarters at the edge of Creag Bheag on 5 March. That calf had been much whiter than the one I had just disturbed so there seemed to be a white calf and a cream calf. But why was the cream calf not with a group, and why was there not a calf with Penelope? More mysteries to be solved, but I had a feeling of foreboding about this wee cream calf on its own.

I walked down the side of Law Wood, amazed at the number of rabbits in the wood, which forms a wide gully with a good view into the wood from the bank on either side. It was already swarming with young rabbits; the mild winter had certainly benefited *Lepus cuniculus.* I stopped for a minute to watch a male bullfinch searching for buds in a rowan tree that was coming into leaf, and noticed in the background a black rabbit; one of the 'known' ones I regularly see near the two small feeder ponds that lie just to the west of the loch at the shooting lodge. It was indeed a black rabbit day: as I continued on down the track between the loch and Loch Wood another of the 'known' black rabbits sat at the edge of the wood watching my progress. It had an amazing sheen on its jet black coat and was clearly in tip-top condition. This is one I have managed to get close enough to on a couple of occasions to photograph, and yet again it obliged. It has no objections to shooting – though only with a camera.

It was a day not just of black rabbits but of puzzles. I encountered another mystery when I got back to my car at the shooting lodge: there was not a house martin or swallow to be seen!

New birds identified: redshank
New mammals identified: none

Chapter 25

Saturday 5 May 2012. Weather: Sunny, but cold wind first thing, with temperature of only 4 degrees. Wind moderated and day had warmed up by 10 am, and was at 10 degrees by midday.

George had told me that when he was mending a fence separating the estate road from Geordie's Moor he'd spotted an oystercatcher sitting on three eggs just 10 yards inside the fence. I saw the bird as I drove up the road, sitting cosily in what looked like one of the hoof prints of the three highland cattle on the moor. Swallow and house martin numbers were recovering this morning. I wondered if this had been a stopping-off point for some of the house martins, which had now moved further north. I know that sand martins, while migrating north or south, can rest in the colonial nest burrows of other sand martins. This had been a crucial piece of evidence from an expert in the trial of a farmer who razed a sand martin colony to the ground, and where the prosecution was required to prove that the burrows were still being used. However I think there is less chance of house martins using old nests on migration north as many will have fallen off the buildings or been removed over the winter. Two swallows landed on the roof of one of the buildings, one on the ridge and one just below its mate, giving me a good photo opportunity.

I checked again for the tawny owl, but there was still no sign. As I was lowering the binoculars there was a flash of red on my left as a male redstart flew off a branch. It must have landed there momentarily, not 10 yards from me, giving me the briefest glimpse of its red, blue-grey and black colours. It was great to see these beautiful birds back, and I was delighted that a redstart was one of the first birds I had seen today. I sat on a stack of slates for 15 minutes to see if it would return. I was regaled by the repetitive but enchanting melody of a song thrush and by the *tea-cher; tea-cher; tea-cher* call of a great tit somewhere just beyond the song thrush. As part of the bass of the orchestra, one of the mute swans on the loch gave a snort not dissimilar to that of an impatient horse, but there was no further sight or sound of the redstart.

I headed down the estate road, hearing the *too-oodle, too-oodle; too-oodle* of the redshank and noticing the oystercatcher come off its nest and run across the moor. It remained on the ground and seemed relatively unconcerned, not taking flight and mobbing me as this species sometimes does when nesting, and certainly with chicks. I watched a lapwing run in a similar fashion; it had probably come off a nest as well. I managed to photograph the oystercatcher nest from the roadside, thus minimising disturbance. I went round by the dam, and stopped for a minute to watch swallows fly in and out of the boathouse. They don't take long to get into action; the two I'd photographed on the roof earlier showed that they were already paired and no doubt some will have started to build their open mud cup and feather-lined nests. I started to walk slowly along the south shore of the loch, seeing a buzzard lift from the top of a conifer and glide silently round over the loch. I'd noticed this bird do the same the last time I'd passed, and wondered at that time if it had come off a nest. In minutes the buzzard was back over my head, still silent and in complete contrast to the one a week or so earlier out near the western march that mewed in defiance at my proximity to its nest. This one definitely had a nest, but despite a scan with the binoculars, I couldn't locate it.

I continued into the grass field beyond, that runs up the south-east side of Law Wood. An oystercatcher rose from an uncultivated, stony corner of the field, and as I passed I saw its nest with two eggs. Three is the more regular clutch, but I was intrigued by this nest for another reason: oystercatchers only make a rudimentary nest, little more than a scrape in the ground and lined – if that is an appropriate term – with some small stones. This industrious bird had gathered literally hundreds of small stones, more than I'd ever seen in a nest before. It was a masterpiece!

I walked on up the fence line, then crossed into Law Wood, where I found a comfortable grassy seat to look down into the relatively open basin of the wood. It was like having one of the best seats at a theatre. Rabbits, large and small, were going about their rabbity business, and I was amazed at the explosion of young ones. Near the bottom of the food chain, they would provide plenty of snacks for a variety of mammalian and avian predators. The wind was still cold and I was thankful that I was sheltered, getting an undiluted value of the sun. Chaffinches were singing everywhere; wrap-around chaffinch song, and yet another song thrush, but there was no sound from the birds I was really listening for: the new migrant arrivals from sub-Saharan Africa. Many of these birds prefer thick bushy cover rather than simply trees, which possibly explained their absence. I enjoyed the 'local' wildlife over a sandwich and drink of red grape juice, reluctant to move from my comfy seat.

I cut through Law Wood, noting the numerous fallow deer tracks, and came out at the south-east end of the Larch Wood. A narrow, damp strip that almost joins the two woods together provided exactly what I was looking for: ideal habitat for warbler species. The strip was mostly goat willow, interspersed with rowan and ash. I had immediate success, hearing a whitethroat, a bird I'd been regularly listening to at home over the past few days. Warblers' songs are almost impossible to describe in words, so I'm not going to try; suffice to say it was a very pleasant series of warbles and trills, given off in short staccato bursts. It took ages before I eventually managed to spot the bird, which perched near the top of a willow for a good three or four minutes; a long time for this type of bird to remain in one place. It had a grey head, so was a male, a white throat, hence its name, brown wings and back and a greyish pink breast. The whitethroat has a longer tail than most of the other warbler-type birds and I always think its tail is slightly darker than the colour of its back.

As I was watching the whitethroat I heard the first cuckoo of the season. The male's *cu-ckoo; cu-ckoo; cu-ckoo* came floating over from somewhere between the Larch Wood and Dank Wood. The cuckoo's visit to this country is short, hardly more than enough time to find a mate, lay a single egg in up to a couple of dozen other birds' nests and head back to far warmer climes, leaving foster parents to bring up baby cuckoo. Individual cuckoos seem to specialise in selecting a particular species of bird as foster parents. I suspect on this estate it will be the meadow pipit.

I cut through the Larch Wood, passing one of George's crow cages and noting a buzzard nest in a larch tree almost above the cage, though I think this was one of last year's. The two captive corvids sat on a perch in the cage and watched me passing. They and the other decoy birds have lured 44 carrion crows and two hooded crows into the traps so far this year. Considering their predilection for eggs and young birds I can't say that I'm sad about that, yet I've no great issue about, for instance, a buzzard taking a young wader chick. I suppose at the back of my mind is the fact that buzzards are protected while carrion crows can legally be controlled under one or more of four general licences. Just before the crow trap I'd disturbed a black rabbit from its form under some rushes. I'd never seen this one before and it crossed my mind it could be the rabbit that I always used to see from my 'comfy rock' overlooking Craigie Face and Eerie Valley. This rabbit seemed to have disappeared though today's black rabbit was only a quarter of a mile away as the rabbit runs from 'comfy rock'. Though I've seen hundreds of young rabbits, there have been no wee black buns yet. I must ask George if he's seen any.

I circled the wood and walked down the dyke-side to Eerie Valley, taking a slight circuit past pegs 1 to 3 of Eerie Return. The face up the north side of Eerie Valley would be an ideal place for ring ouzels, often called mountain blackbirds. I've never seen a ring ouzel for years and would love to see them again, though unfortunately they are in long-term decline and of conservation (red-listed) concern. Still thinking of ring ouzels, I walked along the dyke-side separating Craigie Face from the grass fields. The jackdaws were out in force above The Shudder, mobbing a passing buzzard. There must have been over 100, and even if only half that number have eggs (probably now chicks) on the crags and scree of The Shudder, that will be a massive increase in jackdaw numbers in the area. More prey species, but for a much more limited number of predators than the rabbit; probably only the goshawk, peregrine and maybe the sparrowhawk. Red-legged partridges were calling from Craigie Face, and some of them could now also be on eggs.

I climbed over the dyke at a part well-used by countless numbers of rabbits, the stones stained and scratched by thousands of feet and claws. There is an ideal stepping stone on the field side in the form of a coping stone that has fallen from the top of the dyke. A bounce on this gets them halfway up the dyke, then the gap where the coping stone should be makes an easy passageway to and from the hill. It eased my access to Craigie Face and I sat for a while on a mossy rock with beautiful silver birches with brand new lime green leaves at my back and junipers in front of me. The view down over the birches at the top end of the Henhouse Wood and across to the Ell Wood was incredible. The colours ranged from the brilliant lime green of the birches, to mid green of sycamores, pastel green of rowan, the almost brown colour of oak leaves still unfurling and the dark green of the sitka spruce at the far end of the Henhouse Strip. In contrast (and to some degree contradictory) was the vivid white of the blossom on a row of blackthorn bushes at the side of Law Wood. This was the place for my second – and final – sandwich, savouring the springtime colours even more than the sandwich. The seats I pick now are much more comfortable than in earlier days and, like Law Wood, I was looking down on the variety of birds busying about the junipers – mostly chaffinches and robins – and listening to a blackbird singing from a birch somewhere at my back and part-way up the Craigie Face.

Tearing myself from this idyll, I cut the corner to the sheep fank half-way along Creag Bheag Wood and returned along the track in the centre of the wood, stopping to listen to a robin singing in an old pine tree, and further along to watch a red squirrel searching on the ground for whatever delicacy it could find there. The squirrel hopped down through the wood, then on to a fallen tree, where it ran along the prone trunk almost to my feet, before seeing me at the last minute, giving a snort of alarm, and scurrying up the tree beside me, its claws scratching audibly on the bark at its rapid ascent.

I was keen to see if I could get any more evidence of there being a nesting goshawk in Lament, and made for there, following the burn down on its right hand side, and crossing via a fallen tree in the manner of a very easy tightrope walk. I entered Lament at the high seat, and watched a group of six fallow make their way in single file from the clear-felled and replanted part into the sitka spruce at the top end, stopping only momentarily to look back over their shoulder in unison at me. Just about the point they left the clear-fell I spotted a nest in a spruce tree. I was not sure if the nest was this year's or not, but I knew there was another one about 75 yards to the east in an oak. I checked the oak nest and saw a branch still with dead leaves hanging from it. This tended to indicate it was the one in use, though I still couldn't be certain. I'd seen no bird come off either nest and there was no bird circling above.

I checked the mossy rocks on the top side of the nest and found five that had been used as places to pluck rabbits. None of these plucking posts had feathers, which I would have expected had either of the nests been that of a goshawk. On balance I think that one of the nests I had just seen is in use by a buzzard rather than a goshawk, and the other is last year's. Taking these factors into consideration I would say the plucking posts are those of a buzzard.

I crossed the dyke into Geordie's Moor and walked up the side of the pheasant pen on the moor. The inside and the outside of the pen are a mass of juniper bushes and I could hear two or maybe three warblers singing. One was in a bush just in front of me, with the singer in view: a willow warbler. The song was softer than I expected, this being the first time I had seen and heard one simultaneously. The bird almost seemed to be singing to itself rather than to the wider world, and more specifically to create a territory and attract a potential mate. Like the whitethroat the song came in short bursts, slightly briefer than those of the whitethroat. Its dark eye stripe and pale coloured legs were obvious, though I would have described the breast feathers as white rather than the pale yellow sometimes attributed to this bird. It was puffing its feathers out as it sang, which maybe made the breast feathers look paler than they were, rather in the manner of a carrion crow, whose black breast feathers show the light grey underside if ruffled. The bird moved from perch to perch, still singing but mostly now out of my view. I was lucky with a willow warbler further up through the junipers, which stayed still long enough for me to photograph it.

I had seen a small group of dark coloured fallow sneaking through the junipers, and as I came to the end of Geordie's Moor they suddenly appeared not 20 yards from me. I froze, as did they, and we studied each other. One was a buck, with velvet antler buds only an inch long. Though the deer were dark, they actually looked dappled because of their moult, the remaining light coloured tufts of old coat contrasting with the new, dark, incoming coat. I reached to my pocket for my camera and slowly raised it up, keeping all movement in front of my body rather than to the sides. I took a photo, which remained momentarily on the screen, freezing the image of the deer. If I was being anthropomorphic I could have said they had puzzled expressions on their faces. I kept the camera at eye level for the next photo, but when the screen cleared they were no longer there. In any case, even one photo of totally wild animals at such close range was a fitting end to the day.

New birds identified: whitethroat; cuckoo
New mammals identified: none

Chapter 26

Saturday 12 May 2012. Weather: Sunny, but with occasional cloud cover. Wind brisk though moderated as the day progressed. Pleasant.

The oystercatcher was sitting tightly on its nest on Geordie's Moor as I drove up the estate road. That's good news, and possibly due to the carrion crow control, which the owner told me over an early morning coffee is now over 50, including two that he shot with the rifle. This pair had been determined to raid an oystercatcher's nest on the island on the shooting lodge loch. I was further reminded of the destructive nature of carrion crows when I found a pheasant's egg with the typical hole made by the crow's beak to suck out the liquid (or sometimes not-so-liquid) contents. I'm well aware that it's perfectly natural for carrion crows to eat eggs and young birds, and that they have been doing this for countless thousands of years without, so far as we know, wiping out any bird species. However they are not my favourite birds, and while I often marvel at their guile and ingenuity I don't have to like them. As I went to the estate owner's door, house martins were actively repairing last year's nests, and had a new nesting location in which they were taking a real interest under the eaves of the extension built since the birds left last September. An expanded house facilitating an expanding bird population.

I intended to go to the hill first today, and set off up the road. After 100 yards or so I stopped to scan the fields with the binoculars. It was an unfortunate place to stop, since my change in pace – or indeed lack of pace – made a mallard duck decide to leave its nest not three yards from me. I had not seen the duck, and it would have sat tightly had I not stopped. Its eight blue-green eggs were now exposed, and indeed were shining in the sun. The gleam off the eggs was probably due in part to their imminence to hatching, having been polished by the duck's feathers over a large part of the four week incubation period. They would be a magnet for any passing crow, or even a rook or jackdaw, so I covered them with the down that lined the nest, in the manner that the duck does anyway when it leaves the nest to feed. I made haste up the road to let the duck return as quickly as possible.

When I reached Dank Wood I turned right along the grassy path on the south side, to circumnavigate the wood anti-clockwise. A small bird, facing away from me, was perched on top of the dyke. I could see from the shape it was a young robin; a young robin surrounded by a silver halo caused by the sun glowing on the remaining down that still protruded through its new feathers. I got a better view as I came closer. The robin could have been on its maiden flight; its tail feathers hadn't yet grown and its breast was speckled in the manner of a song thrush. Its beak, as with all young birds, seemed to extend half way back its head; all the better to gape with and to beg for food. The covering of down made the wee robin look as if it had been electrified. Slightly further along the dyke two birds were having a bit of a tussle. When they separated one flew towards me and I could see it was a robin, probably a parent of the electric chick. Its sparring partner flew into the field and perched on a rock. It was a female wheatear, the first I had seen this year. Though the two species are in slight competition for food, both with a predilection for invertebrates, I've no doubt the robin had seen off the wheatear in defence of its chick.

Compared to a smart male wheatear in breeding plumage, the female was much plainer, having a sandy-brown back, as opposed to the slate grey of the male, and not nearly as broad an eye stripe of chocolate brown. As it flew off I could see the white rump common to both sexes, and the main point in identification when the bird is in flight. As I followed the wheatear's flight along the edge of the field I saw a half-grown black rabbit looking out of a burrow. I'd been checking all the known sites of adult black rabbits for young black ones, and here was one in an area I'd never seen a black adult. Observing wildlife often throws up more questions than answers!

This was a busy corner as, three-quarters along the wood, I heard a cuckoo. The sound seemed initially to be coming from nearby Wericky Wood, but was coming closer. The bird was calling in flight, and landed on a fence post just along from me. It sat silently on the post in typical cuckoo pose, with its wing tips drooping much lower than its tail, unlike most birds which hold their wing tips above the level of their tail. It was a slate-grey bird, with a white breast barred with black and looked incredibly hawk-like. The cuckoo moved a few fence posts further up then flew through the wood behind me. It flew fast and low and, had I not known it was a cuckoo, I might have thought the bird to be a sparrowhawk. Its *cu-ckoo; cu-ckoo; cu-ckoo* call then radiated from the west end of Dank, and it may well have been the bird I heard the previous week.

At the south east corner of the wood a red squirrel scurried along the ground and disappeared behind some brushwood. I waited on it emerging but it never did. I'd had only the briefest of glimpses but I was pleased to see a squirrel, as this was the only sighting in this wood since the previous July. I came along the top side of Dank, cutting through a part that had been clear-felled. As I entered the trees again, I became aware of a buzzard mewing in alarm over my head. It was quite low over the trees and I got the impression it had just come off a nest. I checked the trees as I passed through the wood, but couldn't see any nest, though it may well have been further into the wood. After I left the wood and headed out the hill road the buzzard became silent, making me even more convinced it had a nest.

It was a day for deer on the hill, starting with two roe deer trotting to my right towards the east boundary dyke when they spotted me, and another two watching from the horizon to the north. Simultaneously five fallow deer, two light coloured and three dark, filed slowly up the hill ahead of me. I sat on a rock to watch and, true to form, the fallow stopped at the skyline to look back. They knew I was there, though it's doubtful they would see my stationary form. A meadow pipit was giving its *sweet sweet sweet* song behind me, and I turned in time to see it fluttering, almost perpendicularly, to the ground. This is a similar display to that of the skylark, yet another red-listed bird becoming increasingly rare and unfortunately not so far seen or heard on this estate. The hill was alive with red-legged partridges, and I could hear a pair keeping in touch with their quiet *tic, tic, tic* call. Pheasants are nesting and indeed some may have hatched, so I'd be surprised if at least some of the partridges are not on eggs. No doubt the first sign I'll see is a predated egg. The partridges had been quite close to me, and as I rose from the rock they flew off, their call now changed to a *wee-choo, wee-choo, wee-choo* as they disappeared.

I was surprised not to see any buzzards, and disappointed not to see any sign of a kestrel as I approached Middle Hill. Many nesting birds are quite silent at this time of year and it almost seems that they have disappeared, with a re-emergence once their chicks have fledged. I spent some time at a bog on the Middle Hill as George had told me he regularly saw snipe there. No such luck for me, though the area was thronging with meadow pipits. Further along the hill road a hen pheasant fluttered from the heather. It landed only 20 yards away and I was sure it would have chicks. I had a quick look in the area it came from, being careful not to stand on any chicks, but I could see neither chicks nor nest. The pheasant's actions were certainly that of a bird with chicks and I can only assume that there may only have been one or two and they were lying low. Good for them!

Two more roe, one of them looking really scruffy in its moult from winter to summer coat, bounded up the steep face of Grey Crags as I took the right fork. One was making for the overhang where I once had found a dead roe deer, and I thought it would go no further than that as it would be out of my sight. I stopped just after the overhang to admire the natural emergence of plant life growing out of the rocks and scree to my left. Rowan was predominant, even growing out of sheer rock, but there were also mountain ash, birch, juniper, dog rose and of course loads of blaeberries. The gradient of the face will have limited browsing by deer, allowing the seedling trees a better chance, though when I looked through the binoculars at the fierce thorns of the dog rose I was in no doubt as to what its saviour had been.

At the top of Grey Crags I made my way down to a swiped path through the heather that, after the first 100 yards and a right turn, would take me roughly parallel with the march of the estate to the west and gradually down and round towards the eastern estate march. A greyhen, the female of the black grouse, flushed from the path and flew over to the neighbour's side of the fence where there is a stand of young larch trees. When I came further along the path, I could see that what had attracted the greyhen was one of several red trays of medicated grit George had put out for the few grouse that there were. The grit would aid in the production of calcium for their eggs, and the medication in the grit would help combat *Trichostrongylus tenuis*, the intestinal threadworm, accumulations of which can be fatal for young grouse. It was great to see a greyhen as populations of black grouse have fallen dramatically in recent years, though some parts of Perthshire remain a stronghold. The greyhen, as it flew off, was not unlike a red grouse though was larger and had grey-brown plumage, with some white showing under the wings, rather than the much redder plumage of the red grouse. Had it been a male – a blackcock – identification of the glossy black bird with a bright red wattle over its eye and a lyre-shaped tail, would have been much easier.

Further down the hill my 'deer day' continued, as I watched a dappled fallow doe and a light coloured calf climb the hill on the other side of the Chapel Burn. The calf, a young male, had small sharp-looking buds of antlers and rather resembled a wildebeest calf on the wrong continent. The doe was making good progress, but the calf seemed much more intent on looking back to try to understand the reason for the hasty departure from what would no doubt have been a comfy couch in the sun. I sat on a rock, partly to watch the deer and partly to look for any sign of a hen harrier. Another group of fallow deer then filed up the hill from roughly the same area as the light coloured ones. This time there were seven, led by a very rotund-looking doe that seemed ready to drop its almost-developed calf anytime. Tail-end Charlie of the line was again a calf, though this time female. Like its earlier light-coloured relative, it also seemed more interested in what was behind rather than what lay ahead.

From walking parallel with one neighbour's fence, I now gradually turned right to walk parallel with the other neighbour's fence in my clockwise circuit of Connell Hill. I passed a group of larch trees and checked them for carrion crow nests as they were the only trees in the area. No carrion nests, so George's work is definitely paying off. Further round the hill, near the end of my circuit, I spotted fox tracks on a patch of drying mud on the track. They were not fresh enough to have been left the previous night, but had they been there during or prior to the extremely heavy and prolonged rain on Thursday (three days earlier) they would have been washed out. I concluded they had been left on Thursday night after the rain passed. The pads were typical of fox, with the hind foot landing almost inside the mark left by the front foot. George has culled a fair number of foxes this spring, but like the carrion crows, there are always some left.

As I passed the pond on the hill I could hear a hushed willow warbler song coming from within a patch of broom on my right. A willow warbler – possibly the singer – flew from the broom and landed on the track in front of me. I photographed the bird and when I looked at the photo later I was quite amazed at the length of its legs. Perched on a bush the legs appear insignificant, but this bird, standing on the road had its legs, stilt-like, at full stretch and its head cocked to the side scanning for insects. This is all difficult to register even when looking at a bird through binoculars, but can be appreciated at leisure from a photograph. The obliging willow warbler then flew to a small broom bush and inspected it for insects, daintily picking a minute morsel off with some regularity.

I left the hill road and walked across a boggy area where George said he had also seen snipe, but no success for me yet again. Clear of the wet area, I sat on a grassy knoll for my second sandwich of the day. It was a lovely spot at the top end of the clear-felled area beside Larch Wood, with the partridge drive through the clear-felled area simply being called the Larch drive. An old birch tree was close-by on my right. A stand of young birches, now almost in full leaf, was ahead of me in a dip through which ran the embryonic burn that eventually flows into the loch at the shooting lodge. A single roe doe was grazing away to my right, unaware of my presence. She looked rather clapped in at the flanks and I was sure she would have twin fawns hidden in the bracken nearby. Like most animals, roe deer go off on their own to have their fawns, and she is likely now to remain apart from other roe deer until late autumn, when she and her fawns will merge with others into a larger group. The group won't necessarily stay together all winter but will drift apart and regroup as circumstances – particularly disturbance – dictate.

I came through the interior of Larch Wood, keeping to the inside edge of the conifers on the south-west side. There was a huge buzzard nest three-quarters way up a larch tree and to one side on the main trunk rather than in a fork. Initially I thought it was a nest being used this year but when I turned round a buzzard came off another nest in a nearby sitka spruce. Like the one in the larch, this one was also three-quarters way up the tree and against the trunk. The buzzard mewed from above in an alarm call which was more rapidly repeated than the normal communication call. As I left the wood the buzzard was still mewing, but from an incredible altitude. I was amazed at the different reactions of nesting buzzards. Of the four active nests I'd encountered I'd now had one buzzard mobbing me (rather stupidly from a distance that was within shotgun range); two circling and mewing at a height not much above tree level; and now this one, which was little more than a speck in the sky.

I had a listen and a look at the line of predominantly goat willow than runs from the Larch Wood to Law Wood. Almost right away I heard a whitethroat and I tried to get into a position to see it. It had initially been amongst willow but flew to a rowan. I found a comfy seat on a rock and watched the rowan tree, where I had tantalising glimpses of the bird among the branches. It then moved to one of the topmost branches, where I had a good view but for only a few seconds before it flew over my head and continued to sing from within the bowels of a huge rhododendron. Despite sometimes singing from high in a tree, overall they seem much more secretive than willow warblers.

From here I headed towards Ell Wood, stopping briefly to spy up towards Eeerie Valley, where there are normally buzzards circling, though not today. I had high hopes for Ell Wood as I thought it would have been ideal for small birds: mainly youngish birch trees, with a line of mature beech down the west side and a mix of mature trees along the south end and the east side. Apart from pheasant, partridges, mistle and song thrushes, chaffinches and of course the brambling from the winter time, I have seen or heard little else. I decided to sit a while to see what happened and found a mossy tree trunk that suited the purpose. When I sat down I heard a thump from underground, then a three quarter grown rabbit looked out from under the stump, saw me, and bolted into a hole under the next stump less than 10 yards away. Had I been interested in catching the rabbit it would have been no safer there than where it originally had been. The rabbit, and a rather hoarse cock pheasant with a missing tail, was the sum total of 20 minutes on the tree stump. But at least I had tried.

Leaving Ell Wood I cut through the Henhouse Wood to the left hand side of the pond. Half a dozen mallard drakes were on the pond but were reluctant to leave and swam into some rushes at the far side. At the far end I went up the dyke that bisects the pheasant pen, sending wee rabbits scurrying everywhere. A male blackbird on the other side of the dyke busied itself turning over leaf litter in search of the many creepy crawlies that hide under the dead leaves, its vivid yellow beak and eyelids in complete contrast to its jet black feathers. A smaller bird caught my eye as it landed on a branch ahead of me. Though I was looking pretty much due south and directly into the sun I could easily see the red tail of the redstart. It was a female, with unostentatious light brown and cream colouring. It lacked the grandiose brick-red breast, blue-grey upperparts and black cheeks of the male but was still a lovely bird. It flicked its exquisite red tail a few times, then flew into some larch trees just beyond the pen. I sat for a while near where it had been to see if it would return. My patience was rewarded, not by a returning redstart, but by antics of a willow warbler. The bird had flown from the Henhouse Wood to a blackthorn bush some 50 yards outside the wood. It perched there for a minute or two then briefly flew out 10 yards from the bush before returning again to its perch. It did this again, this time flying double the first distance, and back again to the bush. I thought at first I was watching a spotted flycatcher, which launches itself off a branch in this manner to catch a fly, then returns to its perch. I doubted that a spotted flycatcher would be back in Scotland yet, as it is one of the latest migrants to return. At last when I managed to get a good look at the bird through the binoculars and confirm it was indeed a willow warbler I was satisfied, though I was intrigued by activity I'd never seen before.

Turning and moving further up the Henhouse Wood, to the part that is predominantly conifer rather than the birch of the opposite end, I was studying an enormous Douglas fir. Two tiny birds flew from the tree on to the top of the dyke that forms the boundary of the wood. Like the robin and wheatear earlier, there was a dispute over something, but the battle continued down the dyke until they were almost beside me. The flurry of activity was rapid, but one perched on top of the dyke long enough for me to see that it was a male goldcrest, the orange strip on the top of its head bounded by black on each side clearly visible, if only fleetingly (had it been a female, the strip would have been yellow). The two birds continued their skirmish along the top of the dyke, making contact with each other momentarily before one was again in pursuit of the other. It was a fascinating sight and I can only conclude that both were goldcrests and that one was seeing the other off from its 'patch', which I supposed was the Douglas fir. It had been a remarkable day and this was a tremendous finale.

New birds identified: black grouse
New mammals identified: none

Chapter 27

Monday 20 May 2012. Weather: Sunny, no wind; a great day to be out and about.

A day with an absence of wind is a great time to be on the loch, so I made for the fishing loch, which was pretty much a flat calm. I spoke with Craig, who told me there had been a brood of 11 mallard ducklings that was now down to two, and a brood of eight Canada goslings that was also at the same low number. Like me, Craig suspected pike to be the culprits. I was disappointed but my frustration is always assuaged when sad events like this are natural rather than man-induced. Craig also said that the previous evening he saw two great-crested grebes performing their courtship display. This was not a good sign; it was possible that they'd also lost a brood of chicks and were starting again.

A boat was ready for me and I edged it out of the harbour. A quick scan round the loch with the binoculars revealed… virtually nothing. I could see the two pairs of swans in their established territories and a couple of mallard drakes on the south shore, but the loch was unusually bare. Maybe the word 'unusually' is inaccurate, since it could be quite usual for many of the waterfowl either to be on nests round the lochside, or in the case of some species, nesting elsewhere. It was a disappointing start but probably in keeping with the time of year. I cruised slowly up near the south shore, listening in particular for any of the warbler family that was less likely to be found on the hill and in the woods of the estate. What I *did* hear was a real brouhaha coming from within the shore-side trees. A buzzard was rising from ground level and was being harassed by two incredibly raucous carrion crows. I was assuming the buzzard had been eating some carrion, or had caught a small mammal and the crows had harangued it so much it had left its meal; a bit like hyenas seeing off a cheetah. The trio jinked through the trees and into the field beyond, their route still traceable aurally even though not visibly.

As the disturbance calmed down I was able to concentrate on other species. An osprey was circling the loch at a height that I thought might be too high to dive on a fat trout. It seemed a smallish osprey and possibly a male. It was interesting that it kept near the shoreline, mainly on the north and east shore. It gradually lost a bit of height and at one point briefly closed its wings as if about to dive, but quickly pulled out and resumed its search. I watched it for about 15 minutes until my attention was distracted by a great-crested grebe almost in the centre of the loch. I confirmed that the grebe was on its own, then tried to reconnect with the hunting osprey, without success.

I positioned the boat near a reed bed at the south west end of the loch, turned off the engine and sat and listened. It was still and quiet, not even a puff of wind or the quiet lapping of waves against the boat. After about 10 minutes I heard the high pitched and machine gun-like chatter of a sedge warbler. The metallic chatter was quickly followed by an equally rapid *cheep cheep cheep*, not unlike a recording of a sparrow played at the wrong speed, then on an even higher scale, *eep eep eep*. This brisk series was repeated a couple of times, but though I waited a further 10 minutes the bird never broke into its full song, nor, unfortunately, did I manage to spot it.

I did spot the west end mute swans, but they had no cygnets. As if to prove the point they swam closer to me. The last time I visited, the female – the pen – had looked really content on her nest, long neck curled over her back, and it seems a real pity the pair had no family to tend. Round the corner I saw the ripples as something dived. I hoped it would be the otter, but when a magnificent great-crested grebe surfaced near my boat I didn't feel too let down. The grebe dived at various places round the boat and gave some reasonable photography opportunities. As a diversion, nine Canada geese flew honking over the loch and landed in a grass field between the loch and the road.

I sailed down the north shore past the second pair of swans that were shepherding six small cygnets, two of them brave enough to go off a few yards on their own to dabble in the reeds. Unfortunately this is exactly where a large pike was likely to be lying in wait. They would be a fair mouthful for a pike, but then pike have been caught with some remarkably large trout – or other pike – inside them. As another diversion two gulls flew over my head. I paid them scant attention, thinking they were just another two common gulls. The quiet call from one to the other immediately made me take more notice, and when I put the binoculars on them the chocolate brown head, red beak and red legs confirmed them as black-headed gulls. I had all but given up hope of seeing these extremely widespread gulls here. There is no marshy hill pond on the estate where they breed though there must be a suitable breeding site somewhere not too far away.

Strangely satisfied at having seen birds that I see elsewhere almost daily, I headed down the loch towards the harbour. A single goose well ahead of me was honking and my first assumption was that it was the Canada goose that had been steadily losing its brood. There were no goslings with it and I wondered if it had lost the complete brood and was now trying to communicate with its mate. I considered it would be odd seeing the male and female apart when they have goslings as geese are great parents. Getting closer to the goose, I could now see it was not a Canada goose. It had a greyish back, white tail, white head, speckled neck and a smallish darkish coloured beak. I knew there had been three bar-headed geese frequenting the adjacent loch, but I was confused by the absence of the two distinctive black bars across the back of the head that give the bar-headed goose its name, and it had a darkish beak rather than the yellow one of the bar-headed goose. I considered a hybrid a possibility, but later had to seek expert advice from RSPB, who were certain from my photos that the bird was a blue-morph snow goose.

I'd to read up on the snow goose. It has two colour plumage types, referred to as 'phases' or 'morphs' - white (snow) or grey/blue (blue). White-morph birds are white except for black wing tips, but blue-morph geese have bluish-grey plumage replacing the white except on the head, neck and tail tip. They are very vocal, a fact for which I could vouch. The two morphs can interbreed and the offspring can be of either morph. Some snow geese are winter visitors to Britain, though whether this one has been left behind or is an escapee from a collection somewhere will remain a mystery. In any case it was one of my most unusual sightings.

I tied up the boat and drove up to the shooting lodge, noting when I passed that the nine Canada geese in the roadside grass field near the loch had increased to 11. When I parked I was pleased that the first bird I heard was a cuckoo, the sound coming from Dank Wood. I checked the house martin nests at the owner's back door, and they were now completely refurbished. Of two back to back nests, one was half as big again as the other, though I think the additional size was mainly mud underneath and that there would be little difference in the cosy feather-lined chamber inside. The birds went to and from the nests no more than three feet from my head; all hirundines seem remarkably tolerant of humans.

I headed off up the road to see if the mallard duck I had scared off the nest the previous week had returned, or if the crows had dined on embryonic ducklings. Thankfully the duck was back on the nest. It was sitting motionless, with its head and neck stretched out in front of it and encircled by a cushion of down. It looked as if it was sitting on a small grey cloud. I marched smartly past, averting my eyes once I saw it was back and the nest was safe. Further up, I crossed the fence and walked through the sheep field to Wericky. I found a sunny glade and sat on a hummock to watch – and of course to hear – what was happening. A song thrush sang from the top of a sycamore, repeating each phrase three or four times while the cuckoo still fluted its totally different tune from nearby Dank Wood. A woodpigeon *cooed* from some conifers behind me, and I seemed surrounded by chaffinch song. A shrew ran from somewhere secretive among the plantation of Norway spruce, darting across a grassy area kept shorn by the double incisors of rabbits, and took refuge under a pile of pallets. Within minutes its long flexible pink nose poked out the other side, testing the air before its next dash across to undergrowth at the other side of the track. It was very mole-like, maybe the main difference being that it had reasonable sight from its tiny black eyes. A nervous dunnock first flitted among the spruce trees, then hopped about the grass in front of me. It returned to a spruce tree and was joined by a willow warbler, two totally unrelated but equally secretive birds together. With something dry and reasonably comfortable to sit on, unlike the cold, hard rocks of winter-time, I've been sitting for longer periods and letting wildlife come to me. So far the strategy has paid dividends.

I walked up to the top part of Wericky, which is a high mound of mainly giant conifers. Near the very top a buzzard appeared over my head, mewing in the tone I now recognise as that of an anxious nesting bird. I saw the nest high in a Douglas fir; a huge nest that has probably been used on and off over a period of several years. On the ground near the nest tree there was a dead young rabbit, probably killed or had died a couple of days earlier. On some estates this might arouse suspicion of being a poisoned bait. Two factors eliminated this possibility for me: when I turned it over it had no cuts where any pesticide could have been introduced, but more importantly, the integrity of the owner and keeper.

In my next encounter with a rabbit, midway across to Dank, the rabbit was alive. I saw the adult rabbit sitting along the field from me, but sitting in a position that looked much too relaxed for a rabbit that must have seen me. In the proximity of a human, a rabbit claps down, pressing its body as close to the ground as it can manage, until the point where it may eventually have to take flight. I walked closer to this rabbit, and could see that its back feet were pushed forward under its belly more than is normal. This is never a good sign and often indicates a rabbit with a gut complaint, rather like if we had a sore stomach we might curl up for some relief. By the time I was five yards from the rabbit I could hear it wheezing, though there was no discharge from its nose. The very fact I was so close confirmed the rabbit was seriously ill and I raised my stick above my head to finish it off. I still had a couple of steps to go before I'd be in reach, but at the last minute the rabbit hopped off, hunch-backed, and disappeared down a nearby burrow. Wild rabbits get a number of diseases. I suspected coccidiosis or snuffles (pasteurellosis) though I've never seen the latter disease in wild rabbits. Maybe if a vet reads this the answer will be obvious!

I passed along the bottom side of Dank, looking for the young black rabbit from the last visit, but only seeing its grey/brown cousins. The second litters of the season are very evident now, with literally dozens of tiny rabbits just weaned and probably around five weeks old, scattering in front of me like leaves blown in a gust of autumn wind. A heron rose from the pond near to the roundel at the Larch Wood, the ponderous beats of its huge wings progressively gaining the bird height until it could clear the tops of the trees of the roundel and make towards the loch at the shooting lodge. It is only the second of these pterodactyl-like birds I have seen on the estate. I looked in the roundel for the long-tailed tits I had seen several weeks ago, hoping to see their nest, but without success, so I cut over to the damp strip running between Larch Wood and Law Wood, where I knew of yet another comfy seat.

I'd only been sitting for a few minutes, and was awaiting the song of the whitethroat I knew was in that area but, like my earlier encounter with the grebe when I was hoping for an otter, I was surprised – but not disappointed – yet again. Two birds flew into the goat willow beside me: a pair of bullfinches. The female had a beakful of nest material, clearly intent on a nest-building project nearby. Both sat looking at me but of course the handsome male, with his bold black cap, rose pink breast and slate grey back drew my gaze away from the female. By the time my attention had returned to her – or to where she had been – she had disappeared to an unknown nest site. Looking at these willows, almost silver with algae, lichens and mosses, a nest made of the same material would be all but invisible.

I made next for Law Wood, and found a lovely soft grassy seat looking down into the open centre of the wood. I had a sandwich and drink of juice and settled, while the wildlife again came to me. Blackbirds and song thrushes went about their business collecting insects and a variety of worms and grubs. The ground in front of me is damp and an ideal place for much of their food, so they were kept busy. A robin joined them, surveying the land first of all from a fencepost before beginning his invertebrate search. A great tit sang his *tea-cher; tea-cher; tea-cher* song to my left, and a distant convoy of jackdaws made their way to and from The Shudder, beaks no doubt holding as wide a range of food as the parameters of their omnivorous diet allowed. A male orange-tip butterfly danced and pirouetted over the bog in front of me; it seemed to have no clear purpose and looked like a creature demented as it went back and forward, up and down. Red-legged partridges chattered and were *tic, tic, ticking* from areas out of my view as pairs kept in contact. This was one of the most delightful places I have sat on this estate without a doubt. And it got better…

Two garden warblers landed on an alder tree to my left. They hopped about the branches gathering insects for a few minutes, then flew further left out of sight. Five minutes later one landed on a dead tree to my right, perching in clear view, and started to sing. With the warbler family you usually either see them or hear them, seldom both. From my notes (made at the time, M'Lord) it was a brown bird, plainer than some of the other warblers, with a thin, dark eye stripe, dark legs, a light, almost white, breast and with a slightly darker, off-white, throat. Its song was incredible and listening to it was a delight. Like the complex song of the robin and blackbird it is impossible for me to describe. To me it resembled the song of the whitethroat, but much more fluid, with less staccato stops and starts. The bird flew from the dead tree and immediately started singing again on my left, then behind me, then back on to the dead tree again. This had turned out to be a real warbler day.

The garden warbler made me take more notice of the dead tree. It was one of two growing out of an expanse of dense alien and invasive rhododendron, *Rhododendron ponticum*. It seems that little can grow in the shade of this plant and I wondered if it had killed these two trees. There are several patches of this rhododendron in this part of the estate. It is great as cover for foxes, rabbits, partridge and pheasant, and for several nesting birds, but for little else. In many places it is often the subject of intense eradication projects.

After nearly an hour of enjoyment I moved on, passing the delirious but delightful orange tip butterfly still apparently trying to find purpose for its infinite energy. I crossed to the Henhouse Wood and was cutting through the wood next to the pond when I spied a robin with a beakful of moss. Like the bullfinch earlier, it was intent on nest-building. This would certainly not be the robin's first nest and whether its first attempt was successful or failed I'll never know, though I now have seen several young robins on my walks. The bird was aware of my presence but I stood stock-still while it bobbed on a branch like a dipper, keen to get on with the job in hand but reluctant to reveal the nest location. It dipped and bobbed, undecided, while I never moved a muscle. After several minutes it flew to an adjacent tree, landing slightly closer to the ground than on its previous perch. It continued with its hesitant behaviour, then flew to a branch lower still. I looked around for a likely nest spot, knowing that a robin is quite happy nesting almost at ground level or even on the ground. A ditch ran towards the pond, and I thought the banks of this ditch might be the answer. Sure enough the robin flew down to the far bank, slightly out of my sight, to mould its modicum of moss into what would turn out to be a creation of beauty. I decided not to investigate in case the bird deserted. I may look more closely the next time I'm passing. As I turned to go, I almost walked right into one of George's fox snares. What an ending to the day that would have been!

New birds identified: sedge warbler, snow goose, black-headed gull, garden warbler
New mammals identified: shrew

Chapter 28

Monday 27 May 2012. Weather: Sunny, very hot. With a midday temperature of 25 degrees, am I allowed to complain it was really too hot?

A veritable cloud of birds flew from the owner's bird feeders as I went past to where I park my car. A high proportion was house sparrows, which have a safe haven in dense ivy that covers the west gable of the house. The chirping took me back to when my granny lived in an old tenement, where there were innumerable sparrows' nests and roosting crevices under the gutter, and cock sparrows chirped incessantly from their hidden places. Any gaps and fissures still available were claimed by the swifts that screamed round the summer sky, only landing during nesting time since they could sleep on the wing. Farm buildings still seem to hold good numbers of house sparrows, even if they are scarce elsewhere. The ivy would be ideal for nesting tree sparrows, though I've seen none there so far.

When I walked past the mallard duck's nest I was pleased to see it had hatched successfully. The eggs had been painstakingly opened almost round the centre by the small egg tooth at the end of each duckling's beak; a small, hard extension that works rather like a wee can opener as the duckling gradually chips away at the shell, turning in a circle as it does so. Now the smaller part of most of the eggs lay neatly inside the larger part, with the red veins still visible on the inside of the shells, all typical signs of a successful hatching. I scanned the duck ponds for the new family. There was no flotilla of ducklings to be seen, though the female may have preferred the nearby marsh or even the loch where I park my car.

At the top of the road I turned right along the bottom of Dank Wood. It's amazing how one day an area will be alive with birds and the next it seems quiet, as was the case today. The ailing rabbit I'd seen the previous week was certainly quiet. It was lying dead not far from the burrow in which it took refuge seconds before my stick would have ended its suffering in advance of its natural demise. When I got to the far end of Dank Wood I cut back through the centre to rejoin the hill road for a change. I'd never been through the middle of the wood, and the route was frequently blocked with blown trees, which I'd to circumvent or clamber over. There is a large rocky outcrop in the centre, which I also skirted round, passing through a series of lovely patches of wood sorrel, with their trio of heart-shaped leaves and dainty white flowers: five petals surrounding a pale yellow centre giving the impression of a mini fried egg.

Leaving the wood and heading out the hill road, I stopped at the trackside pond, where a willow warbler was singing quietly in golden-yellow broom. When I see broom I'm always reminded of the travellers' song *The Yellow on the Broom* –

> I ken ye dinna like it lass
> Tae winter here in toon
> For the scaldies aye miscry us
> And they try to put us doon
> But it's hard to raise three bairns
> In a sing flea-box room
> So I'll tak ye on the road again
> When yellow's on the broom

I spied another inhabitant of the yellow broom as I turned the corner. A plump and handsome male stonechat sat on the tip of one of the bushes, the yellow of the broom and the azure blue of the sky accentuating his colours: the black head with what appeared a white collar, but not quite fitting and failing to meet either at his throat or at the back of his neck, his speckled brown back and wings, set off by a small white wing patch, and his orange-red breast fading to almost white in the centre. He was a really smart wee chap, but gave me only a minute to study him before disappearing over the back of the broom embankment. I waited to see if he would reappear but was disturbed by the loud *baauuff, buff buff* of a roe doe no more than 100 yards away. She was not keen to leave the area and very obviously had fawns close by. She had winded me but still hadn't seen me, as she was looking in the wrong direction to try to match the scent to a human form. The doe barked again, this time spotting me as I moved forward. Still she stood her ground, gazing at me. *Baauuff, buff buff.* Most of my experience of roe that would have fawns has been in woodland. They would have slunk off, maybe even without a bark, but she just did not want to go. She moved another 50 yards up the hill and remained there as I passed, moving a further few yards to the skyline to watch the dreaded human form gradually shrink as I marched along the hill road. I was amazed, but this was just the first of three similar cervine encounters.

Away from deer for a minute, I heard bird song that reminded me of a skylark coming from heather on the left of the road. I stopped and looked across, though the bird that I saw first of all was a meadow pipit floating down from above in the way that the skylark does. Despite the two being similar in many ways, the meadow pipit will always take second prize to the skylark as a songster. I did see another bird perched on a tuft of heather and didn't immediately recognise it. I walked closer and as I did so the bird gradually edged away from me, though I *was* gaining some ground. It had a mate, and the two briefly chased each other over the heather. Though I was still some way from the birds I could now identify one as a male whinchat; rather similar to the stonechat I had seen earlier, and with a rosy pink breast and partial white collar, but with a wide white eye stripe and very noticeable white feathers at the base of each side of the tail as it flitted over the heather. The other bird – I presumed its mate – was slightly further away and colours were much more difficult to discern, though I was pretty sure they were a pair. I was over the moon that I had seen such beautiful and similar 'chats' within quarter of a mile of each other.

There was a marked difference in the red-legged partridges since my last hill visit just over a fortnight earlier. At that time I saw the birds in pairs; this time it was mainly cock birds that I saw, often on sentry duty on top of a rock or a grass tussock. The females would be on nests close by. I know much more about grey partridges, which are great parents, sharing the responsibility of bringing up the brood. Hopefully their red-legged cousins do likewise. As I passed I could hear their quiet *tic tic* communications. In the distance I could see three fallow deer grazing, but minutes later, despite being nearly half a mile away, they had spotted me and were standing line abreast, heads towards me. The next time I looked they had gone. What had arrived, though, was the Middle Hill pair of buzzards. They mewed as they circled high overhead, though not the concerned mew that they emit when someone is near their nest. I've seen little evidence of them for some weeks and can only assume, if they are nesting, it is among the crags at either side of Middle Hill. A third buzzard – maybe a chick from last year – joined them in their carousel in the thermals.

A lone roe doe ahead of me had also spotted me, and gave a single, deep, *baauuff*. It kept me in sight as I passed along the hill road as it, too, would be close to its fawns. The fawns would welcome the dry spell: lying in the sun is much better than being curled up soaked and cold with rain. The partridges were clearly also taking advantage of the sun, since the heat had desiccated the surface of the hill road and it was pock-marked with their dust bowls, many with a single partridge feather at the rim, rubbed from the bird in its enthusiasm to wriggle in the dust and rid itself of parasites and other biting beasties.

At the Y junction, I went left to go up over North Eerie, spooking another roe doe that was on the shoulder of the shallow gorge leading down to Eerie Valley. The routine was the same: *baauuff, buff buff buff* barked at me, with the doe only moving 150 yards to the first of a line of a dozen elderly larch trees and staring at me from there. I moved on quickly up the steep track to let the fretful doe settle again. With the warning, the fawns would be aware of danger and crouching as low to the ground as they could. I stopped briefly at the pond at the top of the hill, going down to the water's edge. I'd scanned it from some distance away with the binoculars and it seemed devoid of birds, yet when I approached the pond a pair of mallard flew from the reeds at its south east side. I expected to see tadpoles or some form of water beasties in the mildly peaty water, but apart from a handful of pond skaters I could see nothing. No doubt the situation would have been different if I'd been pond dipping.

Over North Eerie I turned left along the bottom of the hill heading for the Hill Loch, passing clumps of tormentil, a plant growing close to the ground with tiny yellow flowers, and another low-growing plant, this time with tiny blue flowers: heath milkwort. Just short of the loch at the small clump of spruce, pine and larch trees on either side of the gully through which the burn runs before entering the loch my attention was taken by a small brown bird perched like a Christmas fairy on top of a spruce. It was too far away to see detail, even with the binoculars, but it allowed me a bit closer. It flew up into the air above the tree and parachuted down, like thistle down that has been whisked into the sky then abandoned by a suddenly abating wind. It landed on the neighbouring tree, where I could see a second bird on a branch near the top. They initially looked like meadow pipits but their behaviour was different, with an obvious preference for trees rather than heather. The first bird rose and parachuted back to the top of the tree again. This time I could hear its *chip chip chip, weech weech, swee-yoo, swee-yoo* call as it fell through the air. I suspected it was a tree pipit and tried to make comparisons with the meadow pipit. The bird had much more white on its breast and had flesh-coloured legs rather than the yellowish legs of the meadow pipit. This, together with its tree-parachuting routine, convinced me I had been watching a pair of tree pipits.

After resting and having my piece in the gully overlooking the loch, I made round the north shore towards Creag Bheag Wood. A cock pheasant was pecking at some grain George scatters daily on the short grass at the entrance to the wood. The shooting season completely forgotten, the bird pecked at grain almost to my feet as I stood watching it. I bet it was glad it was a pheasant rather than a broiler chicken. It took its chance over the guns throughout the shooting season and here it was now enjoying the spring sunshine, not a care in the world. A broiler chicken would have been turned into food for us at 45 days old without ever seeing the sun. An interesting comparison!

From the other end of Creag Bheag I turned left along the bottom of the Craigie Face. A pair of buzzards circled among the jackdaw flock above The Shudder. I'd seen no evidence since the winter of the pair that seemed keen on nesting in Creag Bheag. Several large trees had been blown beside their last year's nest and I suspect this may now be the same pair, nesting on the crags at The Shudder rather than risk a tree nest. Another pair of buzzards circled above Eerie Valley, though this was the pair from the Larch Wood, verified as they gradually drifted over there. A small herd of fallow deer was standing near No 3 peg at The Shudder. They gradually moved down into a shallow gully with some blackthorn as if to hide, but came out the other side. There was one doe that was clear leader and she stood, head up, ears forward, never taking her eye off me and trying to catch my wind. There was a mix of does and last year's calves, and a mix of colours, with the most striking being a doe that was virtually black. As they filed up the hill I counted 16. Four broke to my left back along Craigie Face towards Creag Bheag, while the other 12 went right-handed and stood for a while under the jackdaws' scree. This was obviously taking them away from home territory, and they soon filed back along the face, lissom and nimble as mountain goats on rocks, to join the first four.

When I reached Larch Wood I discovered a pheasant's nest that had hatched successfully, though it was one with a difference. It was under a tussock of grass, and a closer examination of the egg shells showed most to be the typical olive colour. One was greenish, almost like a duck's eggs, and obviously laid in the nest by another pheasant. But the most intriguing aspect of the eggs was that one wasn't a pheasant egg at all: it was a red-legged partridge egg. All had hatched so I can only assume that the hen pheasant was foster mother to another pheasant's chick and a young partridge. Since their diet and habits are similar there should be no problem in rearing all of them (provided there is no mortality to predators or adverse weather). I'll look out for a red-legged partridge that favours the company of pheasants later in the year. I sat nearby for a while overlooking a replanted part of the wood. The birch, sycamore, whitebeam, alder and wild cherry trees were beginning to burst out of their plastic sleeves, crucial for the survival of young trees in a wood full of hungry rabbits. As I sat there, the rabbits only had a wren and a chaffinch for company.

Since I had enjoyed my spell in Law Wood the previous week, I went to have a seat there. To my amazement I found that the two 'dead' trees growing out of the rhododendrons were very much alive. I was wrong on the second count as well: they were pedunculate oaks. Last week no leaves were visible, yet this week they were covered in light green, fingered, leaves. I was flabbergasted! Oak and ash are the last trees to come in to leaf, and the saying goes '*Ash before oak, we're in for a soak; oak before ash were in for a splash.*' Could these two oaks coming into leaf very late mean we might have a decent summer? Their resident songster from last week, the garden warbler, was warbling in the distance, though I couldn't see him. The male orange-tipped butterfly was still dancing; now joined by two females. These were white, as he was, but with black rather than orange tips to their wings. They were all being observed by the robin on the fence post.

I sat for a while but it was excessively hot, so I decided to call it a day. As I cut through the damp wood bottom I heard a very quiet sound, similar to someone blowing very softly. I sat on a stump looking up at some conifers, initially thinking I was being quietly scolded by a red squirrel. The quiet sound came again. It was from my left, at ground level and very close by. As I stood up, a hen pheasant fluttered from right beside me under a root of a tree that at one time had been blown, but later cut, with the root falling back almost to its original position. It was the typical short flutter of a pheasant with chicks, but I could see nothing. I'm convinced she was warning the chicks of danger and as – or just before – she fluttered off they'd taken refuge under the root. I left quickly to allow them to reunite, but as I climbed over the fence from the wood I was met by two very annoyed oystercatchers. These were the pair of the elaborate nest-of-many-stones, and I could see a single half-grown chick running from the field to the stony corner, where it crouched down, almost invisible. The pair *peep peep peeped* at me all the way across the field and halfway across the next, which took me to the shooting lodge loch and almost to my car. A walk in springtime is just magical, with excitement, interest and intrigue round each corner.

New birds identified: tree pipit
New mammals identified: none

Chapter 29

Monday 4 June 2012. Weather: Sunny spells, though never really warm long enough to take my jacket off.

A snipe at last! That sighting made my day, but I'll return to that later.

I headed up the road towards the hill and was disappointed to see 10 lapwings resting in the sheep field (along with the obligatory starling). This was not good news: the lapwings should have been on eggs or brooding or tending chicks. Five pairs, if that's what they were, is a high failure rate. Most will have nested on Geordie's Moor or on a rough patch of ground immediately behind the 'Tawny Owl Wood'. No doubt corvids would have accounted for the loss of some clutches (or chicks), though George has kept the numbers of the worst offenders, carrion crows, pretty low. Considering how lapwing numbers have plummeted over the past few decades this was really depressing, and I'm not sure at this time of the year whether they'll lay another clutch of eggs. I'm quite sure the oystercatcher that nested on Geordie's Moor near the estate road also failed. There has been no sign – or more importantly, sound – of oystercatchers there in the last two weeks. George saw a stoat in the area of the nest, and caught it in a tunnel trap a couple of days later. That's another possibility for predating the chicks. Lastly, there are three highland cattle on Geordie's Moor. I don't suspect the nest or chicks were trampled by giant cloven hooves; Highland cattle are renowned for being extremely careful about trampling nests, possibly because they react to the defensive display that the female will direct towards them if they get too close, and their quiet nature usually means that they move off.

The 10 lapwings flew off as I crossed the fence into the sheep field to walk along past the duck ponds. Six drakes sat peacefully at the far bank, in each case a leg tucked up into their breast feathers and their head beneath a wing. Reluctantly they awoke from their nap and raised heads in unison to watch me as I passed by. Like the pheasants and red-legged partridges, they have long forgotten the shooting season and tolerate humans remarkably close. Along the bank a bit, on a gravel bank near the gate into the ponds, three oystercatchers sat. Unlike the drakes, whose parenting responsibilities cease once they have mated with a duck, both male and female oyster catchers share family responsibilities. They should also have been tending to eggs or downy chicks. They rose and flew quietly over my head, with none of the *peep, peep, peeping* associated with defensive behaviour in the protection of chicks, to land further up the sheep field. As I came closer to the large sandy rabbit warren in the corner of the field, rabbits of all sizes bolted down the holes in a series of disappearing white tails. I walked over the top of the warren and could hear some of the lagomorph denizens thumping with a hind foot in a warning of danger, the sound travelling easily up through the labyrinth of sandy burrows.

I walked up the side of Wericky and followed the boundary fence with the east estate towards Dank Wood. I passed close by the rabbit that a couple of weeks ago had been ailing, last week was dead and now was little more than a skeleton. As I looked up towards Dank Wood a bird disappeared over the tops of the trees, only to reappear minutes later, joined by another. I was a wee bit concerned to see the red kite pair up here. It seemed a long way from their nest site in Lament, though when I looked back towards Lament it was really less than a mile away, no distance to a large bird like a kite. Their eggs should be hatched and the chicks might be of a size they can now safely be left, being too big for most predators. The kites flew above me, occasionally going back over the top of the trees out of sight then reappearing overhead. They seem inquisitive birds and this is quite typical of at least this pair's behaviour. It would also be typical behaviour if they had moved their nesting site to Dank Wood and now had chicks. It is certainly a favourite area of the kites and I made a mental note to discuss the possibility of a nest there with the owner.

I'd spoken to George earlier in the morning. He was telling me about having flushed a snipe the day before as he passed over a boggy bit of the hill in his Polaris. So that was my next destination. I headed out the hill track up past the east side of Dank Wood heading for another Dank, this time the pegs for the Dank partridge drive. The pegs for this drive, and for the adjoining one – 'Victor's Nightmare' – abut, rather like semi circles touching at one end. The partridges go over the guns on Dank from the north-east, and on Victor's Nightmare from the north-west. Both sets of pegs are numbered clockwise, so that number 8 peg of Dank is very close to 2 peg of Victor's. In the gap behind the pegs 5 and 6 of Dank, and 4 of Victor's, is the boggy area to which George had directed me.

I was following George's vehicle tracks from yesterday when a snipe rose from one of the tracks ahead of me, giving a flash of white belly as it did so. The snipe had been feeding rather than having come from a nest. It made the typical single *zeep* call as it lifted off the ground, zig-zagged as it gained height… and emptied its bowels. Snipe is a quarry species and the saying is that you must 'shoot before it shits'. They are incredibly difficult targets and quickly out of range. The snipe flew left initially then gradually circled to the right, gaining some height and flying up over the Victor's Nightmare pegs 2 and 1 and over the short skyline. There are many boggy areas like this on the estate where the snipe can probe for semi-aquatic invertebrates with its long beak. Where I can I usually go round rather than through wet patches but nevertheless I'm amazed it has taken me nearly 11 months to have seen a snipe. I hoped there would be another close by incubating a clutch of four well-camouflaged eggs. They can sometimes be late breeders so I might yet hear their drumming display, when the snipe flies over the nest area continually calling *cheep-er, cheep-er, cheep-er, cheep-er* and generating a loud pulsating *whoooooo*, caused by the wind vibrating the two very stiff pin feathers at the outside of its tail every time it goes into a steep high-speed dive.

As I cleared the bog I heard the sound of a cuckoo. This was not the instantly recognised *cu-ckoo* call of the male bird, but the completely different bubbling sound of the female. I spied in the direction I'd heard the call and saw the bird sitting on top of a rock about quarter of a mile away, high on the shoulder of the hill running from the top end of the Larch Wood. Had I not heard the bird, I may have thought what I was looking at was a sparrowhawk, however even without having heard it, what I saw next would have dispelled any such thoughts. A small brown bird was sitting on a broom bush only a few feet from the cuckoo. I could neither hear nor recognise the wee bird because of the distance but I could see its flutter of wings, its head going forward and its tail going up at it screamed defiance and annoyance at the cuckoo. It was soon joined by another, probably its mate, which fluttered round the larger bird, mobbing it as a crow would mob a buzzard. There is no way they would have dared do this to a sparrowhawk and, though they seemed to know the cuckoo posed a threat, I doubt they knew exactly what the risk involved. I made myself as comfortable as possible on a rock to watch.

The cuckoo sat for about 10 minutes without 'bubbling' again. I wondered if it was surveying the heather below it to spot any comings and goings from a moorland nest, and give it an opportunity to foist an egg onto unwitting foster parents. Between the patiently observing cuckoo and where I was sitting runs a craggy face with several undersized native trees, stunted by the lack of soil on the crags. It would be an ideal place for a nesting ring ouzel, and I'd half an eye on the cuckoo as I inspected and listened, without any luck, for this blackbird-like red status bird. The cuckoo's luck was no better than mine, and it flew off over the back of the hill towards Eerie Valley.

I walked up the track through the heather used by George in his various moorland duties, which has included feeding the partridge stock right from the end of the shooting season so that they are in tip-top condition to breed. I veered right, running parallel with the much narrower top end of Eerie Valley until I was opposite a part where the sides began to flatten out and make access to Eerie Valley possible without crag-hopping. This route took me past dozens of bugle plants, small purplish flowers that resemble tiny orchids. I then cut sharply left into Eerie Valley and started to follow the burn down, now going in the opposite direction to my last few hundred yards. The burn is narrow and I criss-crossed it in accordance with the vegetation and gradient of the banks, picking my way down the easiest route. I stopped to admire a huge spider's web, as perfect in symmetry as webs can be, strung right across the burn. I was puzzled as to how the spider managed to get from one bank to the other to anchor the first strands of its web, and can only assume it was wind-assisted. No spider was to be seen, but the web held a small light-coloured fly at one edge, distorting the evenness of the two outer strands in which the hapless insect was now inexorably trapped. I've no doubt if I had reached across and lightly touched the web its owner would have appeared.

I continued down Eerie Valley, stopping to photograph a group of four early purple orchids standing erect and line abreast like sentinels guarding my way forward. Further on I passed No 6 peg, where I stopped for a minute to yet again reflect on my day's shooting the previous September, paradoxically by far the most demanding shots I've ever attempted yet the best I have ever shot in my life. As I turned away from No 6 peg a bird, which I initially thought was the cuckoo again, crossed my line of vision. The bird was swooping down towards the ground, but when it returned to view I could see it was a male kestrel. The bird came very close to me, giving me a great view of its colouring: light blue head and tail, with a black tip to its tail and a buff coloured belly beautifully streaked with black. In its yellow talons it was carrying a small mammal and it headed across to the crags, just out of my view, at the bottom of Eerie Valley. Minutes later it came back into view minus the prey item, making me think it had just visited a crag nest and fed a chick. I sat on the edge of the pallet used to provide a level surface for the gun at No 4 peg and waited for a while in case it came back with another rodent. I gave it half an hour, but there was no sign. If the eggs hadn't yet hatched or the chicks were very small there would be little pressure on it to hunt extensively, so the next visit might yet be some hours away. In any case the wait had been another chance to look out for a ring ouzel.

I cut across to the Larch Wood and went down the ride through the centre, finishing in the replanted part near the bottom end. I walked through this part and realised that it must be a good vole year as field voles were scurrying everywhere and the grass tussocks were pock-marked with the small round holes they had tunnelled. This will be really good news for many birds of prey, especially kestrels and owls that must still be recovering from the effects of the deep snows of the 2010/11 winter when numbers plummeted due to starvation.

From the Larch Wood I cut across to the Henhouse Wood, as I wanted to see how the robin I had watched building a nest two weeks earlier had got on. The mossy nest in the side of the ditch was well hidden by a curtain of dry grass. No bird flew out and when I gently probed behind the grass screen with my hand I could feel a hole in the bottom of the nest. The nest seemed complete, but whether eggs had been laid and taken by a predator, or whether indeed the female robin had been taken off the nest I'll never know. Small birds nesting at ground level have a fragile and uncertain existence.

I finished my day by visiting Geordie's Moor, walking round to the far side of the marshy area to try to see how the nesting waders were faring. I'd no intention of walking through the marsh and causing mayhem but came in quietly through the junipers and sat on a grassy bank overlooking the marsh. As I arrived, a lapwing rose away to my left. It circled a couple of times, then landed beside a boulder and near to five mallard drakes. Another lapwing was straight ahead, quite near to the fence between Geordie's Moor and the estate road. It was standing quietly, with no sign of chicks. A third lapwing was off to my right. It was sitting on a slightly higher grassy area but not anywhere it would have made a nest, with the cover of the marsh vegetation being a much better option. The lapwing beside the boulder had now moved forward 10 yards or so and I could hear it very quietly calling. *Peeee-weep; peeeee; peeee; peeee-weep.* The bird was obviously calling in its chicks. Suddenly one tiny mottled grey and white form came through the grass on legs that seemed too long for its body, then a second. I waited for the other two, as lapwings have clutches of four pointed eggs that always lie in the nest with the points towards the centre, taking up minimum space. They remind me of four tea cups on their sides, handles hidden in the inside of each neighbouring cup and all placed on a saucer for ease of carrying or storing. No other chicks appeared but two were better than none.

Apart from the five drakes, and a duck and drake near to lapwing No 2 across at the estate road, I could see no sign of sitting or brooding birds. Oystercatchers most certainly would have announced their presence and would have been piping round my head. There was no sign of the redshank pair that had been there earlier, though I haven't given up on them yet. They are much more secretive nesters and even with the binoculars I wouldn't have been able to see the brooding female. It may still be there, or the pair may have moved across to the marsh at the far end of the loch at the shooting lodge, which is also suitable nesting habitat. Of the two other lapwings, might they have been waiting until I went away before they returned either to eggs or to chicks? Just in case, I crept quietly back into the junipers and circled back to my car. Two chicks from all of these lapwings would be a pitiful return, but there's still time yet…

New birds identified: snipe
New mammals identified: none

Chapter 30

Wednesday 13 June 2012. Weather: Overcast, with the sun occasionally breaking through.

I sat for 10 minutes on the veranda of the shooting lodge. There was no wind and the loch was flat calm. The four swans snoozed on a mudbank juxtaposed to the island, heads tucked under massive wings and each with their bulky snow-white bodies balanced on one leg. Two mallard drakes napped on the grass at the far side of the loch, while rabbits grazed round about them. Two more drakes dozed at the water's edge, their full colour images reflected on the loch's mirror surface. The mirror was briefly cracked in places where a trout broke the surface or a swallow skited off it as it caught a fly, though these scars quickly healed. On one of the narrow spits of land running into the loch and created for trout fishers two oystercatchers sat quietly, watching the antics of another black and white bird, a pied flycatcher feeding its two grey and white almost fully-grown chicks. A robin sang in the Tawny Owl Wood on my right and a cock sparrow chirped happily from the ivy on the owner's house to my left. It was a scene of unmitigated tranquillity.

Tearing myself away, I headed up the road towards the hill. A pair of oystercatchers in the sheep field prodded and poked for diminutive titbits, and a single common gull stood as if surveying the scene. I watched a lone duckling, about two to three weeks old, swimming round one of the duck ponds. It reminded me of a clockwork duck in a child's bath, except that every so often its paddling speeded up in an effort to catch an airborne fly, reaching as high as possible to grasp the unfortunate insect. I was concerned at it being all on its own and thought that, for whatever reason, it had been orphaned. I've had ducklings of that age survive at home when their mother is tempted away by a drake and gradually abandons them. I'm not sure if this is a natural phenomenon or only occurs where ducks are semi-domestic. Though these were totally wild mallard they had come to rely on us for much of their food supply and maybe this was an influence that encouraged a duck to try for a second brood, knowing her offspring would be well catered for. Of course this theory could be anthropomorphic nonsense and the continual sexual harassment by the drake may be what really brings the duck back into breeding mode. This wee duck *might* just have been able to survive on its own, but as it turned out there was no need, as its mother suddenly emerged from the reeds to join it. One surviving duckling out of a clutch of 8 or 10 eggs is poor, but birds of all species have many hazards in early life. As I watched the two unite, a common sandpiper called, easily recognisable from its three-note call, *tee wee wee; tee wee wee*. I spied round the duck ponds and the marsh but it was nowhere in sight. I wasn't particularly bothered as it's as satisfying to hear birds as it is see them.

Having given up on the sandpiper I marched on up to Dank Wood. I walked along the narrow grassy track to the south east of the wood, looking over the dyke into the bank that runs down to the field, where there were several groups of meerkat-like young rabbits looking up at me, ready to bolt down their burrows at the first sign of danger. This wood had earlier been the stronghold of the cuckoo, but it was now silent, and indeed it was quiet today so far as other birds were concerned. I turned to come back to join the hill road and noticed one of my inquisitive red kites above me. Its procedure was the same as before: flying over me at about 30 yards up, then dipping back out of sight over the trees again. The kite continued this intermittent surveillance as I walked back to the hill road and even up the hill road for about quarter of a mile, keeping marginally ahead of me. Only when I had left Dank Wood behind did the kite let me continue on my own and return to the wood. I'd discussed this behaviour with the owner the previous week and we were both of the view that it was likely to be nesting in the wood. Despite our conclusion, the habitat was not typical, as the wood is completely coniferous and the kite seems to prefer deciduous or at least a mix of trees. The owner passed this information on to the RSPB kite monitoring officer, who is licenced by Scottish Natural Heritage to disturb nesting red kites, which are Schedule 1 birds. She had visited to make a check of the wood and had found the nest with two well-grown chicks peering over the edge. The conifer was spindly and not suitable for climbing, so the chicks won't be tagged this year.

A young foxy-red roe buck took over surveillance from the kite, keeping ahead of me in the heather and bracken on my left, and giving me the once-over every so often as I caught up with it, when it would trot ahead to repeat the sequence of hide and seek. We parted when I came to the large bank of brilliant yellow broom near the hill pond. A small bird with a black-topped head sat on top of a sprig of broom. When I put the binoculars on it there was a yellow broom flower in front of its head which meant I could only see the black top to the head. I'd recently seen a male stonechat in this bank of broom, but this bird wasn't as brightly coloured. I moved to my right several times to try to get a better view, but still this damn yellow flower was in my line of sight. What eventually solved the mystery was a similar bird with a brown-capped head coming and perching near my first bird. Blackcaps! These are grey-brown coloured warblers, with the male having a jet black crown and forehead, giving the bird its name, while the female has a rusty brown cap and forehead. The male is a fantastic singer; it's a great pity he was sitting quietly rather than in full song.

The blackcap pair weren't the only inhabitants of the broom: at least two willow warblers flitted between the broom and the surrounding heather, actively catching flies. None had a beakful of flies so the chances are any nests will still contain eggs rather than chicks. I settled down in a wooden shooting butt beside the pond, with a panoramic view of the broom bank. No doubt the stonechats were in there somewhere with their fellow summer migrants but they failed to appear. Of the three species, in a singing competition the blackcap would be the clear winner.

The hill was busy today. George was settling the first batch of pheasant poults into their pens. The owner and keeper had recently seen a vixen on the hill and suspect she has cubs. They've tried all the known dens, but there are no signs of occupation. It's a worry for them with a high number of red-legged partridges on nests, newly-released poults – even in a pen – and foxes on the prowl. They hope that either the vulpine family will move on or that they will find them soon. Cubs will be well grown now and might soon be living above ground, away from a den, making them even more difficult to find. It shows that even with the large number of foxes George accounted for in late winter and early spring, their numbers can only ever be reduced, never eliminated.

I walked further along the hill road towards Middle Hill and sat on one of my favoured rocks to see if there was any sign of the kestrels. The owner regularly sees them but, like the golden eagle, somehow they are never there when I visit. As I sat there I heard two birds simultaneously, one behind me and one in front. The one behind was easy: it was an alarm call of a curlew. I'd never seen a curlew on that part of the hill, yet here was one that must have had a nest and had been disturbed, maybe by the proximity of a carrion crow or a stoat. Its *chi wi wi; chi wi wi; chi wi wi* continued while I tried to locate and identify the smaller songster in front of me. I didn't immediately recognise the song, possibly because of my distraction with the curlew, but I could now see the bird 50 or so yards away, albeit just a bit of its orange-brown breast and its head. Its size, plus the white eye stripes that seemed to meet above the beak meant that it was a whinchat. I waited to see if it would give me another rendition of its song but instead it flew off, the white at either side of its tail another identifying feature.

Further along the road, rather than risk disturbing any penned pheasant poults further up the hill, I cut left towards Eerie Valley, disturbing a lone yearling fallow doe as I followed the burn down. I photographed common butterwort, a wild plant that has small purple flowers on top of long stems, and very light green leaves growing almost flat to the ground. I only noticed when I looked at the photo later that there was also a primrose and another small yellow flower (that I couldn't identify) in the frame. I wish I was better at identifying flowers!

I sat for a while further down Eerie Valley. Two roe does, maybe last year's fawns, grazed on the bog near the Larch Wood, where an ensemble of wood pigeons cooed loudly. Chaffinches lower down Eerie Valley joined the chorus, but the graceful rhythm of the orchestra was ruined by the raucous *cuck cuck* of a cock pheasant that erupted from the heather behind me and sailed past me with a whirr of wings across the valley. The other observers were two buzzards, probably from the Larch Wood, circling above the outdoor auditorium and giving an occasional *mew* of approval. There are few trees in Eerie Valley, yet they are as diverse as the wildlife. A rowan tree, now cloaked in white flowers that in time would become rowan berries, was in the gully directly below me. To my left, the slope above the scree was dotted with broom and dog roses, with one rose shrub being the perch of a solitary willow warbler. To my right there was juniper, a pair of really ancient and beautiful birches with leaves resembling a cascading fountain of silver water, though near them was another, much younger and plainer birch with larger and greener leaves. Behind and to my right there were another two old birch tree with a lovely Scots Pine as a companion. I have many favourite parts of the estate, but Eerie Valley is near the top of the chart. I looked again for the deer, which were now, like me, relaxed and sitting down.

Relaxation ended, I headed for Creag Bheag Wood, passing along beneath the Shudder jackdaw colony. Further along Craigie Face, just short of Creag Bheag I crossed the dyke at the rabbits' crossing point where there was a missing coping stone, and sat on the grass above a bank of juniper and among some birch and larch trees. The sun had just come out and I watched a dunnock busy with its preening on a thick juniper branch, framed in an inverted heart-shaped gap by branches growing above. Under the juniper two speckle-breasted young robins were skulking, awaiting food from a parent, and while I watched them the dunnock was replaced in the inverted heart frame by a willow warbler.

Further along the junipers a warbler started to sing. It was a lovely melodic song and I spied the tops of the bushes thinking first of all it was a whitethroat, temporarily forgetting that a whitethroat sings in short bursts, whereas this was a full-blown song delivered with great gusto. I spied a wren right on the tip of a branch, looking rather like a small brown fir cone. That was certainly not the singer. I moved slowly and quietly along the top fringe of the junipers, getting closer to the sound but not yet spotting its source. Eventually I glimpsed the star of the show, a garden warbler. It was halfway up a juniper, on top of a green branch with some dead, grey-brown branches as a backdrop. It was singing its heart out. Its beak was pointing skywards and its white throat feathers were puffed out as it churred and warbled and trilled, the perfect sound resonating across towards me. I edged closer and managed a photo or two, smiling at the thought of how pleased with itself the bird seemed to be. I was in such in awe of the wee warbler that I moved back from it and sat and had my sandwiches, soothed and entertained by its magnificent voice. In fact it got better, as the bird was soon only a few yards away in a birch tree above me, then somewhere just in front of me again. Like the garden warbler to which I had listened a couple of weeks ago in Law Wood the bird was ensuring that any other garden warblers around knew its territory and was patrolling its boundaries. It was just amazing and undoubtedly the highlight of the day.

Moving on from the garden warbler, I headed west along the outside of Creag Bheag, passing one of George's snares lying in wait for the unwary fox (or indeed bird watcher). At the end of the wood I decided to have a look at another of the estate's great juniper stands, Colin's Wardrobe. Two cock pheasants rose together in front of me, tumbling slightly as they clipped each other's wing on taking off. A herring gull flew overhead, maybe making its way from a rooftop nest in the nearby town to someplace unknown in search of food, or maybe even a non-breeder. In any case it was the first time

I had seen this relatively widespread gull (though their numbers are decreasing) on the estate. I sat for a while in a clearing and though there were small birds from time to time flitting along the top of the junipers they would have to land before I could recognise them, and none of them landed where I could see them. Despite that, since the sun had come out again, I was enjoying my seat.

I had been sitting maybe 10 minutes when there was a loud rumble of hooves behind me, so close I could feel the vibration. I'd obviously sat down very close to a deer – probably a fallow – which had decided to stay still and sit out the threat. Eventually its nerve had broken and it had scrambled to its feet and made off with haste. I never saw it but the sounds told the tale. Another sudden sound, this time on my left, was the air whistling through the wing feathers of a young carrion crow as it suddenly changed direction. It had flown almost into my face as it came round a bush, and dramatically altered course. Having done that it landed in a birch tree easily within shot, though a camera is much less deadly than a shotgun. Two of its siblings made the same mistake, though when they changed course in panic it was full speed astern as they made an emergency turn and flew back in the direction they had come. Carrion crows not being my favourite birds, I later let George know where the three catching compartments of his new circular Larsen traps might be filled.

I made my way back along the track running through Creag Bheag, being loudly chided by a wren since I was probably passing near its newly-fledged chicks. I continued via the Henhouse Wood, where a goldfinch watched my passing from a branch halfway up a conifer, then cut across to Loch Wood. I then walked between Loch Wood and the loch at the shooting lodge, spotting a common sandpiper on a rock in the middle of the loch and near the island. The sandpiper flew to the loch shore in a manner very like an oystercatcher, with exceptionally shallow wing beats and appearing to move only the tips of its wings, then landed, wagging its tail up and down in typical sandpiper style. This sandpiper is grey- brown above and on the chest, has pure white underparts, long greenish legs and beak about the same length as an oystercatcher, though a plain yellow-brown colour rather than the much more flamboyant orange beak of the oystercatcher. As I came closer it flew to the dam at the end of the loch.

The sandpiper flew from the dam as I approached, but was almost immediately replaced by a pied wagtail and its chick, the tail of the chick perhaps bobbing in anticipation of food as well as through the characteristic habit of this bird that gives it and others in the wagtail species their appropriate name. Amazingly the wagtails were joined on the dam wall by a male redstart, giving an incredible contrast between the monochrome of the former and the radiance and technicolour of the latter. None of the birds stayed more than half a minute but while it lasted it was a great example of the divergence of colour in birds.

My final stop was at the fence-side of Geordie's Moor. I spied across the moor to see what waders were visible. Where I had seen the lapwing with two chicks on the previous visit a lapwing was *pee-weeping* in warning to chicks, despite my being 100 yards away. She moved away to the right, still alarming, a signal totally ignored by two half-grown chicks that I could see standing bolt upright looking for the danger that the parent had recognised. I spied for signs of any more chicks beside the first two, and was hopeful for a moment, though it was a false alarm in the form of yet another pied wagtail. Behind the chicks I saw a young mallard duckling preening. Intense watching, with arms beginning to ache, eventually resulted in the sight of *two* heads attached to small black and yellow bumble bee-like bodies. Further observation eventually disclosed the mallard duck mother a few yards to the right. Only two ducklings but there was always hope that other siblings were snoozing and couldn't be bothered raising their heads to preen…

New birds identified: common sandpiper; blackcap; herring gull
New mammals identified: none

Chapter 31

Wednesday 20 June 2012. Weather: Mostly sunny, improving as the day went on. No wind first thing, and picking up only to a slight breeze.

Before this year-long survey was over I wanted another quick look round the fishing loch. I didn't expect to see any new birds – though there are always surprises – but I was keen to see what breeding success there had been with the waterfowl there. The loch was a flat calm and as I edged boat number 1 out of the harbour I could hardly believe the amount of flies buzzing over the surface; there were millions. I'm sure a hatch must have newly taken place. It was great news for insect-eating birds and also for the trout in the loch. I thought there would have been more feeding activity from the trout; a hatch like that should trigger a feeding frenzy, but they're fickle creatures. Maybe the flies were too high off the surface, maybe the sun being out put them off feeding, or maybe the flies were not to their liking…

The water was low, and in a part of the loch where there are orange buoys as warning of rocks just below the surface, the rocks were visible today. This was to the delight of half a dozen mallard – four drakes and two ducks – that had claimed them as suitable places to chill out in the early morning sun. A remaining rock was commandeered by a common sandpiper that flicked its tail as I came closer, then flew off round the shore towards the harbour. The mallard were totally relaxed at my approach, still some 100 yards off, and most never even removed their head from below their wing. Their vision of the ducks was almost a blur, partly because they were surrounded by the clouds of flies and also because I was looking into the sun. Light coloured moulted feathers were sprinkled on the mirror surface of the water, looking twice their size because of the reflected image. A pair of swans was behind the ducks. There were no cygnets with them and I could see none sitting on the shore. I made the assumption that this was the pair from the bay at the other end of the loch, who had either lost their brood or the eggs had failed to hatch.

I cruised up the loch near the south shore, seeing a single great-crested grebe ahead. The flat calm was rippled by concentric circles as it dived at my approach. Craig had told me that a few days ago he had seen a grebe with well-grown chicks. This one definitely had no chicks in tow, so I scanned round the loch hoping to see another. If this was the mate of the one with chicks they probably wouldn't be far away. A millpond loch is easily checked, and there were no more grebes to be seen – at least on the south half of the loch. Nine Canada geese flew over, like me, heading up the loch. They were very low and almost skimmed my head, resembling small bomber aircraft. I thought they would land but they began to gain height again and flew over the trees towards the adjacent loch.

I stopped at the reeds where I had heard the sedge warbler on the last visit. A bird was singing in the vicinity but its sound was drowned out by a tractor harvesting silage in the field behind the lochside strip of trees. I listened for a while and gave up, though from what I could hear through the rumpus of the tractor and baler I didn't think it was the sedge warbler. Now that I was up the loch I spotted another grebe in the bay at the top. It had come from the reeds, but had no chicks in tow either. If they were as big as Craig said they could be resting in the reeds; it's a possibility as the grebe don't dally overlong on the water before quickly returning to the reeds. A lone swan was also in the bay. It was tight to the reeds at the very top, and swam further in until it was out of my sight. The reed bed is narrow at this point and it could only have gone on to the bank behind the reeds out of my view. Might its mate have also been there with cygnets? I thought this unlikely as this was probably the pair from the bay, and they had no cygnets the last time I saw them.

As I turned and made my way further down the loch I hoped to see the north shore swans and six cygnets somewhere around the reeds there, but there were none. I can't help thinking the pike have been feasting, but I felt some optimism as a mallard with five ducklings took cover in the reeds at my approach. The ducklings looked at least a week old, still a fine size for pike but at least they had made it thus far. Two small ducks flew over my head, making for further down the loch. I didn't instantly recognise them and before I could lift the binoculars my attention was taken with a single swift on a fly-catching foray, wheeling back and forth above the line of trees behind the reeds. I watched it to see if it was in the company of others, but despite it being in the area for at least 10 minutes it remained alone. Swifts often scream and screech as they feed, which may be a social interaction. This bird was silent, possibly because it had no companions with which to communicate.

Further down the loch I met up with the common sandpiper again, feeding on the shoreline in company with several young pied wagtails, tails wagging frantically as they waited on a parent returning with a beakful of flies. It was a busy corner: next to them stood a young oystercatcher, still ungainly but its grey and brown downy overcoat showing the first signs of feather growth. These birds are more independent than the neighbouring wagtails, beginning to search for food under the parent's guidance much more quickly. The parent was nowhere to be seen. Had I been this close to its chick on land it would have been frantically circling me and *peep-peeping* in alarm. On a boat I was probably just part of the fixtures and fittings and not a human at all.

I tied up the boat for the last time, and chatted with Craig. He told me his son had built a hide to observe yet another pair of swans in the largest reedbed on the loch, which lies between the harbour and Craig's house. Craig confirmed he had seen this swan on eggs, though had never seen it with cygnets. This was a pair that I didn't even see on my last visit, yet it's not easy to hide two birds as large as swans! As we chatted, seven greylag geese approached over the top of the restaurant, circled above the harbour and flew back in the direction from which they had come, as if this loch wasn't to their liking. The Scottish breeding population of greylags was initially confined to the north of Scotland and the Western Isles, but greylags are now breeding in many other parts of Scotland rather than heading back to their Icelandic breeding grounds. My observations here were complete, yet without satisfactory answers to all the puzzles. I now headed for the estate.

A mallard with eight newly hatched ducklings sat at the side of the estate road, slipping quietly through the fence onto Geordie's Moor as my car came closer. Eight or nine is the normal clutch size. These ducklings would have hatched the previous day but the duck sits on them for around 24 hours, allowing them to dry, before leading them away from the nest. This would be their first outing, but they had many dangers yet to face before they could be considered large and strong enough to be safe.

I parked and headed up the road towards the hill. Apart from three oystercatchers and some rabbits, the sheep were the only occupants of the sheep field today. A single red kite soared over Dank Wood, coming down the road to meet me as if in greeting, though with a nest of chicks in the wood that wasn't the reason for its interest at all. I went round Dank Wood in an anti-clockwise direction, noting a female wheatear watching my progress from a rock in the field. Two buzzards were calling from the tall conifers at the top of Wericky. The chicks from their nest near the top of a Douglas fir should be nearly ready to fledge; in fact it will not be long before family groups of three, four or five buzzards rather than pairs will be circling above my head in different parts of the estate. Let's hope, like last year, they behave and don't bother the partridges too much. On the subject of predation, I've seen no more than half a dozen eggs on my travels that have been picked by carrion crows. That's a really small number and in no small measure attributable to George's purge on them through multi-catch cage traps and Larsen traps. I once saw nearly a hundred picked pheasant, duck and wader eggs during a spring time walk on a 1000 acre farm where there was no crow control.

As I orbited Dank Wood and crossed the clear-felled part at the far end, two lovely dappled fallow deer bounded through the bracken. One was an adult doe and the other a yearling calf with short buds of antlers in velvet. They stopped to look back at me when they came to the march dyke, then bounded on again. Their presence, and mine, went un-noticed by a roe buck grazing at the other side of the dyke in a field that seemed to have more nettles than grass. He was intent on filling his belly and obviously felt relaxed, though his relaxation is maybe misplaced since the season during which bucks may be shot began on 1 May. Though this buck was on the other side of the dyke, the owner had told me the previous week that he was cutting back on the roe deer shot during 2012 as he felt they still hadn't recovered in numbers after the effects of the horrendous winter of 2010/11. Good wildlife management means being aware of the numbers and condition of the wide range of animals and birds, the suitability of the habitat to support them, and taking appropriate conservation measures to maintain the species. As far as deer are concerned, in some years this might mean culling the older or weaker beasts in quite high numbers, exactly as wolves would have done centuries ago.

The kite had moved to the top side of Dank Wood to keep an eye on me and, like last week, it fell back once I started heading out to the hill. Where there was a roe buck on the left of this part of the road last week, it had been replaced by a doe, which stared at me with ears forward and nose in the air as I approached. I didn't see its departure as a resplendent male whinchat was sitting on top of a small broom bush. It *cheeped* at me, as did a willow warbler with a beakful of flies that came on the scene, both now probably feeding chicks. They kept their distance, but fluttered nervously from bush to bush until I moved on. I was hardly up the road 50 yards when I spotted a glint from something polished under a trackside broom bush. I lifted a small branch of the bush, and underneath was a pheasant's nest that had successfully hatched. Shells of seven eggs that had hatched remained, and another which was intact, either being infertile or from which the chick failed to emerge. It was a smallish clutch for a pheasant but if it reared them all successfully it will have done well.

As I passed the first hill pond I caught sight of what on some other estates would have been highly suspicious: an egg on top of a rock just out from the shore. I have found many eggs in the past that have been laced with pesticide and this would have been a perfect place for one. The egg in fact was a duck's egg without a shell, laid on the rock probably in the evening by a duck resting there. Only having the membrane and not a shell for protection, it had begun to dry out, with part of it now being concave rather than rounded. This is quite common, and my own ducks from time to time lay one of these shell-less eggs. They desiccate very quickly so I suspect this egg had been on the rock less than 24 hours.

I sat and had a sandwich at Middle Hill, watching – and listening to – the pair of buzzards that circled on the thermals and mewed incessantly while I was there. Chances are they are nesting on the crags on the west side of Middle Hill, though it's a fair trek through high heather and bracken to get there. At one point a large bird dived down with folded wings just like a peregrine on a stoop. It travelled easily quarter of a mile at an incredible speed, losing height rapidly. It was so fast that by the time I got the binoculars up it had gone out of sight behind a rise in the ground. I turned my gaze back to the Middle Hill, expecting to see only one buzzard… but there were still two. Buzzards can stoop at speed as well, and while I suspect it *was* a buzzard I had seen, there remains the outside chance it was a peregrine. Peregrines don't nest here, though they are frequent visitors. Just not on the days I've visited!

At the fork in the road I journeyed left up through North Eerie, this track seeming to get steeper every time I climbed its rocky surface. I passed the hill pond, with only one drake in residence, swimming into the reeds as I passed. It will be unable to fly just now as it will be moulting. Most bird species moult a few feathers at a time so that they are always able to fly. This is crucial in birds that depend on flight either to escape predation or to search for food. Ducks, on the other hand, complete their moult over a very short period, losing all their flight feathers simultaneously, and making them flightless for about three weeks. This different moulting strategy is facilitated by being able to find food and refuge on water, with the drakes moulting first, then the ducks moulting after their brood has fledged. Three common gulls flew over the pond, this being the last wildlife I saw until a mile and a half later when I reached the sheltered gully above the Hill Loch. There was no sign of the tree pipits, but a wren chattered at me from the root of a blown tree as I passed and a willow warbler softly sang a few bars of its repertoire from somewhere within a birch tree. I'd seen the wren in this area every time I'd been in this gully and knew it would be nesting somewhere within or near the blown root. From its reaction I was sure it had well-grown chicks in the nest. The visit to the gully was completed by a single dark coloured fallow deer springing out of the bracken ahead of me and running off through the trees.

I cut past the west end of the Hill Loch, watching a red squirrel with the most gloriously silver tail, shining in the sun, as it scampered about the edge of the huge West End woodland I was about to enter. As I reached the quad bike track into the first part of the wood – a mix of larch and sitka spruce – the squirrel raced up a tree and watched me from the first fork. I followed the track, taking a wrong turn to the right first of all, which took me into a clearing with an incredibly old granny pine to my right and a fantastic view down over a number of lochs below. I went a bit further than the end of the track to see if there was a route through the trees, and stumbled on a fox den, though one that hadn't been used this year. It seemed to consist only of a single entrance hole and I'd be surprised if the owner and keeper don't know about it as I suspect visits to the den in spring to be the reason for the spur off the main track.

The track I was on took me back to the main woodland track that runs from the Hill Loch to the public road, though just before I reached it my route took me past another really old pine, this time having probably one of the widest girths I've seen on a Scots pine. The diameter of the tree exceeded the length of my extended walking pole, so is well in excess of fix feet. I couldn't help wondering what age it was and how many different centuries it had seen. I followed the woodland road down, marvelling yet again at the diversity of trees in this unique woodland and stopping for a minute to try to spot a whitethroat that was singing (though not nearly so well or with so much gusto as at the beginning of spring) somewhere behind a large *Rhododendron ponticum*, that out of control foreign invader. The purple Asian interloper blocked my view and the bird was reluctant to move, so I carried on, intent in due course on deviating from the main track through the area of wood nearer the public road that is part of the Fallow Rutting Stand pheasant drive.

Half a mile on I made my right turn, leaving the main track and following the subsidiary track that goes round the Fallow Rutting Stand. There was a thunder of hooves as seven dark fallow deer that had been resting round the first corner took off. One yearling doe was a bit confused and stopped, looking in the opposite direction to the potential threat – me. I took my camera out of my pocket but she heard the faint whirr as I put it on to almost maximum magnification, and she took off to join the remainder of the deer, which had stopped 100 yards away. In another few hundred yards I came into a large clearing with a high seat from which deer could either be shot or watched, depending on the intent of the occupant. It was a lovely open part in the woodland, the variety of types and density of trees in this woodland being much better than the regimented monocultures in some forests. I was taken by the beauty and symmetry of a half-grown Norway spruce. Its topmost branches grew upwards, and as my eye came down the tree the branches came straight out from the trunk, then nearer the bottom hung downwards touching the ground. The new growth on each branch tip was light green and made the tree a real gem in the woodland. Another admirer of the tree, this time for its shade, was a dark fallow deer that bolted out from under its branches and stood for a minute with just its head visible over the top of the bracken while it decided on the best direction in which to make off. The silence was suddenly broken by the deep roar of a plane high above. When I looked up there was a pair of buzzards that seemed almost as high as the plane. They must have caught a really good thermal to gain that height. They circled without a sound; at least that's how it seemed to a tiny human hundreds of feet below.

I briefly joined the public road before leaving it again as I entered the drive to the estate house, the part of the estate retained by the original owner. A part of the hillside near the house was alight with rhododendrons – and some azaleas – of every colour. It was a glorious feast of colour in the early afternoon sun and no doubt would have been even more magnificent a few weeks earlier. The huge mansion, until recently looking decidedly dejected, has had a facelift. It has been repainted, slates replaced and the stonework has been cleaned and repointed. Old-fashioned climbing roses adorn each side of the door at the top of a flight of wide stone steps and the lawns are beautifully manicured. It probably now looks something like it did when it was built, apart from the height of the Wellingtonias behind it, which would be mere saplings at that time.

I crossed the burn that ran from the shooting lodge loch via a wooden bridge over a very deep ravine. There was a waterfall directly under the bridge cascading white water into the foamy pool below and even creating some fine spray. The route to the bridge was concealed by bushes, then a patch of dog's mercury, and had I not been looking at the burn for evidence of dippers (which I never found) I would not have known of this hidden gem. From there I walked along the replanted part of Lament, disturbing yet another pair of fallow deer and noticing a buzzard fly quietly from an area I knew there was a nest. Once airborne and away from the nest the buzzard began to mew at me, and kept track of my movements through a sea of foxgloves to the nest tree. Bracken under the nest was soiled with the droppings the chicks had scooted out after first reversing their backsides to the edge. I left them in peace, my route away from them including stepping over a log from which the bark had fallen with age. Its surface bore a myriad of parallel scratches from the sharp claws of rabbits scrambling across it in either direction and over many years. A jay flew silently away, with none of the screeching that is the norm at other times of the year when not needing to conceal the presence of a nest.

I noticed a month ago when driving up the estate road that Lament was carpeted with bluebells. It was now a nightmare of bracken, each frond trying to out-compete the oaks and reaching chest height already. Unless looking up all the time I'd see nothing. A roe buck rose almost at my feet, running off through the wood with a loud *baauuff, buff buff.* This angry call got even more intense: *baauuff, baauuff, baauuff, buff, buff.* The sound reverberated through the woodland, with the buck still giving vent to his anger – or the fright he got – even when he must have been several hundred yards away. For my part I'd had enough of sprachling through bracken and made for the top of the wood. I deliberately went past the mysterious plucking post on the moss-covered rock. This time another young rabbit had been plucked. The diner had been there recently as two fresh and bloody chunks of a rabbit skull remained, along with copious amounts of plucked fur. I'll definitely settle for a buzzard as the predator.

I finished my day walking through Geordie's Moor, also now rather awkward with high bracken, though at least at a height I could see above. I skirted the wet part with the nesting waders and ducks, circling round to come in from the north end and sit on a small crag where I could see across the wetland without unnecessarily disturbing the birds. I watched a redshank rooting about in the sodden ground, and was pleased to see they were still here. Despite trying not to disturb it I did so in an indirect way. My route through the bushes on the top of the crag had obviously disturbed resting rabbits. These rabbits now wanted back to the main part of Geordie's Moor and the cover of the junipers. Their route was past the redshank, with a succession of rabbits scooting past the bird a few feet away from it until it abandoned its former peace and quiet and flew further down the marsh to continue its probing. A lapwing *pee-weeped* quietly from the far end of the marsh, and another from my right near to George's house, welcome sounds and maybe an indication that there could be two pairs with chicks.

New birds identified: swift
New mammals identified: none

Chapter 32

Thursday 12 July 2012. Weather: Dry, though overcast till late morning, then intermittent sunshine. Light wind.

Three weeks since my last visit, with a sprained right ankle and twisted left knee (done on the steps from our conservatory, not on the hill) and almost incessant rain keeping me at home. The weather was far better in March! I set off down the estate road past the bog on Geordie's Moor. The ground cover on the wetland had grown slightly and it seemed abandoned by the ducks and waders. There is no doubt that some would still be there, but it was even more wet than normal after the previous day's torrential rain, and in any case I don't like to panic any birds that might have chicks and risk them getting lost and abandoned. I continued on and entered Geordie's Moor further down, meaning to cut through and have a last look at the plucking post at the top of Lament.

I struggled through the shoulder-high bracken at the bottom end of Geordies Moor, quickly attracting the attention of the pair of buzzards nesting not far from the plucking post. They circled above me, mewing relentlessly. The chick (or chicks) would have either left the nest by this time and be in the nearby trees, or would be ready to do so. The *baauuff, buff buff buff* of a roebuck ahead of me broke the rhythm of the mewing. I couldn't see the buck but knew from his barking that he was getting near to the Lament boundary dyke. He barked a few more times and eventually quietened as he ran deeper into the huge oak wood. I gingerly climbed the fence which was tight into the dyke, not seeing what was on the other side for the density of the bracken. I didn't want another injured ankle or knee, so prodded with my walking pole and identified a small square of ground free of large stones that had fallen from the dyke, where I could jump down safely. My efforts were in vain, since there had been no more activity at the plucking post since my last visit to it, and the remaining parts of rabbit skull had been cleaned of any vestige of meat by the myriad of wee beasties that inhabit any square yard of ground – or of moss-covered rock in this case.

I returned to Geordie's Moor and was disappointed at how few small birds were visible. None were singing now, as it was getting late in the season, but I thought that an odd one might have been alarm-calling at me if I passed too close to a nest. It was as if they had all abandoned Perthshire and moved to somewhere that it didn't rain every day, as had pretty much been the case in most of the UK apart from the Western Isles these past few weeks. There is no doubt that many nests will have failed and young birds perished. Insect-eating birds will have struggled some days to get enough food for their chicks, and would have been unable to leave them unprotected in the nest during the very many downpours as they would die of hypothermia. The same would apply to ground-nesting birds that leave the nest after the first 24 hours. Newly-hatched waders, pheasants or partridges are often okay as they are small enough that all can get under the mother, but as they get older and bigger there's no longer enough space. In any case this year a large proportion of the invertebrates on which they depend will have themselves been drowned, died off or simply been unable to breed and increase their numbers. The owner was telling me that this year has had the best hatching success for pheasants and partridges since he took over the estate, but that the chicks were being killed by the weather within a very short time. It's a real pity, both for the birds and for all the work George has put in over the winter keeping the birds fed and keeping at low numbers any predators he can legally control.

I left Geordie's Moor and headed up towards Wericky, noting a roe doe in its foxy-red summer coat and a dark coloured young fallow buck standing almost together on a ridge ahead of me. The doe at least must have been disturbed from an early morning rest: it stretched and its back gradually became concave as it arched its head back over its shoulders. It then proceeded to stretch its back legs, pushing them straight out behind it one at a time. It was now ready, if need be, for flight. It was an unusual pair, and I assumed it was just coincidence they were together rather than any inter-species partnership.

I could now see that there were over 100 lapwings and a handful of oystercatchers in the sheep field. Of the lapwings, there was a good proportion of young birds, and if they had all been hatched on this estate I had missed them somewhere. Irrespective of where they were hatched, I was pleased to see such a large number of one of my favourite birds. Surprisingly they seemed to have been abandoned by their diminutive friends the starlings. Thirty or so mallard were in the duck ponds but I was too far off to be able to recognise any as this year's young. In any case the early-hatched ducklings would now be almost adult size.

I walked up the outside of Wericky, and was surveyed by the Wericky pair of buzzards. The female had flown quickly over from Dank Wood to join the male, which had raised the alarm from near the Wericky nest. They were as vocal as the Lament pair, though remained higher in the sky. By the time I had cut across the field to Dank Wood the buzzards had landed in the trees in Wericky and I was sure I could hear three different birds calling. Probably their chick or chicks had fledged as well. I watched out for the kites from Dank, which were bound to have been alerted by the noise, but they never showed. The owner had never seen the chicks on the wing yet, but had regularly watched the adults over Dank Wood. I had a sense of foreboding.

As I headed out the hill road the usual roe buck was on my left. He was busy feeding and I managed to pass him unseen. Small birds were still scarce, and even when I came to the large patch of broom near the pond it was – or at least appeared to be – devoid of birds. A mallard drake lifting off the pond was the only sign of life. Once round the corner I sat on a flat-topped stone and spied the hillside. Two roe deer, about 200 yards apart, were feeding near the top of the hill, and a pair of meadow pipits flitted anxiously around in the heather near where I sat. At least one nest seemed to have survived. I considered that there were far fewer wheatears than last year. Whatever had caused this, the recent atrocious weather could well mean there will be even less next year.

I moved on, spying a roe doe along with a buck further ahead on my left. We were almost into the roe deer rutting season, that possibly being the reason they were together. They were near the brow of a hill, and they slowly disappeared over the crest without having seen me. I stopped at the Middle Hill, at last seeing a kestrel high in the sky on the west side. It was mobbing a soaring buzzard, though rather half-heartedly. The kestrel was a male and looked tiny compared to the buzzard, the contrast more exaggerated if the buzzard was a female, since with birds of prey the females are bigger than the males. The buzzard seemed unconcerned at my presence but, just as I was beginning to think that the Middle Hill pair had failed to breed this year, two buzzards (presumably this one and another) appeared over me, mewing apprehensively. By this time I was nearly at the bottom of Grey Crags. A third buzzard then rose from the rocks on Grey Crags and flew low over my head, landing rather unsteadily on the top of a larch tree down towards Eerie Valley. It would seem that this was a chick, and my proximity to it the reason that the Middle Hill parents suddenly took an interest in me.

I walked up the side of Grey Crags, returning down past one of George's pheasant release pens. Well-grown pheasant poults fluttered out of my way, landing after only a few yards. It was maybe this food source that had attracted a golden eagle that the owner had seen here the previous day, though unfortunately there was now no sign of it. He had been pleasantly surprised that the presence of the eagle had not scattered the pheasants; in fact he said there had been very little predation on the poults from birds of prey this year. I retorted that I had the avian predators well warned to be on their best behaviour. As I looked over to North Eerie I could see a roe doe feeding on a patch that was bare of heather, and with a single calf with her. I was surprised how large the calf was, but of course with being born in May it would be somewhere around the eight-week mark. They appeared very relaxed, and were yet more deer that I had seen today without being seen by them.

Coming back down to the slightly lower ground beside the hill road, I could hear a bird scolding me from somewhere among the bracken and heather. There was a quiet *chit chit chit chit,* then a louder single *cheep,* which I at first thought was coming from a different bird in a different part of the heather. When the bird eventually perched on top of a frond of bracken I could see it was a male whinchat. Another one, probably the female, was alarming somewhere behind me and I was obviously close either to their nest or to recently-fledged chicks in the heather. So another nest had survived the rain.

I made for Larch Wood, cutting through the Victor's Nightmare partridge drive on one of George's Polaris tracks. There was plenty of mud to examine for tracks made by the range of wildlife that take advantage of these roads, but there was nothing more exciting than pheasant, red-legged partridge, rabbit, roe deer and fallow deer. Once in the Larch Wood, I was spotted by the resident buzzard – only one this time – which circled over me mewing in unease. I checked under their nest and there was an absence of 'whitewash', so it was likely that their nesting attempt had failed at some stage. From there I moved out of the wood and round the corner to sit on one of my favourite rocks (when not in toiletry use) looking out to the Craigie Face. One or two small birds were fluttering about the bracken ahead of me, though I was never quick enough with the binoculars to get identification. A young roe buck with single spike antlers was grazing in Boggy Bottom, though he spotted me when I rose to go to Law Wood, and he entered that wood ahead of me.

I sat for a while in Law Wood, but the foliage on the trees was now really thick and making out the few birds of which I did get a fleeting glimpse was extremely difficult. However I could now see the trees in full 'bloom', and I admired the blend of oak, alder, ash, rowan, larch and sitka spruce. The sun had come out, my jacket was deposited in my rucksack and I sat for half an hour in the sun. I've no doubt that there were as many birds in the wood now as there had been a month ago but they were eerily silent and hard to see, a good survival strategy! I saw that many of the nettles in front of me had their tops eaten off, clearly a delicacy for the deer, yet something I'd never noticed before. Half an hour with no birds or mammals focusses the mind on trees and plants, and there is always something to learn.

I left Law Wood and walked round towards Loch Wood. The black rabbit that lives in Law Wood was at the mouth of a burrow in the adjacent grass field. In the past when it has spotted me, the rabbit runs the 200 yards to Law Wood rather than diving down the first available burrow. Today was no exception. I spied round the other burrows looking for any black offspring, but there were none, though plenty of the 'normal' colour.

It's amazing how often my day has finished on a high. Today was no different as not one but three young herons flew off from the marsh at the top end of the shooting lodge loch. There would be no trout in the marsh but maybe frogs and certainly slugs and other creepy-crawlies that herons might relish. The three, all still without the glorious crest they grow in later life, flew as if in slow motion in a semi-circle, then headed up in the direction of the small pond near to Larch Wood. They were probably from the same brood and it was remarkable to see that they were keeping together rather than dispersing. Despite the weather-induced devastation to young birds that there had obviously been, there are always survivors.

New birds identified: none
New mammals identified: none

Chapter 33

Wednesday 25 July 2012. Weather: Dry, sunny and only a light breeze – perfect for my last walk.

What a surprise – another daytime-hooting owl. I had just parked my car and went to check at the former perch of the tawny owl in the small wood beside the shooting lodge (it wasn't there) when I heard an owl hooting. It was a long *hoooooooooooooooooooooo*, followed a few seconds later by a *hoo hoo-hoo-hoo-hoooooooooooooooooooooo.* I couldn't make out if the hooting was much quieter than normal or if it maybe was coming from further away – maybe the east end of Law Wood. I stood silently for five minutes but the owl had gone silent. It was a great beginning to my last official survey day as the year was now up, but it had knocked my theory for six that tawny owls hoot in daylight at nesting time to keep into touch; we were long past nesting time and the owlets would have fledged some weeks ago.

I headed up the road towards the hill, noting about 40 lapwings in the sheep field and scanning about without success for the remaining 60 or so from my last visit. Two buzzards circled above Wericky, and there was definitely another in the wood answering. My theory – if I be so bold as to theorise again after my tawny owl failure – was that this was a fledged chick ensuring the parents knew its whereabouts for when food became available. I suspect one chick (if any at all) will be the norm this year after the diabolical spring and early summer weather. I saw that in 2012 in Norway only six nests of white-tailed eagles from dozens visited had more than one chick and that from those 'twin' nests only six chicks rather than the target of 20 could be collected to finalise the reintroduction of this iconic species to the east of Scotland.

When I got to Dank Wood I was hoping to have confirmation that the two red kite chicks had fledged. There was no sign of a parent over the wood but when I walked along the front edge of the wood a red kite flew quietly from a tree ahead of me and quickly slipped over the top of the trees out of sight. Had this been one of the parents, their trait in the past had been to keep an eye on me, so this *may* have been one of the fledged chicks. I stood for a while to see if there were any developments, a wait that was worthwhile. A redstart, either female or immature, perched on a branch near me, eyeing me up and giving me that distinctive flash of red when it eventually flew off. Dank Wood seems popular with redstarts, yet as a completely coniferous wood, doesn't have the holes in trees suitable for this species to nest, especially compared with the mature oaks in Lament, where I have never even seen a redstart. When I returned to the corner of the wood I was pleased to see a large tortoiseshell butterfly busy feeding on some thistles. It is one of our more common butterflies, (though its numbers are declining) orange-brown with black spots and iridescent blue round the trailing edge of its wings. Butterflies in general have been scarce this year, though I'm not too sorry about the lack of cabbage whites and the corresponding absence of caterpillar damage to my brassicas.

As I headed out the hill road a flash of white caught my eye. It was a very light dappled fallow doe running downhill in my direction and disappearing into the bracken. It hadn't seen me and I could see nothing uphill from it that would spook it. Deer don't usually take off like this for no good reason but what caused its panic remains a mystery. Further up the hill I could hear – but not see – one of the Middle Hill buzzards. As I got closer I spied it on a rock almost at the top of the hill. Its call seemed immature and its bright yellow legs tended to back up my view that this was a young bird. As I got closer to it another buzzard appeared, then another, which I took to be the parents. The two new arrivals circled and the young buzzard flew short distances from one rock to another on the hill, continuing to mew loudly. This seems to confirm that the Middle Hill buzzards have only one chick. I sat for a wee while hoping to see the kestrels, though they never made an appearance. I expected by this time of year to have seen the family flying round, but their breeding success may unfortunately have been no better than many other species. There was a good stock of red-legged partridges, and they were now forming small packs rather than the pairs of the springtime. Unfortunately none of the packs had young from this year.

I cut down through Eerie Valley and was enthralled to see a pearl-bordered fritillary butterfly. It was on the leaf of a foxglove when I saw it at first, with its wings open. It is a lovely orange-brown colour with an amazing pattern of black spots and chequering, and some white shimmering round the trailing edge of its wings. I tried to get closer but it lifted off and flew round me, close to the ground as this species seems to favour. It landed on another young foxglove, then a thistle, and from there into the bracken. It was a great sighting for me as I think it is only the second one I've seen.

As I continued down Eerie Valley I gradually climbed up the right flank, gaining height as I approached Craigie Face with, surprisingly, no jackdaws. I almost walked on top of a mid-brown coloured fallow doe that barked loudly at me as it sprang out of the bracken, a bark that could easily be mistaken for that of a large dog such as a German shepherd. It stopped 50 yards away, broadside, and as I was motionless it seemed momentarily unsure of where the danger lay. It ran off a further 20 yards to the top of the ridge, where it stopped to look at me again, before barking and making its final exit into the dip beyond. I watched for it reappearing to the left, right or above the ridge, but it never did. The older fallow are as wily as a fox and it would sit tight once it was out of sight.

I came down to the grass field below Craigie Face, where the walking was much easier. My attention was drawn by a movement which seemed to be on top of the dyke just at the entrance to The Shudder. I thought it was a stoat, but when I saw it again it was the tail of a dark fallow, regularly switching from side to side to keep the flies off. I moved a couple of steps to the right to get some cover from the dyke and quietly moved closer. Even though I moved soundlessly, it must have got my wind and I saw it bounding ahead then stopping to look back to allow its eyes to confirm what its nose had told it.

I went through the gate to the second grass field and at the far end leaned on the fence to have a good look into the junipers at the end of Craigie Face. Willow warblers were in good numbers feeding on insects on the junipers. Many had the typical yellow, more fluffy, breast of young willow warblers, though there was an occasional more dishevelled adult bird with a white breast. They fed busily on the junipers but seemed disinterested in the nearby birch and larch trees, so I assume that insects are more attracted for some reason to junipers. I watched a wee brown bird skulking about in some bracken and eventually got a view of its orange-brown wing feathers, distinguishing it easily as a whitethroat more so than its white throat, which in truth I can't recollect noticing. As I watched, I heard a roe buck loudly barking 500 yards away at the bottom end of the Ell Wood. Something, probably something insignificant, had disturbed it in its highly-charged rutting state, or maybe it was seeing off a rival buck. The *baauuff, baauuff, buff buff buff* echoed through the woodland and made me realise, with the sounds I had heard over the past year and what they meant to me, how much more they mean to wildlife that depend on all of their senses to survive from one day to the next.

I cut through the east end of Creag Bheag Wood and came out of that wood on to the track running between Pheasant Wood and the marshy rectangle between Craigie Face and Henhouse Wood. This is all the territory of the white fallow deer: Penelope, Sandie and the cream-coloured calf. I was walking down the track thinking that I hadn't seen the cream calf since about April and hoped that he (or she) was alright. At that I was suddenly aware of a white fallow on the marsh area near the Henhouse Wood. It had a calf beside it, but not a white or cream one: a brown calf. This answered my query from early in the survey as to whether fallow calves are always the same colour as their mother. They stood for a few seconds but had spotted me, at 200 yards away, and they trotted in to the safety of the Henhouse Wood, the doe leading her calf through a well-used gap in the fence. Further down the Henhouse Wood I cut through past the pond, noticing a nice brood of mallard ducklings a week or so old trotting behind their mother at the far side. I exited the wood through the kissing gate and cut over towards Law Wood. I passed under the tree in which I had during the winter watched the flock of crossbills, reliving that fantastic experience. It was only then that I noticed that the tree (which I at the time thought to be an ash) was in fact a small-leaved lime tree, with its huge crop of fruits hanging in threes and the leaves near the fruits being a long narrow shape, as opposed to the more common heart-shaped leaves on the remainder of the tree. I walked past where the oystercatcher had nested in the rough stony corner of the field. The nest was still identifiable, but was now a tiny flat raft of small pebbles in a sea of larger stones. The fluttering of a pheasant poult in the adjacent Law Wood made me look round… in time to see a small black rabbit scurry under a blown tree. In the last minutes of my last day I had seen evidence of the progeny of one of the four (or maybe five) adult black rabbits I had watched over the past year. The year had turned its full circle.

New birds identified: none
New mammals identified: none

APPENDIX 1

Topography of the Estate

Larch Wood, including the adjacent small roundel and pond

This medium-sized, almost square, mature woodland is mainly conifers, including larch, to the south and west, with a mix of deciduous trees, mainly sycamore, in the remainder. A small corner of the wood has been replanted with native deciduous trees, and the east side has a thick covering of *Rhododendron ponticum*, the invasive rhododendron. There was moderate damage to this woodland during the winter gales of 2011/2012.

For some reason this woodland is very attractive to the thrush family, with all species seen in decent numbers, including the redwing and fieldfare in winter. The song thrush is particularly common, yet the habitat is not that normally favoured by these birds for nesting, with few bushy areas apart from the rhododendron.

The less common birds seen in this woodland are bullfinches and goldcrest, with whitethroat and willow warbler seen and heard regularly in a damp strip of goat willow that runs from Larch Wood to Law Wood. Great-spotted woodpecker and green woodpecker have been heard – though not seen – in Larch Wood. This wood is extremely popular with buzzards, with a pair nesting in a conifer there in 2012, though no chicks seemed to fledge.

Roe deer are commonly seen, and while fallow are no doubt present from time to time there were no sightings. There was a single sighting of a red squirrel.

The small roundel juxtaposed to Larch Wood was badly affected by the winds of winter 2011/2012, and many trees were toppled or had the tops blown off. It is a haven for rabbits; more so now that there are blown trees. It is a favourite wood for the tit family, with great, blue, coal and long-tailed being seen there. The pond adjacent to the roundel was quiet for much of the year, though in spring there were mallard, goosander and a single heron using it.

Law Wood

This is a delightful medium-sized rectangular wood, comprising some mature conifers at the north-east end, and a mix of deciduous trees in the remainder. The wood has moderately steep sides and has a shallow burn running through it, making the centre damp though open and attractive to wildlife. This wetter patch has young oak, ash and alder trees growing. *Rhododendron ponticum* is beginning to invade parts of Law Wood.

Sitting near the top of the banking on either side and looking down into the woodland is like being in an amphitheatre. Rabbits abound and there was considerable evidence in spring 2012 that this was a valuable food source for buzzards, with partially-eaten carcasses being regularly seen. This part of the estate has several pure black rabbits, those being seen in this wood, the Larch Wood, Loch Wood and Dank Wood.

Of the less common birds seen in Law Wood was a flock of common crossbills on a lime tree in winter, and a pair of garden warblers in summer. A pair of oystercatchers nested on some rough grassland just outside Law Wood and fledged two chicks. The nest was unusual in that it was 'lined' with hundreds of small stones, despite most stones nearby being quite large.

Law Wood is extremely popular with fallow deer.

Ell Wood

Ell Wood, now almost triangular but named as such because of its original L shape, is a small wood of young birch, though there are mature beech trees on the longer edges, particularly the west. It is a wood with a damp floor and, despite being quite open, doesn't seem to be popular with wildlife. The main birds in Ell Wood are blackbirds and thrushes, with the only less common bird being a male brambling feeding in snowy conditions with a small flock of chaffinches at a pheasant feeder. Roe deer were also visitors to this feeder, and while there were no sightings of fallow in Ell Wood, their cleat marks were frequently seen in the mud.

Henhouse Wood

This is a medium-sized rectangular coniferous wood with mature Douglas fir at the north-east end, which were badly windblown over the 2011/2012 winter. The flattened trees are now a harbour for the already sizeable stock of rabbits. Midway through the wood there is a pond and marsh, graduating into goat willow and some alder at the north end of the wood.

The conifers are not conducive to a wide variety of wildlife, though they are seen to be popular with birds such as goldcrests and goldfinches, which are probably nesting there. A redstart was seen in the south-west end of the wood, though with the trees in that part not being mature there may not be nest holes available. Willow warblers were regularly heard at this same part of the wood

Henhouse Wood is popular with fallow deer and, along with the Pheasant Wood and Creag Bheag, is the main territory of the white fallow, Penelope, and her cream coloured calf. Strangely, since I saw the calf with Penelope and other fallow in autumn 2011, I have only seen her (or him) on his own, never with other fallow.

Pheasant Wood

This is a small to medium rectangular coniferous wood, mainly sitka spruce. It was unfortunately badly affected by the storms and many trees are now down. Because of its monoculture of trees and scarcity of undergrowth (apart from the now fallen trees) it has limited attraction to wildlife. Finches are the most common birds, especially chaffinches, and many were seen feeding on grain scattered on the rides for the pheasants in winter. The least common bird seen in the Pheasant Wood was a spotted flycatcher on its eastern side. The bird regularly flew off its perch on a branch and caught a fly, returning to await its next dipteran victim.

Roe and fallow deer commonly use this wood, and it will be even better for deer with the fallen trees providing more cover and better shelter from the wind.

Creag Bheag Wood

This is a long narrow wood of predominantly conifers, though those are mature and are a good mix of larch and Douglas fir. One or two Douglas fir trees at its eastern end were blown down during the storm, though the damage is not too severe. The eastern end is part of the territory of a pair of buzzards, though the blown trees (including a tree in which they nested in 2011) may have put them off nesting there, and there is a high probability they nested in 2012 on the Craigie Face near the jackdaw colony, since the more recent sightings have been there. If so, they should be well-fed on young jackdaws.

The limited ground cover restricts the variety of bird life in Creag Bheag, though there is no shortage of the more common birds – robin, wren, song thrush, blackbird, chaffinch. It also held a flock of around 12 bullfinches during the winter and, if not a resident, was at least visited by a female or immature goshawk during the autumn of 2011. It is an ideal wood for red squirrels, and at the beginning of spring 2012 there were at least two pairs present; one pair near the west end and one near the east end. It is also a popular wood with fallow and roe deer.

The West End

The West End of the estate is a huge mixed wood comprising mainly Scots pine, larch, Norway spruce, oak, ash, juniper, birch and rowan. Most of the trees are mature and there are also some ancient Wellingtonia near to the estate house. It is interesting that in parts less accessible to deer there is good natural regeneration of trees. There is little doubt that this is one of the most beautiful woods in Perthshire, if not in Scotland.

Because of the variety of habitat, most of the woodland birds that can be found in any or all of the other woods can be found in the West End. All of the more common birds are regularly seen, and of the summer migrants there were sightings (or the songs heard) of willow warbler, garden warbler and whitethroat. Other less common birds seen were the tree creeper and bullfinch, with the great-spotted woodpecker and the green woodpecker being heard in springtime. As in most oak woods, jays are common.

Roe and fallow deer are plentiful in this woodland. There was only one sighting of a red squirrel but it is likely that this could be one of the strongholds of this delightful mammal. There is a fox den near the eastern boundary.

Lament

Lament in winter and early spring must have one of the most diverse range of bird species. It is a large wood of mature oak with some sitka spruce at the north west corner and a clear felled and replanted area of oak below that. The wood is interspersed with wild-seeded holly trees. The mature oaks are well spaced and the breakage and splitting of branches over the years means that there are now countless nesting places for hole-nesting birds such as woodpeckers and tits, and the cracks in limbs and in bark no doubt accommodate nesting tree creepers. As in the West End, jays are common.

There are several resident pairs of great-spotted woodpecker and at least one pair of green woodpecker. The latter are seldom seen but their loud yaffle call is a regular aural treat. A mixed flock of redwing and fieldfare visited in winter and a flock of long-tailed tits kept me entertained. A pair of red kites fledged two chicks in Lament in 2011 and at least two pairs of buzzards nested in 2012. A 'plucking post' on a moss-covered rock *may* indicate that a goshawk is nesting, though with only young rabbits being the prey – never birds – a buzzard seems much more likely.

Roe and fallow deer were commonly seen, with most of the fallow being the dark variety. Red squirrels were seen several times in the north-west corner near the conifers.

Geordie's Moor

Geordie's Moor, adjacent to Lament, is a large open area interspersed with juniper, oak, alder and birch. It is incredible nesting habitat for small birds and is bounded on one side by a burn running through a shallow gorge, widening its appeal to even more species. In spring and summer there are vast numbers of chaffinches, and also bullfinches, siskins, tits and willow warblers. With this food supply it is hardly surprising that this is the place I had the only sighting of a sparrowhawk during the year.

Many of the ancient birch trees have holes suitable for tits and other small birds nesting and of course oak and birch have a myriad of insects and caterpillars as a food supply for this thriving bird population. A pair of dippers was seen several times in the burn and over adjacent loch beside the shooting lodge in autumn 2011 but, despite a search for sightings along the burn in 2012, they were not found. In spring, a redstart was seen near the overflow of the dam into the burn. It was next to a pied wagtail feeding a chick and provided a contrast between glorious technicolour and monochrome.

Part of Geordie's Moor is bog, and is extremely suitable habitat for waders. Oystercatcher, lapwing and mallard were seen nesting there. A pair of redshank and a common sandpiper (probably one of a pair) were also seen and it is likely that they nested in this area.

Of the more unusual sightings, a white-tailed eagle overflew Geordie's Moor, having come from the direction of a neighbouring estate.

Loch Wood and the shooting lodge loch

Loch Wood is a small, almost circular, wood with an amazing variety of mature trees. These are mostly conifers and include several giant firs, one of which unfortunately blew down during the winter storm of 2011/2012. The trees are widely spaced and there is plenty ground cover, giving this wood a good variety of birds for its size. Of the less common species redstart and willow warbler have been seen in Loch Wood, and a buzzard twice showed concern at my presence in early spring, indicating that it was nesting (though I never found the nest). The absence of buzzards circling and mewing at me during late June and July tends to indicate their nest failed.

Though mallard (and the four semi-domestic mute swans) are the predominant wildfowl on the loch, a pair of Canada geese took up residence in early spring 2012, but did not nest. A single wild mute swan was seen in winter at a time when many lochs were frozen or mainly frozen. An adult heron and a trio of immature herons have been seen on the loch and the marsh at the top of the loch. In the small field between the loch and the shooting lodge a small group of twite was seen feeding on grass seeds in late winter. Oystercatcher and lapwing regularly use the grass spits of land round the loch, the marshland to the west of the loch, and some rough, rocky pasture just beyond that.

In summer the loch invariably has a cloud of swallows and house martins hunting flies over its surface, regularly making contact with the water and competing with the trout in making splashes and concentric rings on the surface. By early September 2011 nearly 100 were perched on the telephone wires at the side of the estate road in advance of their journey to sub-Saharan Africa. This included at least two that had just fledged and were sitting on the wires still being fed by the adults. It is doubtful if they would finish their epic journey.

Wericky

Wericky, like many of the other woods on the estate, is mixed woodland of medium size. At the lower end of the wood the trees are mainly deciduous – ash and oak, with a sprinkling of conifers. The centre of the wood is young spruce trees, while the high roundel at the top end, also coniferous, is mainly mature Douglas fir. There is a good mix of birds, though they are more difficult to see with the perpetual cover on most of the trees. The willow warbler is common here in summer, and there is a surprising number of dunnocks in the young spruce. A pair of buzzards nested in one of the mature Douglas fir trees and reared at least one chick to fledging.

There was one sighting of a red squirrel and with this being an ideal habitat, there are likely to be several more.

Dank Wood

Dank Wood is a small wood of sitka spruce, many of which were broken in the winter storms. There is a rocky knowe in the centre of the wood, which gives it some character and prevents it being the barren type wood that so many of these sitka plantations are. Of all the woods, it was the one most favoured by the cuckoo in springtime, though it may have been the springboard for the cuckoo accessing the hill beyond and the considerable number of meadow pipit nests. Of the less common birds seen here, the redstart is the most memorable, and the wood is particularly popular with coat tits and robins. Sightings of wheatear, willow warbler and a single chiffchaff (though the distinctive song of the chiffchaff was never heard in springtime) were made in the rough land to the west end of the wood. In the spring of 2012 a pair of red kites nested and fledged 2 chicks.

There were two sightings of red squirrels, and, given the proximity of Wericky, it is likely that the red squirrels will travel between the two, using a connecting drystane dyke as a corridor. Roe and fallow deer were sighted in and around Dank Wood, with some of the fallow being dappled and including a mature buck with a lovely set of palmated antlers. A single cast antler of a red deer stag was also found.

The Hill, including Hill Loch and ponds

The hill is mainly a mix of rank heather and bracken, with the bracken particularly suiting red-legged partridges and pheasants as cover, and allowing them to be flushed more easily than from rank heather. Two large areas of formerly rank heather were burned by fires that got out of control, one in 2010 and the other in 2012. Neither fire appears to have burnt into the peat and it is likely that the heather will regenerate in both areas. Regeneration is underway in the area of the earlier fire, with large amounts of blaeberry already in evidence. Apart from deer and wheatears, the burnt areas are meantime largely devoid of wildlife.

On the remainder of the hill wildlife abounds, and this includes a variety of wild flowers – chickweed wintergreen, bugle, common butterwort, heath milkwort, tormentil and early purple orchid being the most abundant. Of the larger birds, buzzards are commonly seen, with at least two nests in springtime, one on Middle Hill and the other in a larch tree near the western march, where the female was particularly bold. Kestrels were sighted on Middle Hill and may well have nested there in 2012. There were two sightings of the same hen harrier in late winter, either a female or an immature male. Despite observations from late April to mid-May for the skydancing display of a male harrier, which is a prelude to nesting, there were no more sightings.

Though the habitat is suitable for merlin and short-eared owls, none were seen, nor was there a sighting of a peregrine. Occasional sightings were made of a golden eagle (though never, unfortunately, by me). A single raven, or occasionally a pair, were seen passing over the estate, though there are no known nesting crags or trees. Carrion crows are at tolerable levels, and an occasional hooded crow is seen on the hill. Despite my searching, no nests of either sub-species were seen, and only one brood of carrion crow fledglings was seen in springtime.

Apart from wrens, some meadow pipits and a flock of bullfinches, small birds were uncommon on the hill in winter. The situation changed in summer, with a considerable increase in meadow pipit numbers, and good quantities of whinchat. Where there were patches of broom, willow warblers were common, and a pair of blackcaps and an occasional stonechat was seen.

A large stock of pheasants and red-legged partridges remained from the 2011/2012 shooting season and many nested. Unfortunately the extremely wet weather in late June and early July coincided with the hatching of many of these nests and a high proportion of the chicks will have perished. There seems little doubt that the same fate will have befallen the chicks of small ground-nesting and/or insect-eating birds, such as meadow pipit, stonechat, whinchat and warblers. On the small ponds on the hill mallard were the only wildfowl sighted. The Hill Loch seemed only to attract mallard, despite the number of other duck species on neighbours' larger lochs. Occasionally red grouse were seen, mostly singles but in the summer of 2011 there was a pair with one well-grown chick, and another pair just prior to nesting time in 2012.

Adjacent to the Hill Loch is a gully with a mix of a hundred or so larch, spruce and fir trees. It is a great area for wrens, which nest either in the rock face of the gully or in the roots of the few blown trees. The most interesting sighting there was a pair of tree pipits, summer migrants from Africa. There was also a single sighting of a red squirrel. North-west of this area there was a sighting of a greyhen, which had been taking grit from a supply provided for red grouse, and which flew over the western march.

Roe and fallow deer are regularly seen on the hill. The roe have their favourite areas where sightings are almost guaranteed, but the fallow are wider-ranging. There is a good mix of colours of fallow, with more dappled ones being seen on the eastern side of the estate and almost exclusively dark ones on the western side. Dappled does were always seen with dappled calves, and dark does with dark calves, though in 2012 a white fallow had a dark calf.

Craigie Face and Eerie Valley

Craigie Face is a craggy north-facing slope running from Creag Bheag Wood to Eerie Valley, a valley through which a small burn flows. Eerie Valley runs north-west to join the hill road at North Eerie and Grey Crags. At Eerie Valley, red-legged partridges driven in either direction over guns placed in this valley provide possibly the most challenging birds of all the drives on the estate. There are crags and scree on the north-east side of Eerie Valley, with a sporadic mix of trees and shrubs – larch, birch, rowan, juniper, broom and dog rose. It is ideal habitat for small birds, especially blackbird, robin, wren, chaffinch and willow warbler, There have been frequent sightings of kestrels in Eerie Valley and, at the far end of the Craigie Face. Fallow deer are commonly seen in Eerie Valley, though there was only one sighting there of roe.

Craigie Face itself has steep crags with scree below. Some trees, mainly stunted rowan and larch, are growing from the crags and around 50 to 75 pairs of jackdaws live and nest here. A pair of buzzards is also in residence and may also have nested on the crags in 2012. They probably deserted their 2011 nesting site in nearby Creag Bheag Wood because of some of the mature conifers being blown down. In September 2011 the presence of the jackdaws attracted the attention of either a female or immature male goshawk. The jackdaws would be easy pickings and I was surprised that I did not see it in that area again, though it may just have been passing through.

Craigie Face creates great thermals and I have seen seven buzzards soaring above it. The south and east slopes have a peppering of trees – birch, rowan, junipers and larch, some of the larch being really ancient and gnarled. This is an incredible habitat for birds, with high numbers of robins, wrens, blackbirds, song thrushes, mistle thrushes, willow warblers, at least one pair of garden warblers and a single sighting of a yellowhammer. In winter a flock of fieldfares were seen feeding on juniper berries, with a cock and hen pheasant underneath awaiting any berries that fell. Though there are probably roe here, all my sightings have been of fallow, including the cream coloured calf.

The fishing loch

Considering the number of boats on the loch, it remains rich in wildfowl, though lacks some of the duck species that tend to be more wary of humans. The highlight has to be the numbers of goldeneye on the loch in early spring. Other interesting sightings were the family of goosanders, the brief springtime visit by a family of greylag geese, the single blue-phase snow goose, the regular fishing forays to the loch by ospreys and the resident otter or otters.

APPENDIX 2

Summary of birds and mammals identified

Birds

The birds seen on the estate can be classified as (1) Resident all-year-round – at least in Scotland if not on this estate (2) Winter visitors (3) Summer visitors. The birds can be further classified as red-listed (R) – of highest conservation priority, those that are amber listed (A) – of next conservation importance, and those that are not currently under any conservation threat and not included in these listings. A total of 89 species of birds were seen.

Resident in Scotland all-year-round:

Blackbird; Bullfinch; Buzzard, common

Chaffinch; Coot; Cormorant; Crossbill, common; Curlew (A)

Dipper; Duck, goldeneye (A); Duck, mallard (A); Duck, tufted (A); Dunnock (A)

Eagle, white-tailed (R)

Goldcrest; Goldfinch; Goosander; Goose, Canada; Goose, greylag (A); Goshawk; Grebe, great-crested; Greenfinch; Grouse, black (R); Grouse, red (A); Gull, black-headed (A); Gull, common (A); Gull, herring (R);

Harrier, hen (R); Heron

Jackdaw; Jay

Kestrel (A); Kite, red (A);

Lapwing (R)

Moorhen

Owl, tawny; Oystercatcher (A)

Partridge, red-legged; Pheasant; Pipit, meadow (A)

Raven; Redshank (A); Robin; Rook

Sandpiper, common (A); Siskin; Snipe (A); Sparrowhawk; Sparrow, house (R); Starling (R); Swan, mute

Thrush, mistle (A); Thrush, song (R); Tit, blue; Tit, coal; Tit, great; Tit, long-tailed; Tree creeper; Twite (R)

Wagtail, pied; Woodcock; Woodpecker, great-spotted; Woodpecker, green (A); Woodpigeon; Wren

Yellowhammer (R)

Winter migrants

Brambling

Fieldfare (R)

Goose, pink-footed (A); Goose, snow

Redwing (R)

Summer migrants

Blackcap

Chiffchaff; Cuckoo (R)

Flycatcher, spotted (R)

Martin, house (A); Martin, sand (A)

Osprey (A)

Pipit, tree (R)

Redstart (A)

Stonechat; Swallow (A); Swift (A)

Warbler, garden; Warbler, sedge; Warbler, willow (A); Wheatear (A); Whinchat (A); Whitethroat (A)

Passerines

Of the passerines (perching birds), chaffinches and bullfinches were regularly seen, with small flocks of bullfinches a regular feature in winter.

Siskins, goldfinches and goldcrests were present but uncommon, and surprisingly there were only a couple of sightings of a small group of greenfinches. On one occasion, in winter, a single male brambling was seen at a pheasant feeder with a small flock of chaffinches. Four tit species were regularly seen, as were other woodland birds such as the tree creeper, song thrush and mistle thrush, though less so the blackbird. The thrush family was augmented in winter by large flocks of fieldfares and smaller flocks or redwings. There was only one sighting of a yellowhammer, possibly reflecting its red listing. House sparrows were abundant around the owner's house and farm steading. This is probably accounted for by the suitable habitat of buildings and ivy, plus additional year-round feeding from bird feeders (which attract a wide range of small birds). A highlight was the sighting of a large flock of common crossbills and a smaller flock of twite in late winter, though none of these birds was ever seen again.

It was good to see that the redstart was fairly common, though surprisingly seemed to be absent from the mature oak wood with the most suitable nesting habitat for it by way of tree nest holes (Lament). It could be that it prefers smaller blocks of woodland, though Lament is extremely open and the oaks will produce plenty of insects.

On the hill and moorland, and even over some of the permanent pasture, meadow pipits were present all year round, though less so in winter. In spring and summer the willow warbler and the wheatear were the most common of the summer migrants, though there were good numbers of whitethroat, garden warbler, whinchat and stonechat. There was only a single sighting of a pair of blackcap, a pair of tree pipits, a spotted flycatcher, a yellowhammer and a chiffchaff.

Great-spotted woodpeckers were seen and heard with regularity, especially in early spring when the birds were drumming. Green woodpeckers were regularly heard, though seldom seen. There seemed only to be a small number of cuckoos in late spring. The most common area to see or hear them was in the vicinity of Dank Wood and the area of hill between that wood and Larch Wood. In this area it is likely that their preferred 'fosterers' will be the meadow pipit.

Corvids

There were high numbers of jays throughout the estate, and a large colony of jackdaws that nest among scree and rocks on Craigie Face. Rooks visit from a rookery on a neighbouring estate though none nest on this estate. Carrion crows and an odd hooded crow were present only in moderate numbers, probably due to the unrelenting trapping and shooting regime carried out against them because of their predation to ground nesting birds' eggs and chicks (100, including five hooded crows, were trapped in spring/summer 2012). No occupied carrion crow nests were seen, and only one brood of fledged carrion crows was sighted. Single ravens or pairs were seen over-flying the estate on many occasions though do not appear to nest here.

Waders

Oystercatchers and lapwings were present in good numbers and nested on various places within the estate. The 2012 nesting season for these two species did not seem particularly successful, with only a handful of nests known to have fledged. The fact there are many immature birds of both species present in summer and autumn suggests that some *may* be fledged elsewhere and move to this estate. A pair of redshank and a pair of common sandpiper were present and probably nested. Another single common sandpiper was seen at the fishing loch and may well have had a mate on a nest round the shoreline.

Curlew were heard round the fringes of the fishing loch, on the hill land above the shooting lodge and one was seen at the back of the hill near the eastern march. From the warning call given by a curlew in early June 2012 (probably in the Dank partridge drive) it is likely the bird had chicks, though the bird was not seen because of the topography.

Waterfowl and birds with a water-related habitat

Most of the birds in this category were seen on the fishing loch, though in some cases were on the loch at the shooting lodge or the Hill Loch. Three pairs of mute swans bred on the fishing loch, as did at least one pair (possibly two pairs) of great-crested grebe. Mallard were abundant and also nested round the shore. At least one pair of moorhens frequent the reeds at the east end and a single coot was seen at the west end. It is likely that they all nested on or near the loch, though survival rate of chicks of all species was extremely poor, believed to be caused by predation from pike. Large rafts of tufted duck were present from summer to winter, though did not breed here. At one point in early spring there were at least 60 goldeneye. They do not seem to breed here either, requiring suitable holes in trees or nest boxes to do so. It may be possible to encourage them to breed by the erection of nest boxes, though with the current pike predation issue it seems hardly worthwhile.

Of the pescivorous species, cormorants visit the fishing loch in small numbers. A family of goosanders was present in autumn 2011, though it is not known if they bred locally. Since there were six immature birds plus both parents, it seems more likely they bred elsewhere and moved here when they fledged, by that time being too big for pike predation.

A flock of 30 or so Canada geese frequently visit the fishing loch, and a pair settled for a time on the loch at the shooting lodge. None appear to have bred successfully. A small group of greylag geese flew over the fishing loch in June 2012 so must have been some of those that remain in mainland Scotland to breed rather than returning to Iceland. Pink-footed geese were frequently seen over-flying the estate, though were never seen landing. A blue-phase a snow goose was seen on the fishing loch in late May 2012. Its origin is not known.

Snipe are present in low numbers, which is rather surprising considering the amount of suitable marshy habitat for them. It is likely at least some of them breed on the estate, though I never encountered their drumming display. (One was seen with a chick in early August 2012.)

Herons were seen occasionally both on the estate and on the fishing loch. Lastly, a pair of dippers was seen several times in 2011 on the burn running from the loch at the shooting lodge, though they were not seen during 2012.

Hirundines

Swallows and house martins nest in high numbers in the area of the owner's house and the farm steading, and are regularly seen feeding over the loch at the shooting lodge and the adjacent marshland at Geordie's Moor. On suitable days weather-wise they can be seen hunting flies on the hill, often quite high in the sky. There are no nesting sites for sand martins, though a flock was seen hunting flies over the fishing loch in late March 2012. Though swifts are not hirundines it is worth a mention that a single swift was seen hunting round the north edge of this loch in late June 2012.

Birds of prey and owls

Buzzards are commonplace on the estate, with eight pairs confirmed in early spring 2012. Nests of four of those pairs were found, though there is nothing to suggest that all eight pairs did not nest. Four red kites (two adults and two young from a nest in Lament) were regularly seen from midsummer right through to mid-winter. It seems that the two immature birds left the estate before the spring breeding season, as one which was radio-tagged was located near Crieff. The adult pair bred again in 2012, this time rearing two chicks in Dank Wood though they may not have fledged due to extremely inclement weather.

A female (or immature) hen harrier was seen twice on the hill in February 2012. Despite regular observation of suitable nesting areas no other harriers were seen and it is unlikely that they bred on this estate in 2012. Though the habitat is suitable, there are so few hen harriers remaining in the eastern half of Scotland because of persecution that recolonisation would take some years even if the persecution stopped now.

Kestrels were seen in low numbers, their limited presence probably being due to starvation during the very severe winter of 2010/2011. It is possible that a pair nested on crags on Middle Hill and another either on crags in Eerie Valley or in a tree nest in Larch Wood since a male was seen carrying prey in that direction. Short-eared owl numbers will be low for the same reason, and none was seen. Sparrowhawks, as predators of birds rather than small mammals, should have fared better, yet over the course of a year I only had one sighting. Peregrines were not seen.

A white-tailed eagle was seen over-flying the estate once in the course of this survey. Golden eagles were seen by others, though unfortunately were absent on the days I visited. There was one sighting of a female or immature goshawk in August 2011. Soon after this a predated pheasant was seen that could have been attributed to this raptor, though could equally have been killed by a collision with a fence. A moss-covered rock in Lament was seen to be used regularly as a plucking post, a feature of nesting goshawks. What was unusual about this was that the prey species was always young rabbits; never birds, making its use by a buzzard much more likely.

Tawny owls were present in reasonable numbers, one being seen regularly roosting on the same branch of a large conifer beside the shooting lodge. At three separate locations during March and early April 2012 tawny owls were heard hooting during the day. On the first occasion the gurgling call appeared to be a female, though on the subsequent occasions it was without doubt a male. After the last springtime occasion (9 April) only one daytime-calling owl was heard (25 July).

Lastly, ospreys were frequently seen over the fishing loch, to the delight of the anglers when they were seen catching a trout or pike. It is not thought there are any nesting on the estate, though they were sometimes seen over-flying the estate in the direction of the neighbouring estate to the west, where there are several nests.

Other birds

There are a few red grouse on the estate, and efforts are being made to boost the numbers by supplying medicated grit. Black grouse are sometimes seen on the marginal land between this estate and the western neighbours, where they probably nest among young conifers. Several successfully-hatched pheasant nests were seen. One nest had also hatched a red-legged partridge egg. Extremely wet weather during late June and early July is likely to have had a catastrophic impact on nesting birds of many species.

Woodcock were seen from time to time over the winter, but not in high numbers. Unusually, gull species were uncommon, with the common gull the most often seen, especially in the fields above the shooting lodge. There was only one sighting of a pair of black-headed gulls (at the fishing loch), and a single sighting of three herring gulls. It was amusing to see that a small flock of starlings regularly mingled with a flock of lapwings above the shooting lodge, lifting, circling and landing with them in unison.

On my visits to the estate since the survey I could add a grey wagtail, merlin, peregrine and golden eagle to the list of birds I have identified, making a total of 93 species.

Mammals

Deer, red; Deer, fallow; Deer, roe; Fox; Hedgehog; Mole; Otter; Rabbit; Shrew; Squirrel, red; Vole, field; Weasel.

Fallow and roe are the most common deer species on the estate, with many of both species regularly seen on the hill as well as in woodland. The fallow deer are predominantly dark, though with some of the light dappled variety present. There are two pure white fallow doe (known as Penelope and Sandie). Penelope had a cream coloured calf in 2011. There were no sightings of red deer, though I found a cast red deer antler.

Strangely I had no sightings of foxes during the year, though frequently found their scats and saw many of their tracks in mud or in snow. In one unusual incident after a snowfall I had been following a fox's tracks and saw where it had deviated to pounce on and catch a small mammal, which it then proceeded to eat – but only after sitting down. The marks in the snow of its front paws, back legs behind them in almost V formation and the circle of its backside behind that were testament to its comfort while dining!

Red squirrels are extremely common on the estate, with sightings in every wood except Henhouse Wood, Ell Wood and Pheasant Wood. Even without sightings it is likely that they are there given the proximity of other woods where they are present.

Compared with some areas, mustelids are relatively uncommon. During the year I only saw one live weasel (though saw a few dead ones caught in tunnel traps) and no stoats whatsoever; unusual considering the high rabbit numbers. Like on all estates, otters will pass through from time to time, and evidence in the form of two trout with their heads eaten off was found near the edge of the loch at the shooting lodge in November. A large otter, possibly male, was seen at close quarters on the fishing loch. The otter seemed relatively unaffected by the proximity of my boat and dived several times in search of food, its bubble trail showing its direction of travel. When it was on the surface I was surprised to see that its tail was sticking up clear of the water. Though I didn't see them, there are believed to be pine martens in the large woodlands at the west end of the estate. Neither badgers nor feral ferrets appear to be present.